EUROPE AND EUROPEANS

Europe and Europeans

A Study in Historical Psychology and International Politics

By

COUNT CARLO SFORZA

THE BOBBS-MERRILL COMPANY

Publishers

INDIANAPOLIS   NEW YORK

TO ALL THOSE
WHO STILL WANT TO HOPE

CONTENTS

PREFACE

This book aims to present a synthesis of the historical and psychological characteristics of the European peoples with respect to their fundamental international problems.

Its defect or its advantage—the reader will judge—lies in the fact that it is not based on books, but rather it is based entirely or almost entirely on the author's personal experiences and observations through a long contact with many nations and with all sorts of political problems, first as an Ambassador and a Foreign Minister and later during a voluntary absence from his country.

It is for this reason that the author does not make a special apology if he appears occasionally by name and in the first person in the pages that follow. For, if he appears therein, it is only for the purpose of offering his personal testimony; and when he comes forward, he does so as an additional guarantee of intellectual sincerity.

Impartiality in historical writing probably does not exist, and the historians who boast of it, such as the pompous Macaulay of our grandparents' time and the pedantic Taine of our fathers', should arouse even more suspicion, precisely because of their claim. But what a writer of history can give, and therefore is under a duty to give, is the authentic source of facts, and in the case of this book, those events above all which the author has witnessed or in which he has taken an active part.

In writing the various chapters of this book, the author very often had to make a special effort to recall the political and diplomatic events in which he took a part and which seemed at the time of their occurrence to be of such feverish concern to the quarrels and prestige of the Great Powers, but most of which a few years later seemed to him lost in the clouds of a distant past; while the human personalities who took part in them have remained vivid in his mind.

May not such subjective impressions help to prove that so-called political events are but the toys of history, while what really matters is traditional psychological tendencies behind them—human characters in a word?

If, as the author believes, there is some foundation for this impression, it would offer a lesson in human tolerance and healthy skepticism in viewing historical "events."

Old wise Greece had felt so when Heraclitus said: "Everything flows; no one has ever crossed the same river twice." And one of his disciples, correcting him: "No, master, not even once; by the time one has crossed it, it has already become a different river."

Carlo Sforza

EUROPE AND EUROPEANS

I

THE EUROPEANS AND THE WORLD WAR

BEFORE the World War, there was only one autocratic government in Europe: the Russian Empire. We should not forget, indeed, that the Germany of the *Junker* and of William II, as well as Austria-Hungary, recognized the freedom of the press. And where there is freedom of the press—or even a certain amount of it—it is impossible to speak of dictatorial autocracy.

What characterizes the post-war dictatorships in Germany, in Italy and in Russia is essentially this: all newspapers, all books, all printed matter become instruments of governmental propaganda, with the same result everywhere—intellectual debasement.

It has been fashionable for years to say that democracy is a form of mob-rule, while dictatorships offer government by the best. But it is now obvious to everyone that it is the dictatorships that are organized on the basis of mob-rule and often on the basis of lynch law. All the European dictators have proved to be demagogues and first-rate showmen. No prime minister in pre-war Europe was so prodigal of ready-made, catchpenny phrases as the dictators of post-war Europe—except Stalin, because he is the only dictator who is sure of his own strength.

One understands now what Cavour meant when he said that any fool can govern by martial law.

How is it, then, that such a lowering of the intellectual and moral atmosphere of Europe has been possible?

In my opinion, those who answer by citing armaments, feverish nationalisms and trade barriers as causes of the world depression are certainly right; but they forget the main human reason: that during the four most horrible years in the history of the world the flower of European youth fell in battle. Does not each of us who lived during or fought in the war, remember that it was on the Carso and on the Alps, in Flanders and in the pestilential trenches of Macedonia that two or three of our best friends died—friends whom we considered as the purest promises for the scientific and moral life of tomorrow? How many times have I seen their shades and bitterly felt their absence in the sessions of the Italian Parliament in which I took part, or later as I observed the proceedings of the French Chamber of Deputies from the ambassadorial loge.

Another thing we forget: those four years of war taught too many survivors the vicious lesson that violence was bravery and duty, that blind obedience, even spiritual obedience, was a moral virtue, that "patriotism" explained and excused everything, even spying on a friend on what was called the "home front," very far from the fire of the enemy. . . . If the greater part of acts of violence committed by Fascists in Italy and Nazis in Germany is characterized by base cowardice, it is because their authors believed or wished to believe that after all they were committing acts of war—where all is permitted.

The dictators accelerated the process of moral debasement, for everywhere, Russia included, they favored the flatterers, the so-called experts (who under the pretext of doing their technical work have lent themselves without conscience to serve everybody and everything), but they eliminated all the courageous servants of the State,* the most reliable critical minds, the original brains. Years of dictatorship have proved that capable servants stood no chance unless they debased themselves by a simulated servility and never ventured frankly to disapprove policies they considered baneful. But the acceptance of rule by fear ends in the degradation even of those who prudently think that they might obey or feign to obey the demagogue in power, while keeping free, at the same time, their inner conscience. The coward begins with a resigned silence; but passes very soon to demonstrations of respect and even enthusiasm for those whom he still loathes from the bottom of his soul. Shortly after he has begun to compromise with himself, even this secret feeling disappears. Such is human nature: when one is forced to endure bitter humiliations without possibility of rebellion, one ends by trying to forget all that; very soon one begins

---

*I am not thinking in the least of myself. Ambassador to France when Fascism went into power, I was not "eliminated"; I resigned at once—and maintained my decision in spite of written entreaties by the leader of Fascism to keep my post with him. I went to the Senate, in Rome, and there opposed Fascism as long as public discussion was allowed (end of 1925).

to say that the position is not so bad, after all.   One step more, and men who live under humiliating political conditions do not complain to even their trustiest friends. That would mean acknowledging the depths to which they have sunk.   They prefer to forget.*

He who has traveled in the ancient East has seen nations which seem to have been everlastingly degraded by long generations of despots into serviles races without hope and without faith.

No people can survive constant, forced submission to dogmas, formulas and men—and they have even less chance for survival when formulas and dogmas change all the time and men are exalted today by order and forgotten tomorrow by order, as happened in Russia to Trotsky and in Fascist Italy to so many shallow but noisy "hierarchs."

What is to be feared is that such moral evils threaten

---

* And it is the same thing everywhere even when dictators are intellectually powerful as perhaps was the case with Napoleon I and Bismarck. The following description of the Napoleonic days in France is not from a radical but from catholic and royalist Chateaubriand: "The whole country has become an empire of lies; newspapers, speeches, prose and poetry, all distort the truth. If it rains, we are assured that the sun is shining. Everything leads to the Master alone. We must above all yell applause when a mistake or a crime has been committed. No book may appear without having pages in it given up to praise of him. The crimes of the Republican Revolution were the work of passions which always leave certain moral resources. But how heal the wound made by a government that has established despotism as a principle? A government that, talking the whole time of morality, is constantly destroying it? A government that mistakes a terrified condition of slavery for the calm of a well-organized society? The most terrible revolutions are preferable to such a State."

Chateaubriand's words are a perfect description of post-war European dictatorships.

to remain, in part at least, even after their causes have disappeared.

There was good reason for the ancient motto: "The strength of a city is not ships or walls but men."

II

THE REALITY ABOUT THE RESPONSIBILITIES
OF THE WORLD WAR

THE lowering of intellectual standards in post-war Europe has rendered even more difficult the study of a question as complex as that of the responsibilities of the World War—a question which necessarily arouses so many passions.

And yet, if real peace is ever to reign once again in European minds, it will be necessary that, on both sides of what used to be the trenches, this grave problem be faced with a historical equanimity which has hitherto been lacking almost everywhere.

Men with grand political views are often dangerous— I mean those who, being but literary imitations of the rare ones who are real makers of history, try to lay on some *grand dessein* their problematic statesmanship.

Mazarin, Richelieu, Frederic II, Cavour, probably harbored plans less complete than the history school books would have the children of France, Germany and Italy believe. Cavour certainly desired the independence and freedom of Italy; but he would have been hard put to it to say, when Garibaldi landed in 1860 at Marsala, whether he would choose a centralizing system, as actually happened a few months later, or federal unions. Indeed, this improvisation of political genius may be noted more or less everywhere, even outside responsible governments; Marx wrote the *Communist Manifesto* a good many years before he had found its communistic reasons in *Das Kapital*.

Only those who want to heighten their stature, artificially set up for themselves grandiose aims in which extravagant fantasy outstrips the real; such was the case with Holstein in Germany and possibly with Delcassé* in France.

General Rochs, in his illuminating book on Schlieffen,† the famous chief of the German General Staff from 1892 to 1913, revealed that, in 1904, the latter declared, at a confidential meeting headed by Bülow:

"The only solution, from a military point of view, lies, as I see it, in immediate war with France; England is still weakened by the Boer War; Russia has the War with Japan on her hands; France is isolated. . . ."

It became known later that Schlieffen's purveyor of political ideas was Holstein, the Gray Eminence of the Foreign Affairs Office. The two men used to meet at least once a week, but always in secret. Holstein was of the kind who liked the shade. Baron von der Lancken has told in his *Meine Dreissige Dienstjähre* how Holstein admitted to him that he had resolutely urged on the war.

---

* He was French Foreign Minister from June, 1898, to June, 1905.
† *Schlieffen*, Berlin, Vossischer Verlag, 1920-1926.

"When I perceived"—so Lancken relates Holstein's words—"the danger of England participating in the Franco-Russian Alliance, my predominant idea was that we must break the circle before we were completely shut in; that we must break it with such energy and skill as would not fear to face the worst extremities. Hence the Kaiser's journey to Tangier."

This was at the time when Schlieffen had declared himself in favor of war.

Holstein added that he had only come to realize later that a policy of such scope was impossible because "the Emperor would never make up his mind."

At the Algeciras Conference on the Moroccan question, the German policy was dictated by Holstein; and Holstein's instructions and forecasts always derived very logically from his rational premises.

All those who went through the long weeks of the Algeciras Conference, and who were placed in such a position as to know everything, must have gone away from it with a weakened impression of German moral strength, the only strength that counts, after all. Even German discipline was a myth at Algeciras. The French often attributed to perfidious Machiavellism the difference in the language used respectively by the two German delegates, Radowitz and Tattenbach. Nothing is further from the truth. Radowitz carried out the formal official instructions of the Wilhelmstrasse, the ones which were meant to be known by all the Cabinets, whereas Tattenbach stood for Holstein's style and secret ideas. Failing to realize that, by his very outbursts, he was all the time exceeding and missing his aims, Tattenbach, whose blunt ways had first made him rather popular with the younger members of the Conference, always went about confiding to them and to all the neutrals that Germany certainly did not want war, but that if she were obliged to enter into it, she would .squash the French "like bugs." He liked this simile.

One day he complained to Marquis Visconti Venosta of the coldness of the attitude of the Italian delegation. The first Italian delegate reminded him that this attitude was inspired only by the reserve dictated by the ties of the Triple Alliance on the one hand and, on the other, by the Italo-French agreements about Morocco, which had been known in Berlin since their origin.

Tattenbach, not realizing that the old man with whom he was speaking was the living honor of European political thought, began to lecture him on Italy's real interests, as if Visconti—the old disciple of Mazzini, the old friend of Cavour—did not know them.*

---

*Tattenbach, to belittle Visconti Venosta, termed him a Francophile. French political writers said the same thing of him to exalt him. Both sides were equally wrong, but with this aggravating circumstance for the French: they thereby unwittingly diminished the import of Visconti Venosta's thought, even as regarded France herself.

Visconti was convinced—I quote his words—"that the interests of Italy are closely allied to the general interests of European peace"; that the Italian people desired "to live in good harmony and on good terms" with France; and that "to foster, to keep alive the germs of antagonism and of hostility between the two peoples is not to work in conformity with the great cause of civilization and of human progress." (His speech to the Italian Senate, February 10, 1899.)

Visconti listened to him with long-suffering courtesy; but finally he said:

"Would you tell me, my dear Count, whether you do me the honor of speaking to me on instructions from your government?"

Tattenbach admitted that he had not this authority.

And then Visconti, putting an end to the conversation, said:

"I might be your father, my dear Count; allow me therefore to make a remark. Your idea of diplomatic negotiations is to hurl yourself on your adversary, to throw him on the ground and trample him down, then to say to him: 'Let us agree.' This method, if it becomes general with you Germans, will bring you to a bad end."

I had been a silent bystander. Tattenbach gone, the Marquis looked at me; I was smiling. He only said:

"You are right. Let us go for a walk; if we put it in a telegram, the whole thing might become serious. Only it will be for you not to forget."

The political methods of the Holstein style had, in Algeciras and in London, the opposite result to that expected in Berlin. The British delegate, Sir Arthur

---

Count Robilant, who renewed one of the treaties of the Triple Alliance, did not think otherwise than Visconti Venosta who laid the foundations of the Italo-French Entente. I quote both, for they always seemed to me the best of all Italian Ministers for Foreign Affairs, after Cavour. Their defense, at once calm and haughty, of the interests of Italy was all the more effective since they always avoided the dangerous phraseology that leads to war. Bismarck used to say that, of all the European Foreign Ministers of his time, Robilant was the most indifferent to threats and flattery (in which Bismarck's arsenal was so well stocked).

Nicolson, accentuated his support of his French colleague, Revoil—and God knows he liked him little, so much was Nicolson the old reserved and laconic Englishman and Revoil the French barrister with an abundant and flowery flow of language.

In Berlin Germans realized, late, that they were steering the wrong course, and Bülow asked Vienna to have a compromise on the thorniest questions suggested by the Austro-Hungarian delegate. This was done; and for good or evil, we got into port.

And then, the Conference over, came Kaiser William's turn to create further animosities. By way of thanks to Austria-Hungary who had got her ally out of a dangerous corner, he wired to Francis Joseph to express his gratitude for the services rendered by the "brilliant second"; a qualification every one in Vienna resented, from the Emperor and his Foreign Minister Goluchowski down.

It will be a sign of great political progress in Germany when German historians realize the harm William II's semi-romantic, semi-theatrical language did to his country; a great progress, because one is sometimes inclined to fear that the whole paraphernalia did not spring from the depths of his morbid brain alone; but that the disease pervaded almost the whole of Germany. Had not Heine ridiculed the *Gothischer Wahn* (Gothic delirium) of his day?

At least, about Holstein a unanimous opinion has been reached in Germany; his long and mysterious influence has been generally recognized as harmful.

In France, opinion is divided as to Delcassé—which is quite natural. Delcassé's career is made up of two historical moments: the creation of the Entente Cordiale, and his attitude during the Moroccan crisis.

Where is the Frenchman who might have disapproved, or might disapprove, the agreements with England and with Italy?

If the reversal of the Alliances under Frederic II was such a great event, there is no reason to stint the admiration which the results achieved by Delcassé deserve. Even if it were proved—as I am convinced it might be—that two men, Barrère* in Rome and Paul Cambon† in London, were the great craftsmen of this policy, Delcassé would still always keep the merit of having understood and supported his most important collaborators.

May I be allowed to point out—the most limpid facts are not necessarily the least useful to state—that the key to the success of both Ambassadors lies in this initial starting point: clear-sighted Frenchmen, they always perceived where it was necessary that France should give in; they grasped, and led Paris to grasp, that sound understandings do not go without sacrifices? In this lies the chief merit of professional diplomats; being used to silence and secrecy, they are not urged on by the desire for immediate and loud success; they are accustomed to labor for ends of which they know well that the successful achievement will be credited to their government, and that any blame

---

* French Ambassador to Italy from 1897 to 1923.
† French Ambassador to London from 1898 to 1920; died, 1924.

or disavowal will be for them.   This helps to make a man—
when man there is; which is not always the case.

The embassy of Barrère's predecessor in Rome, Billot,*
is a case in point.

Billot had devoted himself with admirable patience and
foresight to preparing the ground for better relations
between France and Italy.   He had collaborated with
Visconti Venosta—who came back to power in 1896 after
Crispi's defeat and thought very highly of Billot—in the
preparation of the Tunisian agreements and of closer
trade connections.   Within sight of the goal, he became ill
and asked to be recalled; and with stoical equanimity he
passed on the arduous task to his successor and retired
in silence.   Billot knew Delcassé well.   Although it was
not generally known, Delcassé had, about 1884, asked
Billot for an appointment as chancellor in some French
consulate in Germany.†   What a career did Billot's refusal
open up to Delcassé!

The final judgment on Delcassé will one day probably
be this: he succeeded in forging an excellent tool, the new
Ententes; but the tool was too big, or too dangerous in
his hands.   Besides his gifts of optimistic courage and
Gambettian patriotism, was the man also too blind and
too thoughtless?   I should not dare to say; but when
one turns to facts—strangely forgotten—one finds that his
management began with a burning humiliation of the type

---

* French Ambassador to Italy from 1890 to 1897.

† Billot was then a high official at the French Ministry for Foreign
Affairs.

which his resignation on June 6, 1905, imposed by Germany, drew on France. I refer to the close of the Fashoda incident, an affair for the beginning of which he was not responsible; indeed Captain Marchand's expedition had been decided under Hanotaux, whom Delcassé had succeeded.

Delcassé, on September 8, 1898, with the first diplomatic contacts for the solution of the unpleasant adventure, could write with great serenity to the French Ambassador in London:

"It does not lie either with Captain Marchand or with General Kitchener, to draw the political consequences of the expeditions they had to lead."

But the French press had once again taken up the same style of language it had used on the eve of the 1870 tragedy, and Delcassé gave in.

On September twentieth, his manner is already reminiscent of the Duke of Grammont, the 1870 Foreign Minister of Napoleon III: "We could contend that we have no lesser rights to Fashoda than England has to Khartoum."

Thus, having embittered the incident, he prepared his own mortification by declaring, on October fourth, to the English Ambassador: "To ask us to evacuate Fashoda prior to any discussion would really amount to an ultimatum. And who, knowing France, would doubt her answer?"

Lord Salisbury, who was little concerned with newspaper success, was willing to make some concessions; and, in a conversation with the French Ambassador on October twelfth, admitted that the question of the Bahr-el-Ghazal, the main affluent of the Nile, should be reserved.

What should a prudent and intelligent minister have done? Seize the opportunity and even turn it into a success for his country.

But Delcassé repeated what he had done a few months earlier with regard to certain German overtures about colonial agreements, overtures to which he had not even answered. He did not condescend to notice Salisbury's conciliating words; he continued to insist on his theses, and on his theses alone.

The results, which Frenchmen sixty years old have not forgotten: Marchand sent away on a brutal ultimatum, with no compensation whatever; and a few months later, when the delimitation of the Chad territories took place, the loss to France of the whole Nile basin—including the Bahr-el-Ghazal that Salisbury himself had been willing to leave to her.

Another grave error of Delcassé was that he did nothing to prevent the Russians from getting too much involved in the Far-Eastern quarrels which were inevitably bound to bring about a war with Japan. The case is made worse by the fact that eminent Russians, Count Witte for instance, always thought and said that serious opposition on the part of the French Government would have made the Czar understand the dangers of the mad enterprise: an enterprise in which "Willy" was engaging "Nicky" with all his might; William II dangled before

Nicholas's eyes the glories of a crusade against the "Yellow Peril," out of sheer levity probably, rather than out of a desire to weaken Russia. Delcassé kept silent and let things go their way, convinced—what other explanation is there to give?—that imperial Russian military laurels would enhance the prestige of the alliance—and his own.

It is therefore permissible to believe that no more than Bülow and Holstein did Delcassé, in 1905, perceive the danger there was in brandishing the bugbear of war in order to insure the triumph of one's policy; naturally, like all diplomats, he believed that his policy and the interests of his country were at one.

Unfortunately the use of the war threat automatically increases the probabilities of war.

Cabinet meetings, in France and in England, leave no traces; there are no minutes.* Two ministers, Chaumié† and Thomson,‡ have published their recollections of what happened at the Council of Ministers which met at the Elysée on June 6, 1905. But the most complete evidence is probably that given by Paléologue, Delcassé's intimate collaborator at the time.§

Here, according to Paléologue, are the words of Delcassé; but to appreciate them accurately it should be remembered that they were spoken to ministers who, with

---

*Minutes were always drawn up in Italy; but in a very summary form.

† Minister of Justice in the Rouvier-Delcassé Cabinet.

‡ Minister for the Navy in the Rouvier-Delcassé Cabinet.

§ Later on French Ambassador to Russia from January, 1914, until the advent of Lenin to power.

the exception of Prime Minister Rouvier,* were unaware of the sudden gravity of the situation although they shared with the masses the vague anxiety which had prevailed in France since the Tangier speech.

"Germany threatens us," declared the Foreign Minister. "For my part, I think it is mere bluff. Therefore, we must resist. Now, England is offering us her alliance; we must immediately accept it. For either Germany is bluffing, and she will all the less readily keep up her bluff if she sees England ready to defend us; or Germany really wants war, and in that case the co-operation of the British fleet is of vital interest to us. I have finished. Weigh carefully, gentlemen, the decision you are about to take. Today England boldly stands by us. But tomorrow, if she sees us weaken, tremble before the boasts of Kaiser William, she will no longer rely on us; and, shifting her ground, she will soon negotiate with Berlin a reconciliation of which our colonial empire will bear the expense. . . ."

Delcassé's supreme argument, therefore, was that England was offering her alliance. On what did he base his affirmation? On a letter which Lord Lansdowne had sent a few days before to the French Ambassador, Paul Cambon, inviting the French Government "to discuss with the British Government the various complications which are to be feared during the rather alarming period we are going through." A document of capital importance, undoubtedly. But here should be placed—before the

---

* Prime Minister, 1905-06.

meeting of the Cabinet—an incident which shows what great servants France then had abroad. Delcassé, on receipt of the letter from the British Secretary of State, had immediately ordered Paul Cambon to hasten the discussion.

The Ambassador refused; or at least, he sent his chief at the Quai d'Orsay this preliminary lesson:*

"A conversation of this kind may not be entered into before all the consequences have been faced nor without the consent of Rouvier.† . . . It seems to me some-

---

*I am in a position to assert that Barrère, more than once during his embassy in Rome, refused to take steps which might have looked unduly pressing and thereby have spoiled the work of Franco-Italian *rapprochement.* He was probably, at the time, sometimes accused in Paris of being lukewarm or over-careful; but, as a matter of fact, it was then that he was serving his country best.

The Germans should ask themselves if an imperial Ambassador would have dared to do the same. No; the German Ambassadors were too much in fear of the sarcastic marginal notes of their imperial master.

To explain Barrère's success in 1914 and '15, the legend was spread in Germany of the floods of gold he had poured on the Italian press. Nothing is more exaggerated; the serious Italian press was, before the Fascist régime, one of the most honest in Europe; nobody in the world could have dictated a single line to papers like the *Corriere della Sera* or the *Stampa.* This was proved by the German Embassy itself, for when it had millions to spend in the campaign for the maintenance of Italian neutrality, it had to resort to publishing new papers which hardly anyone read and which irritated those who read them.

May I recall that in 1921 Barrère came to see me on certain plans for the creation of institutes of French culture which had been suggested to him from Paris and were, in reality, to be nothing but propaganda centers?

"Don't do anything of the sort," I said; "at least, you should not in your own interest. There will never be in Italy better French propaganda than that done by the German propagandists."

I was alluding to Bülow's and others' campaign in 1914 and '15. Barrère understood at once.

† Then President of the Cabinet.

what difficult for you to answer overtures which will lead you to an alliance. . . ."

And simultaneously Cambon wrote to Loubet, the President of the Republic.

This is the answer Rouvier made to Delcassé at the meeting of the Cabinet, according to Paléologue who had it from Delcassé:

"Do not believe Germany is bluffing. She is as anxious as mortified by the isolation you keep her in, by the circle you have managed to circumscribe about her. She sees in the Moroccan conflict an excellent occasion to break through this blockade and she will, in order to break through, go to the last extremities if needs be. On the other hand, she knows that England has recently offered her alliance to us. Germany knows of the English offer. . . . Bülow sent one of his friends to me a few days ago to warn me that if we accepted the English offer, Germany would declare war on us. Are we ready to face war with Germany? No, no. Even with the co-operation of the English Navy, we should run to disaster. It would be criminal to start on an adventure of this kind."

The Cabinet believed Rouvier rather than Delcassé. All the Ministers fell in with the views of their President. Delcassé was left alone.

There is no doubt that Rouvier helped his country at the time. If war, so be it. But how could anyone have wished to embark on a terrible war on account of Morocco?

Everybody understood then, in France.

The only thing I should feel inclined to admit if I judged matters from the standpoint of the most ticklish French patriotism, is that Rouvier exaggerated in form and in appearances; he might have avoided giving Bülow the dangerous impression that he had won even in French domestic affairs. But he did not: it was the price France had to pay for the somewhat Balzacian vulgarity of its 1905 Prime Minister.

That day, Delcassé, beaten, said the most cruel things against Rouvier: "This man would sell France for a lucky stroke on the Stock Exchange!" And: "He told Radolin* that he cared nothing for Alsace-Lorraine!" It was mere lobby talk, repeated from group to group. Nothing to stop at: home politics. But it is worth while pointing out—as a lesson in tolerance—that Delcassé joined Clemenceau's name to Rouvier's: two traitors according to him.

But another doubt remains: I do not know whether it is to Delcassé's honor or not. One of the keenest and most outstanding public men of France once told me that, as he saw it, the truth was not so tragic; that Delcassé, boastful but wary like all good Gascons, had, at the famous Cabinet meeting, declared himself for war simply because he knew he would be put in a minority; he ran no risks for France and for himself, but was taking an attitude of cheap heroics. The fact is that, reading the diary Paléologue kept at the time, in which he recorded all

---

* The German Ambassador in Paris, 1900-1910.

Delcassé's sayings, one feels that they are inflated, strained, theatrical; they lack the accent of sincerity.

Be it as it may, Delcassé had only his legend and his panegyrists much later, and as the years went by, after the war, they increased in importance. One even saw men of real political and intellectual value maintain that France had better have risked her all in 1905. . . .

But in Germany, mistakes began immediately. If, in default of the statesmanship he never had, Bülow had been endowed with at least half the diplomatic ability he was credited with, he would have seen that it was in his interest, and in the interest of Germany, to smooth the way for Rouvier; he should have wished that the French be led to believe that Delcassé's successor was winning success after success. It might possibly have helped to set up a new atmosphere. But nothing of the sort happened. Intoxicated by Delcassé's fall, Bülow and Holstein multiplied the difficulties in the path of Rouvier, who, heroic in his coarse way, fought in silence, only to burst out sometimes to his faithful Moreau: "The dirty beasts!"

A short while after Delcassé's fall, Holstein came to Paris to relish his triumph in secret. He saw there only Radolin, the Ambassador, on whom, for that matter, he set little value. Radolin was scared by the violence of the ideas and plans Holstein nurtured in his troubled brain; he went for help to the Spanish Ambassador, Leon y Castillo,* who enjoyed exceptional standing in

---

* Spanish Ambassador to France from 1887 to 1890, from 1893 to 1895, and from 1897 to 1910.

Paris and whom Holstein, with his rather mechanical notions, considered was not, at bottom, very friendly to France. Was he not the Spaniard, the neighbor, who had been in such fear lest Delcassé should not respect Spain's old mortgages on Morocco? And Leon y Castillo went to the German Embassy and explained at great lengths to Holstein that his was not the right way to handle France, that he would end by driving her to hatred and dangerous rancor. . . .

"Frenchified!"

This was the sole contemptuous remark that Holstein, speaking with Radolin, found to oppose to Leon y Castillo's objurgations.*

Six years after the fall of Delcassé, war was avoided a second time, thanks to Caillaux, helped by Jules Cambon,† and to Kiderlen-Waechter.

---

*Prince Radolin confided the story later to Marquis Visconti Venosta, who told it to me. Radolin's was no great brain, but he had tact and moderation as often happens with professional diplomats. When he was quite young, when imperial favor had not yet shortened his name and he still went by his old Polish one, Radolinski, he had known Visconti Venosta well in Rome. On his way to Algeciras, Visconti stopped one night in Paris, and received only two visits: first one from Rouvier and, immediately after, one from Radolin: "Do not believe, Marquis," he began, "that I have come as counter-poison to the Rouvier venom." And indeed, his whole conversation, at which I was present, was nothing but a lengthy disquisition on a very simple and "diplomatic" idea: that, in vain perhaps, and a little through everybody's fault, we had brought a hornets' nest about our ears and that the important thing was to get out of the trouble without creating too much discontent on any side.

†Younger brother of Paul Cambon; Ambassador to Washington from 1897 to 1902, to Madrid from 1902 to 1907, to Germany from 1907 to 1914; one of the French Delegates at the Peace Conference; French Representative at the *Conference des Ambassadeurs* for the execution of the Versailles Treaty which met in Paris for a few years every week at

Kiderlen had been so rash as secretly to give German nationalist and militarist circles the assurance that southern Morocco would come into the hands of the Reich. But as soon as a danger of war appeared, he fell in with Caillaux. With a Duke of Grammont in Paris, a Jagow as tool of the military in Berlin, who knows whether the fateful hour had not struck three years earlier?

Kiderlen's periodic fits of violence were due only in part to his Bismarckian temperament; he often gave way to them knowing they were excellent devices to continue to impress the *Jünker* and the generals, who were beginning to be suspicious of him; they felt that, notwithstanding appearances to the contrary, he was not entirely one of them.

When, in 1910, after a long exile there, he left Bucharest where I knew him intimately and where all his colleagues reveled in his sallies, Kiderlen declared to Take Jonescu, who repeated the words to me:

"If Germany does not begin war, nobody else will. The French Republic is essentially pacific. The English do not want war, whatever our papers may say. As for Russia, she knows too well we should beat her hollow."

But the naval craze went on in Berlin; and Take Jonescu, when he met his old friend there the following year, could not help saying to him:

the Quai d'Orsay, the British Ambassador representing Great Britain, the Italian Ambassador Italy, and Foch and Weygand attending as military advisers; died, 1935.

"As long as you Germans wanted to become the second naval power in the world, I could see your point. But now you have got there, you still keep pushing farther. Do you want to become the first on land and on sea? You must know that would mean universal domination; and that such a thing shall not be."

Kiderlen, with his usual frankness, replied:

"I said all that myself; I said it to Tirpitz. . . . But I did not convince him. . . ."

"And the Emperor?"

"Oh! He has been won over body and soul to Tirpitz's views. You can make him waver on anything; but not on that."*

It was asking for war; and it is an absolute fact that William II talked of war, talked too much of it, but he did not want it.

Never will a collection of diplomatic documents, however complete and honest, disclose the deep reasons and unreasons that brought on a war. The most essential diplomatic dispatches are never anything but fragments of truth. First of all, they do not take into account the psychological imponderables which evolve little by little among the masses and even in the heart of the leaders.

The myth which, as 1914 drew on, materialized for the French masses was called "fear of German provocation."

For the German masses it was "encirclement."

---

* Take Jonescu left me a summary of these conversations when he came to see me in Rome in 1920.

Had the imperial diplomats had eyes to see, they would
have realized that the French people—whom Berlin
thought rotten and ready for revolution—were being more
and more united by one common anxiety. When, in 1912,
a Zeppelin having lost its way landed undisturbed before
Nancy, an immense uneasiness spread even among the
peasants who still are much nearer in France than in Italy
to that old Roman tradition which made of the boundary-
stone a god, the God Terminus. No one has ever thought
of adding to William II's liabilities the medal he had
struck to commemorate the landing of the Zeppelin at
Nancy. And yet it contributed toward making the French
peasants feel—I noticed it personally—that the Germans
wanted to be "the masters."

On the other side, I am convinced that certain needlessly
resounding, loud-spoken attitudes taken on sometimes by
the Entente contributed far more than the speeches and
articles of the Berlin nationalists toward making the
Germans believe in encirclement.

Viviani's* decision, on the eve of the war, to withdraw
the whole French Army ten kilometers behind the frontiers
may have made Germany smile, because the gesture proved
nothing. Of course, it proved nothing. But for the
French peasants, the most convinced devotees of the God
Terminus, the point that the German patrols were the
first to cross over the border constituted the essential proof
of the fact that the Kaiser had wanted to invade France.

---

* French Prime Minister from June, 1914, to October, 1915.

And again: a few capital documents of 1914 were necessarily missing from the beginning; the telephone has altered the value of the "document"; one dares more in spoken words than in words written and signed. If fatal words of encouragement were given by Berlin to Vienna immediately before and after the ultimatum to Serbia, one may be sure they were exchanged over the telephone between one General Staff and the other; that there are no traces of them left; and that Bethmann-Hollweg knew less of them at the time than was afterward believed in the capitals of Europe. Bethmann-Hollweg, for German military psychology, was almost an enemy: the spokesman of conceptions of which one should beware.

And as for men, what collection of diplomatic documents will ever throw light on those depths of conscience we ourselves sometimes hesitate to explore?

Sonnino, for instance, thought it was his duty, and in the interest of Italy, to follow the policy which crystallized in April, 1915, in the signature of the Pact of London. But, before and after, he never ceased harboring in his secret self an instinctive distrust of anything that came from France or England. Suspicion breeds suspicion; and a good many Italo-Franco-British misunderstandings during four years of war had no other origin.

French revisionist writers have launched the most fantastic insinuations concerning Poincaré "who wanted the war." The more documents are published, even on the German side, the more proof there will be of the utter baselessness of the legend of *Poincaré-la-Guerre*. But if only one could strike the psychological balance of a man—and documents are dumb on this score—one would find this: that Poincaré always did all he could to ward off causes of war; that he certainly was not swayed, as some would have it, by the influence of Izwolski,* whom he knew to have received large sums of money from his Italian colleague Tittoni† during the Italo-Turkish War, a fact which Giolitti, Prime Minister of Italy at that time, later confirmed to me; but that if he mistrusted Izwolski, he never questioned the reality of Russian military forces. When he returned to Paris after his 1914 journey to Petersburg, he spoke to French Ministers, to Malvy for instance, of the wonderful strength represented by the Russian Army; he considered the doubts which Malvy expressed, quite scandalous. It was only natural that he should have been dazzled by the ostentatious display which Petersburg could put up for distinguished guests.

A far-seeing French Ambassador to Russia, General Le Flô, in 1873, informed the Duke de Broglie, Minister for Foreign Affairs, that the British Military Attaché, Wellesley, had visited Nicolaïeff and found the arsenals "empty"; and he added:

"Today, as on other occasions, France has overrated the forces on which Russia could draw in case of war; and serious investigations into the state of the land forces would possibly lead to discoveries similar to those recently made by Captain Wellesley on the Black Sea. . . .

---

* Russian Ambassador to France from 1910 to 1916.
† Italian Ambassador to France from 1910 to 1916.

"In Petersburg . . . one never sees anything but picked troops; but observations should be made everywhere . . . ; in a country where one may not safely believe anything but what one has seen."

Paris had forgotten that nothing is secure where prevarication prevails. Aerenthal, who returned to Vienna from his embassy to Russia convinced that the strength of the Romanoff was only apparent, drew better conclusions. This is well brought out by the success of his bold policy in the Balkans, in 1908, a policy built on contempt of the Russian threat.

In all this, where do the responsibilities begin, and where do they end?

No history book, no international court, will ever be able to tell.

From the international point of view, the study of the responsibilities of the World War will never serve anything but the purposes of those who speculate on insatiate grudges and hatreds.

This study might be useful if it were made independently by a people wishing to discover merely the mistakes made at home. But this could be done only in an atmosphere of international calm; meanwhile we shall have to resign ourselves to admitting—whenever responsibilities are mentioned again—that, before the Kellogg Pact, there was no reason to condemn a government which resorted to war. There have been, in the past, wars that were willed; and they made the glory of the man who willed them; as a case in point, let Cavour's immortal name suffice.

The World War was really the War of the Austrian Succession.

If we realize that, the problem of war responsibilities is shifted and loses something of its moral import.

Not that the leaders of old imperial Austria are excused when they say: We were fighting for life. There was one Austrian among them who thought that the danger might be put off by a radical transformation of the monarchy, which was to suppress the Magyar-German hegemony over the Slav and Rumanian subjects of the Hapsburgs. The man who had perceived that the Danubian monarchy might find a new reason for life by changing itself into a sort of gigantic Switzerland centering on the old imperial myth, was no ideological dreamer: he was Franz Ferdinand of Hapsburg—Lorraine—Este, the heir to the throne, the man murdered at Sarajevo.*

The German responsibility must be ascribed to another type of blindness: the fear of losing the Austrian ally, of being left alone. Germany has, since the war, paid the price mainly because she let herself be led by men so stupid they did not see that Austria was dead.†

---

* One of the worthiest political personalities of pre-war Vienna, Doctor Baernreither, wrote in his diary on June 20, 1911:

"It is evidence itself that our Southern Slavs and the Serbians tend to unite. Our unfortunate attitude against Serbia sins against nature, against geography, against community of language, against instinctive inclinations, against the natural relations between our Slavs this side of the Save and those on the other.

"Can we still make up for our mistakes, for the mistakes committed on both sides, which have caused so much bitter lack of comprehension?

"That is the essential question."

† Nothing is more fantastical than the legend of "Germanic fidelity"

Bismarck himself has his responsibilities, for he helped to create the insoluble problem by having Austria cast out of Germany. None of his panegyrists can quote one sentence of his to prove that he had sensed the imminence of the threat. But the man, as I have said before, had wonderful technical reserves, and as long as he was in power, he always worked on the following three principles: to assert that Germany was *saturiert* (full, crowded); to refuse to collude in any way with an Austrian policy of aggression in the Balkans; to avoid giving Russia the impression that Germany would always stand in her way to Constantinople.

Bismarck's successors, except the wise Hohenlohe, took the very opposite stand on each of these three points. It spelled war: the war Bismarck had always wanted to avoid.

But in this war Austria-Hungary was fighting for her very life; she was right, if by life she meant her old feudal and unliberal order. Germany was fighting for the life

which William II enjoyed attributing, in his customary romantic style, to his allies in Vienna.

Let one—unknown—example suffice: one of the most alarming pre-war Moroccan incidents occurred through the vain efforts of the German Consul at Casablanca to have six deserters from the Foreign Legion— Germans it was said then—deported. Recognized by French officers, the men were torn from the hands of the officials of the German Consulate.

The affair finally came before an arbitration court; but while it was being discussed in Paris, the Austro-Hungarian Ambassador, Count Khevenhüller, went to the Quai d'Orsay and declared that one of the deserters was Austrian, but that Vienna entirely washed its hands of his fate; this without informing, either before or after, his German colleague for whom the whole business was, in those days, exceptionally important.

Had Italy done anything in the least like this, the German press would have raved for months about "Latin disloyalty." But Austria was the sacred ally, this Austria of all betrayals; and Germany kept silent.

of her ally, fearing lest she remain encircled and isolated if Austria were to disappear. Russia defended, or said she defended, Serbia, and, in any case, strove for the future of Slavism. Italy was fighting to eliminate the danger of Austro-Hungarian pressure and complete national unification. England was fighting to avoid the eternal danger of a continental hegemony. France defended herself, imperial Germany having achieved this masterpiece of diplomatic clumsiness: the accomplishment of "sacred union" in one of her chief adversaries. One element they all had in common: fear; fear of the neighbors, of their encirclements, of their armaments. If the World War had lasted a few months only, if it had not heaped up so much ruin and hatred, no one would have thought of making a moral case of the responsibilities.

No one thought of doing it when Japan, a few years earlier, attacked Russia; when Italy decided on the Lybian war; when the Balkan States waged war on Turkey and thereafter on one another.

None of these States had ever undertaken never to wage war; a Kellogg Pact would have seemed inconceivable.

The same thing was true in 1914.

The only responsibilities of the World War which the peoples have a right to find out are those incurred by their respective blind shepherds, responsibilities which the naïve masses have paid for with long years of misery and of blood.

III

WILSON'S FOURTEEN POINTS AND THE PEACE OF VERSAILLES

THE German troops, coming home in perfect order after the Armistice, were greeted in certain towns with ori-flammes bearing these words: "Brave soldiers, you have done your duty; God and Wilson will now save us!"

In a concord as exceptional as it is dangerous, France and Germany seem today to agree on one point—one only: to abolish all remembrance of the state of mind and of the hopes which expressed themselves at the time by this linking of divine mercy with the intentions of the American President. The point thus condemned to oblivion is nothing short of essential: the moral bases of the agreement which put a stop to hostilities on the German front in November, 1918.

I have said "an essential point," for what does count in the long run is always the moral law; far more so than economic and political factors.

Indeed, the Armistice was asked for, and granted, at the end of the war, on the grounds of Wilson's Fourteen Points.

There is no possible doubt on this score: not only did the German Government declare on October 12, 1918,

44

that it accepted "the points formulated by President Wilson in his speech of January 8, 1918"—the Fourteen Points
speech—but it added: "The aim of the transactions to be
entered into would thus be only to seek an agreement on
the practical details of enforcement of these points."

Wilson who, on October fourteenth and twenty-third, had
already acknowledged the German overtures "unrestric-
tively," solemnly declared in his final note of November
fifth, in his name and in the name of the Allied Governments, that they were prepared "to conclude peace with
the German Government on the conditions laid down in
the President's address to Congress on January 8, 1918":
the Fourteen Points address.

It was on the grounds of the Fourteen Points that
Germany capitulated and surrendered the greater part of
her war material.

Let us examine the Fourteen Points and their fate as
serenely as if we were studying an historical problem of
the Middle Ages.

The first point recommended: "Open covenants of
peace openly arrived at . . ."

Quite undeniably, the Germans may claim that, as far
as they were concerned, the Treaty of Versailles was not
"openly arrived at," seeing that, through a psychological
error which the spirit of revenge, then called justice, explains but does not excuse, the Germans were not admitted
to serious discussion of any of the treaty clauses. This,
incidentally, should make them recognize in all humility
that they owe the word *diktat* (dictation), so useful for

propaganda, to Clemenceau. But, from a permanent and
general point of view, it may be said that the first point
was observed, since all the States which became members
of the League of Nations were compelled to communicate
to the League all and any treaties or agreements to which
they became a party.

The second point, Freedom of the Seas, fell through at
once, the British Government having opposed it and the
United States having given in to Great Britain.

The third point dealt with the removal, as far as possible, of all economic barriers.

Now, economic barriers have never been so hateful
and harmful as since the Great War, Wilson's Republican
successors having been the first to set the example in this
field. But one may say that the Treaty of Versailles is
guilty by omission of one aspect of the problem in that
it failed to prescribe certain limits to the protectionism,
which was easy to foresee, of the new States, limits which
would have been a boon for each one of them and a first
step toward a better organized, less anarchic Europe.

The fourth point provided: "Adequate guarantees
given and taken that national armaments will be reduced
to the lowest point consistent with domestic safety."

Sterile years of discussion at the Geneva Disarmament
Conference, the Japanese invasion of Manchuria, the
declaration of rearmament on the part of Hitler's Government, the Ethiopian war, constitute a series of ironic
denials of the hopes which Wilson alone, probably,
nourished in 1919. Undoubtedly, this pledge was among

the most difficult to keep in an atmosphere which, already in 1919, was again full of fear and mistrust. But the point holds, nevertheless, that Germany will always be entitled to maintain that no disarmament was undertaken, after Versailles, but the one-sided disarmament of the vanquished Germans, Austrians, Hungarians, Bulgarians.

The fifth point demanded an impartial adjustment of litigious colonial claims, with due regard for native interests.

Nothing could foretell that this was to mean essentially: complete exclusion of Germany from any colonial possession.

The sixth, seventh, eighth, ninth, tenth and eleventh points concerned Russia, the reconstruction of Belgium, the restoration of the devastated regions in France and the restitution of Alsace-Lorraine, the national boundaries of Italy, the autonomous development of the nationalities of the Austro-Hungarian Monarchy, the evacuation of the Balkan States and an outlet to the sea for Serbia.

All these points have been more or less carried out. Germany might have complained that the costs of "restoration" provided under points seven and eight had been unduly raised by the addition, mainly owing to British proposals, of all kinds of reparations. But the reparations agreement reached at the Lausanne Conference in 1932 fortunately ended this vexatious controversy.

The thirteenth point declared: "An independent Polish State should be erected which should include the territories inhabited by indisputably Polish populations, which should be assured a free and secure access to the sea, and whose political and economic independence and territorial integrity should be guaranteed by an international covenant."

As a whole chapter of this book will be devoted to the Germano-Polish relations, it will suffice to state here that the thirteenth point was, if not violated, at least badly enforced through a needlessly irritating demarcation of Poland's outlet to the sea.

The fourteenth and last point provided the foundation of the League of Nations.

There is no doubt that four of the fourteen points, the third (economic barriers), the fourth (disarmament), the fifth (colonies) and the eighth (Poland) have been violated, or forgotten, or adjourned, either deliberately or through the force of circumstances.

Revisionist literature, even the French, has always held that the harm done to Germany must be redressed.

The truth is that the observance of the Fourteen Points, which constituted the basis of the Armistice, was as much to the economic and national advantage of France as of Germany; at any rate if one chooses to look a little further ahead into the future of both countries and of Europe.

After Hitler's advent to power in Germany it seems risky to talk of possible discussions between Germany and France in the more or less near future. But, after all, nothing is impossible in a Europe which was never so unsettled. And it might be wise for the French to get used to remembering this: that the Fourteen Points were accepted, even solicited,

by Germany, and irrevocably, at a time when she had not
yet surrendered her arms; that not only did Prince Max
of Baden's Government and the Reichstag consent, but
with them, and in full freedom, the Emperor himself and
the principal chiefs of the German armies. There is
no question here of a treaty signed by the Socialists and
later rejected by public opinion; no question here of dictation.

France—I mean the great masses of provincial France,
so healthy and pacific, who express their opinion every
four years only, on election day—this France has dreaded,
in the velleities of revision, the chaos in which she might
eventually sink with Europe, with Germany herself. It
is not that she was so deeply attached to the Treaty of
Versailles; but with the Treaty she felt herself to be on
some firm ground and feared that, by foregoing it, she
would slip into the quicksands of the unknown. Hence her
policy, as well-intentioned as it has been sterile and lacking
in courage and frankness, of partial concessions to Germany—from her renouncing the extradition of the "war cul-
prits" up to the anticipated evacuation of the Rhineland—
concessions not one of which appeased Germany, for each
was made too late; and always in a clumsy way and in
gross defiance of the most elementary sense of the psychology of peoples.

Some clear-sighted minds in France—but in the provinces, not in Paris where opinions are so frequently too
artificial—have sometimes noted this error; the Governments, save Poincaré's, probably perceived it too; but

they were shackled by the nationalistic furore of the Parisian press.*

A return to the solid rock constituted by the Fourteen Points as basis of the Armistice, might one day eliminate all danger of chaos. They once saved the Entente countries when, during the last twelve months of the war, they gave them a new reason for faith and hope. It would hardly tell in favor of the moral courage of the political writers of a country to continue to hush up—even though the sacred reasons of defense are no longer in question—those critical months when it was asked in English: "How many thousands of lives must we still give for Alsace," and in French: "Must we really go on dying for Poland and for Trieste"; and when only the Fourteen Points succeeded in bringing a new element of moral resistance.

May I own that, even now, I feel more national satisfaction than sadness at the candor, sometimes cruel and painful, which, between 1919 and 1920, characterized parliamentary discussions in Italy regarding the causes of the 1917 French and Italian setbacks? It is to the honor of the Italian democracy to have admitted the new force which Wilson's ideals brought to four million Italians in arms.

The fashion is now to belittle Wilson not only as negotiator—one can understand that—but as statesman. To grasp the value and scope of the Fourteen Points it should

---

* I am referring especially to Arthur Huc's admirable articles in the *Dépêche de Toulouse,* which his son, Paul Huc, collected in one volume: *Hommes et Doctrines,* published in 1935.

be borne in mind that here was the first document the strength of which lay in this threefold fact: that it was meant simultaneously for both enemy groups; and simultaneously for governments and peoples; and that it relied as much on the radio and the daily press as on diplomatic communications.

I, for my part, shall never forget how it stirred the Italians and the French huddled along the Eastern front; and the German and Austrian prisoners with whom I discussed it freely on the Macedonian front.

Justice has not been rendered either to the deep bearing of each word of the Wilsonian document. For example, in the eighth point, concerning France, this simple sentence: "the wrong done to France by Prussia in 1871 in the matter of Alsace-Lorraine" noiselessly excluded any secret agreements which might have been made regarding the Saar on the grounds that the Saar had been part of France in 1814.

The victory of the Entente should have been the victory of the Fourteen Points.

But Lloyd George and Clemenceau "did" Wilson.

Lloyd George first secured a withdrawal of the second point—the Freedom of the Seas—failing to understand that he thereby possibly hit a dangerous stroke at the life of the United Kingdom; for he should have felt that nothing was less certain than the permanent maintenance of British superiority on the seas; and that consequently an international sea police might one day mean a precious means of defense for the English.

Clemenceau, who was more of a journalist, began by sarcasms. On December 29, 1918, he said in the French Chamber of Deputies:

"We are told: you will make a just peace and, if you do, everything will be easy. You have heard many strains on this score," etc.

"President Wilson is a man the noble candor of whose mind inspires us with respect," etc.

Clemencism was triumphant already. Can we wonder if it was thought in Germany that all the high-sounding words of the Entente statesmen during the war were simply masterpieces of hypocrisy?

France long stuck to the Treaty of Versailles. Today everybody recognizes that it was only a gigantic armistice formula. President Hoover went so far as to define it, in a speech he made in Washington on August 11, 1932, as the "poisoned springs of political instability." English and Italian opinions are well known.

As regards Italy (I am not referring to the somewhat versatile manifestations of Fascism), I shall recall this: when the Treaty of Versailles was presented to the Chambers for ratification, Luzzatti was chosen to report on it. Luzzatti was one of the Italian statesmen most in sympathy with France. The French Ambassadors, Billot and Barrère, at the Farnese Palace, always found him a precious friend; both have testified to it in their memoirs. The words "pro-French," "pro-German," "pro-English" have no sense for statesmen. But if ever a word fitted a man, "pro-French" fitted Luzzatti. And he had put in his report a

few very hard criticisms. I was Under-Secretary of State
for Foreign Affairs and alone in Rome, Tittoni, the Minister, being still in Paris. Showing me the proofs of his
report, Luzzatti said: "It is also for the good of France;
I do not want to betray her during the most critical of her
trials." He consented to suppress the bitterest sentences
only when I told him that each country should find out its
own errors for itself; and that all lessons coming from a
foreign parliament would only cause—we were in 1919—
needless irritation.

What kind of moral authority can a treaty preserve
which is harshly criticized not only by those on whom it
falls but by its very authors?

This was admitted, indeed, by a Frenchman who is,
wrongly, considered to be responsible for some of the
worst errors of the Treaty, Tardieu. In his speech at the
Disarmament Conference at Geneva, on February 8, 1932,
Tardieu, whose pugnacious dispositions are recognized
even by his adversaries, owned to the following:

"Even though the summits of this treaty be lighted by
a luminous ideal of co-operation, certain of its clauses could
not but have been inspired by the needs of the hour in
which the treaty was negotiated. By the nature of things,
provisions were made which were the result of a recent
past and which every end of every war has always entailed.

"It is a fact, and to deny a fact has always been entirely
useless. International contracts are like private contracts:
they take circumstances into account and certain of their
stipulations are based on these circumstances."

It is impossible, when the speaker is the responsible head of a government, as Tardieu was in 1932, further to recognize the frailty of the work elaborated in 1919.

After a first period of conviction more fictitious than real, the French nation, with its solid common sense, had, even before Hitler's accession to power, come to feel that it might have been better to secure bulwarks more modest but also more effective than titles which, beneath their pompous wording, are nothing but speculative deeds guaranteed by the pitiable hazard of alliances.

The situation is full of dangers, just as it seemed to be in Europe after the 1815 treaties against which France and Italy protested. But with what a terrible difference!

Fifteen years after Waterloo and the Treaty of Vienna, toward 1830, it was felt that one day war would inevitably break out; but that was all. Today, everybody knows that a new war would constitute a mortal danger not only for Germany and her old enemies alike, but for the whole of Western civilization.

Republican and democratic Germany was wrong in leading a campaign against all the treaties as a whole; wrong in her own interest.

If Germany in the days of Ebert and Brüning had made up her mind to demand amendment of the treaties on the basis of the Fourteen Points which she had freely accepted when she had not yet laid down her arms, an agreement with France had been much nearer. If anyone feels to the contrary it is because all he has known of France is the artificial France of the Parisian boulevards.

The Treaty of Vienna was still-born in 1815 because it failed to recognize a dawning truth: the rights of nationalities.

The 1919 treaties failed to see the new law which is forcing itself on the world: development of nationalities but within the bounds of a higher law common to them all, binding them all and organizing them, and preventing them from rising against one another.

When this essential law shall have been admitted—the greatest Italian minds from Thomas Aquinas to Mazzini always advocated it—then shall the fiercest grievances and problems lose the greatest part of their acuteness.

IV

FRENCH AND GERMANS

BOOKS are the fashion now which, in scientific manner, describe and define the English, the French, the Italians. . . . They are nothing but novels prompted by a somewhat pedantic imagination. From the very first page of an essay on the French we learn that they are pre-eminently intellectuals, logicians, Cartesians. The painters of this schematic France forget that the written constitution of the country, and its geometrical divisions, date from the *Constituante* only and, after the Revolution, from a despot of Italian origin, Bonaparte. The slow and spontaneous creation of French history before 1789 reveals nothing but centuries of a political organization as empirical and as irrational as in arch-empirical England.

But the game of defining a people—and literary magnifying alone distorts every feature of these definitions— is not only illusory; it is also dangerous. Dangerous, because journalism has put science and pseudo-science into everybody's mouth; and at the very moment when in the field of serious historical research one no longer dares speak of races, the pedants of nationalistic literature at three cents a day have taken up the old poisoned lay again.

The striking point in the evolution of the relations between French and Germans is the deep contradiction lying between the relative closeness of the two peoples at their origin and the estrangement which barely a few centuries of more and more diverging histories have succeeded in begetting.

The two peoples, equally mingled with Germans and Celts (the contribution of Latin blood is not greater with the French, language and tradition set aside, than the Slav contribution with the Germans), sometimes seem so close to the origins of their history that one is tempted to wonder whether they are not still at the time of the old war for the Kingdom of Austrasia. In spite of the hatreds aroused by invasions and wars, they are the only two peoples in Europe where even the most violent and most childish nationalists unconsciously own the links between them. The one dream of Irish nationalists, of Yugoslav nationalists, is to eliminate, to expel the English from the North of Ireland, the Italians from the Dalmatian cities. The French nationalist thinks that France might settle down and be loved on the Rhine; and the nationalist maniacs of the Wilhelmine era considered the annexation of certain parts of France as the repatriation of Germans ignorant of their origin. Nationalists believing in the myth of the purity of their race would not wish to incorporate by force minorities which they are supposed to despise.

The divergence between the two nations increased more and more rapidly in the wake of the two historical trends which led the two peoples apart like two streams flowing from the same valley into seas far distant from each other.

The Capetian monarchy is the kernel about which France builds herself up: work of the people more than of the kings, as shown by Joan of Arc who, indeed, began the first nationalist mysticism if it be true that she exclaimed: "They who fight against the holy kingdom of France fight against King Jesus." The rising French patriotism killed the old universalist ideas of the Middle Ages and finally achieved under Louis XIV a national state as complete, powerful and exclusive as China in the days of Chen-Lung.

The Germans, on the contrary, preserved the universal and Roman conception of the empire until the end of the eighteenth century. The formula is majestic, but the ideal too vast and too diffuse for a people, and the nineteenth century finds Germany broken up into hundreds of principalities, the people viciously divided by two Christian creeds which mistrust and despise each other.

Nineteenth-century Germany decided to do in two generations what the French had taken centuries to achieve. Slight wonder, then, that the Frenchman today seems static and the German dynamic.

But they who mistake French statics for permanence fatally doomed to rapid backwardness are misled by wretched outward appearances. France, gigantic hexagonal crystal, does not even conceive she might become bigger. She is what she is. Never does a Frenchman wonder what it is to be French; the word, for him, is in itself its best definition. The Germans have spent a century theorizing as to what *Deutschtum* (German nationality) is, or is not. No people in their daily life show themselves linked to their past as do the French. During the long night of their divisions, the Italians found in incomparable songs of poets like Dante the script and rallying cry which they held in common and which made them feel still and ever Italian, from the Alps to Sicily, despite German and French conquests, despite Spanish kings and viceroys. But in no country in the world, save China, are the classics as popular as in France. A verse from La Fontaine, Racine or Molière is a live entity for millions of Frenchmen; it is still as if it had been written yesterday. Devoid of music, or at best parsimoniously musical, the French language secretes in itself all that constitutes the life of its people.

This language is the emblem of French solidity in all the forms of national life. Those French traits which sometimes seem defects to strangers are in reality only the resultant of a perfect, that is a complete, civilization.

France's economic autonomy is sufficient explanation for the little interest she shows—except in periods of international readjustment—in what happens far away from Paris. Selfishness, indifference? Not in the least; merely the natural consequence of the fact that France finds within her frontiers practically all she needs.

The same applies to individuals, in France. What strangers often term as excessive passion for money with the average Frenchman, is but the passion for his own independence. If wealth for a German is a dynamic force he gladly makes use of, it is generally for a Frenchman a useful fortress with which to safeguard his personal freedom.

The result is a solid social structure, as in China, where revolutions may shake everything except what counts: the conception of life. The French citizen has had his fits of madness; the individual Frenchman, registered yesterday in corporations, today in the *Bottin* (Directory), never. The political ideology of the average Frenchman is often Left; but his banker and his notary must be Right; and the secret of Poincairé's long success lay in feeling this and in having himself also been, and very sincerely, simultaneously Left and Right; like a certain old five-francs coin which had *Napoleon empereur* on one face and *Republique française une et indivisible,* on the other.

One might say of France that her idea of the Fatherland is synonymous with a certain style of life freely accepted by all. Nothing is more French, therefore, notwithstanding appearances and legends to the contrary, than Clemenceau proposing the cession of Corsica to Italy after 1870. It was a Bonapartist Department; what was it doing in the great republican family? Similarly today, strangers do not even suspect the bitterness with which the French complain of the persistent particularism of the Alsatians; complain among themselves, for a sort of French reserve prevents the echo of their grievances from reaching the press, which is all to the good. It would be a pity if wrong conclusions were drawn in Germany. The truth is that France regards herself as a happy family whose every member must be glad to belong to it. If ever Renan's definition of a nation: *"Le désir de vivre ensemble et de continuer indivis l'héritage qu'on a reçu"* (the wish to live united and to carry on jointly the heirdom which they have received) fitted a people, it fits France. *Héritage,* heirdom, joint heirdom. The French master-piece is solid, because it was made slowly; it would be a mistake for the French to be shocked by the story of the two Archdukes of Hapsburg-Lorraine who, shortly before 1870, were welcomed at Nancy by enthusiastic demonstrations and cries of: "Long live our dukes." For it was only after 1870, and in the throes of defeat, that Lorraine Nancy felt entirely French. The intoxicating draughts of victory are not always, far from it, the safest bond for the moral oneness of a people.*

Excesses, natural and inevitable perhaps after four years of suffering and of blood, and, before the 1914-18 years, the froth and bubble of Déroulède's gab and of Boulanger's swagger, have accredited throughout the world the fictitious myth of French militarism. Undoubtedly, the old tradition of imperialism in its humanitarian style of Year II of the Republican Calendar—far more than imperialism in the style of the sterile victories of the Empire—can still be found, sometimes unconscious, even among Frenchmen who are sincerely convinced of their democratic love of peace. The Socialist, Jules Guesde, an old rigid Marxian formal-

---

* Never were the Italians so united, nor so determined to resist the enemy, as after Caporetto, at the end of 1917, with Germans and Austrians masters of the Venetian plains. In proof of the blindness of Berlin and Vienna, they believed that the invasion would break the fighting spirit of the Italians.

Fascism, which has confused patriotism and theatrical gestures, always failed to understand that those sorrowful days are also among the most beautiful in the history of Italy during the war.

ist, probably felt the Hoch's leaven working in him, when he joined a bourgeois Cabinet during the World War.

But whoever dips below the surface in his study of the French people will find a passionate love of peace, equaled but not surpassed in others. Time and again, under the old régime, did the *Etats-généraux* endeavor to prevent the kings of France from waging war. Commines, speaking of the first great invasion adventure, that of Charles VIII into Italy, said that every wise and sensible man condemned it. If the French people gladly welcomed Louis-Napoleon, it was because it mistrusted social agitations, but the first Bonaparte's nephew had to turn to the peasants of France and say to them: *"L'Empire c'est la paix"* (in the Empire lies peace); the people were indifferent to the *honte* (disgrace) of the 1815 treaties.* And if in 1871 all Frenchmen were for Thiers, it was because Thiers wanted peace. If the greatest man of the Third Republic, Jules Ferry, was so unpopular, it was because he had forced a colonial war on his country. One might even say that the whole magnificent colonial empire built up by the Third Republic, was built up in spite of voters and of Parliament.

May one note too that, except for the two Bonapartes— both accepted at the beginning as pacifiers of the internal situation—this French people of militarist renown has never tolerated either soldiers, or a military cast, at the head of its government? The lack of influence of the

---

* Napoleon I, hated by all the French after his downfall, only recovered his popularity about 1830, more as a liberal myth to oppose the Bourbons than in remembrance of his military glory.

victorious generals after 1918 merely follows the rule.   All
of them, for that matter, showed the most deferential
obedience to civil power; all except Mangin; but Mangin
found support only in very restricted political nationalistic
groups.

Granted this, how is it that the myth has gone round
the world of a French people with whom military dogmas
would secure unanimous national consent more than in
any country where public opinion is free?

It is because in no country is the breach so wide between
French security in its incomparably autonomous economic
life and the vague anxiety which the French have often
felt over their frontiers: it is the price they have to pay
for the geometric perfection they achieved in the building
up of France from which they have excluded all vague and
universalist ideas.   Anything like Article II of the Weimar
Constitution providing that "other territories may be admitted within the Reich if their population so desires it"
would today be quite inconceivable in France; just as the
slow and wise evolution of the "British Empire" into a
"Commonwealth" of independent nations, which the English have almost pretended not to notice, would have constituted a real tragedy for France.

Before formulating psychological laws, one should remember that the vital interests of certain countries do not
necessarily identify themselves with their national territory.
Goldoni tells the story of an English lord who, having,
from his gondola, dipped his finger in the Canal Grande
and tasted the water, exclaimed: "Oh, it is salt, therefore

it is English here!" And of course England cannot but find herself on all the waters on which her ships and cargoes sail. Therefore, when she proclaims her interest in the prosperity of the whole world, her generous ideal is strongly colored by the incentive of an essentially British interest. In another field, deprived by fate of minerals and of raw materials, Italy should identify her efforts toward prosperity with an ever wider achievement of international solidarity.

Alone in Europe, France, as I have said already, might isolate herself economically behind an impassable wall, like that China enjoyed for centuries, and be self-sufficient. A unique case in Europe, it is matched only by the United States which has almost a continent to draw on.

But whereas the United States has, to the south, neighbors from which it has nothing to fear, and to the north the only frontier in the world which is entirely devoid of guns—the Canadian frontier—France is everlastingly on the alert as to what goes on not only in Germany, but in Italy and even in Spain and in Belgium. Compared to France, Italy and Spain are, politically, islands as inaccessible as Great Britain.

In fact, and in spite of certain periods, some rather recent, during which the governments of France seemed to make it their special duty to put all the semblance of wrong on the side of their country, one should beware of all facile generalizations regarding the militarism of the Third Republic. If one régime in Europe is to be associated with the idea of peace, it is indeed the Third Republic.

Could it not be that the Germans are pacific militarists whereas the French are antimilitarists with a warlike spirit when necessity thrusts war upon them?

Certainly, the efforts of Bismarck who, in his pride, believed that he could achieve in Germany the unification which had exacted in France the labor of thirty stubborn generations, reveal a personal genius who doubted the collective action of his compatriots.

Succeeding to his brother Frederick William IV, who died insane in 1861 having, in 1848, refused the imperial crown which an elected Diet offered him, William I, from the very first years of his reign, had been faced with a momentous choice. The faithful Roon had drafted a military reform bill which would have increased the military force of Prussia enormously, but the Chambers had rejected the bill. King William, as obstinate as he was honest, held that he must not give in; but even the most feudal among his ministers hesitated to countenance his resistance; they thought it was unconstitutional.

A diplomat, little known to the public, was in Berlin at the time. The King summoned him and asked:

"Is it true that you feel ready to undertake the reorganization of the army without and against Parliament?"

And the diplomat, Herr von Bismarck-Schönhausen, replied:

"I am, Sire."

"Then my duty is to try you and go on with the struggle. I shall not abdicate as I thought of doing these last few days."

Thus it came about that Prussia's representative in Paris became Prime Minister in Berlin.

With the brutal frankness which he used to advantage all his life long, he went to the parliamentary Finance Committee and declared:

"Germany does not count on the freedom of Prussia but on the strength of Prussia. It is her own strength which Prussia should increase. Our frontiers are bad and we must change them; our future will not be built on speeches but on iron and blood."

One of the members of the Finance Committee wrote in his own secret diary that evening: "King Frederick William was not so mad when he wrote in the margin of Bismarck's name: 'To be used only when governments will rule by bayonets alone.' We have come to that."

The time has perhaps come for the world, if not for Germany, to pass an even judgment on Bismarck's action.

Bismarck found Germany entirely wanting in political education; like Bonaparte, and more deservedly than Bonaparte did, he despised the "ideologists" who considered themselves the guardians of university and academic culture; he had seen them at work in the church of St. Paul's in 1848, and he had weighed their mandarin vanity, their political naïveté. But a Cavour, in his place, would have understood that one must not alienate or ridicule these forces and these flames; that, on the contrary, one should use them in practical life, give them the civic sense and responsibility they lacked, mainly owing to the Reformation after all. For it is impossible to forget, when one notes the failure of the intellectuals in Germany during the Bismarckian era, during the coarse and materialistic period of William II, and, worse still, under the Nazi régime, that the Reformation favored freedom of spirit only in the—wholly theoretical—sphere of philosophy. But the blind respect for the Prince which it imposed turned, more than any other cause, the Germans into cringing subjects rather than free citizens.

Bismarck plowed the old furrow even deeper. How dared he, when he became Chancellor, complain in his letters to his wife that none of his subordinates ever made the smallest decision in his absence? He it was who by his policy had, more than anyone else, made a great Germany, but very small Germans. Cavour was always anxiously seeking around him for those who, one day, should succeed him; Bismarck never once contemplated the problem; he probably never suspected, at least while he was in power, how great a loss of force and expansion the State underwent through having as subjects only marvelous specialists but no really free men.

I am used to believing more in what I see, than in what I read. I must own therefore that Bismarck's responsibilities toward Germany never seemed so heavy to me as during my visits to American universities, which I undertook to escape from the stifling Fascist atmosphere. Wherever I found groups of American citizens of German origin, from Wisconsin to Connecticut, I found the highest intellectual and political standards among those descended from Germans who, after 1848, had failed to resign themselves to a life without freedom. Germany felt losses in human values then none too different from those France incurred after the revocation of the Edict of Nantes.*

Too often did Bismarck, during his long all-powerful years, incline to consider, whenever a serious obstacle lay in his way, that the Constitution was but a form of procedure. It has been proved that he wondered more than once whether the "Nuremberg toy"—as he termed the Constitution—should not be replaced by a union of the German princes on the basis of a simple military and customs fusion, with no collective representation of the German people whatever. It was just a case, with him, of reversion to the old Prussian 1848 *Junker* for whom the very word "Germany" savored of liberal heresy. With all the limitations which his practical turn of mind accepted, Cavour thought always of Italy, always ready to melt his own beloved Piedmont in a united Italy, Bismarck never regretted that the unity he achieved was heavily maimed, owing to the expulsion from the Reich of the oldest and most German part of the Germanic body, Austria.

Bismarck's end is a great lesson. He had been a great diplomat, a great handler of men; he had twice boldly cast the dice of history, but he had remained deaf, and blind

---

* France believed too well in the German propaganda in the United States. I am convinced that the propaganda of William II's agents was so coarse and so clumsy that it finally did more harm to Germany than to France. It was rather the rashness of certain French generalizations which prevented belief in "German barbarity" in a country where the German-Americans of 1848 origin happened to be among the most justly respected for their high moral qualities.

to the supreme problems of a country. Is it strange if
he did not find a single friend, when William II's vanity
could stand the giant no longer?

Am I wrong in limiting Bismarck's greatness to a sphere
of immediate action? Here are some examples: he understood that it was useful to leave the French Republic free
to build up a colonial policy (no small thing if one considers the stupid blundering of French and British against
Italians and Germans fifty years later); but he had entirely failed to grasp the marvelous swiftness of reconstitution which the French democracy was showing; did
not he, the *Junker,* believe that it was enough to let the
country be under a republican rule to insure its total collapse?

And again, he had for Italian unity, for an Italy built
out of plebiscites, nothing but sarcasm and suspicion. He
never believed in the vitality of Italy; he had a horror of
the men of the Left who had come to power in 1876; he
thought they were "Reds," dangerous and hateful. But
in practical life, he saw the advantages of a Triple Alliance,
and concluded it with those men of the Left whom he had
so reviled.

Finally—for the list of examples might be much longer
—in his struggle against the Roman Church, which the
German professors, who had become courtiers of the
master, pompously christened *Kulturkampf,* he saw nothing but the old imperial fight of the Prince against the
power of the priests. Not for a moment did he suspect
the reasons for victory he might have found had he placed

the struggle on wider and newer ground. His Canossa, which surprised him so, was henceforward inevitable. He might have been saved from it had he lifted himself to heights where he would have become unassailable—but that was Freedom, and, worse even than hating it, he did not even understand the concept. During the conflict with the Vatican, he lost his self-control to the extent of one day demanding satisfaction of the Italian Government for the sayings and doings of a Pope whom liberal Italy had made truly free and intangible* by taking from him all the qualities of a territorial sovereign.

The professors of the Bismarckian and of the following periods decided to reduce to system and theory the political conduct of the great empiric, thereby earning the latter's most sarcastic contempt. The man never stooped to defend his ideas; he was too proud and too sincere for that. But in a country essentially didactic, the intellectual harm done by the professors was very deep. By Treitschke especially. On the eve of the war with Austria Bismarck had invited Treitschke, then a young professor at Friburg, to come to General Headquarters to draw up propaganda manifestoes. He offered him a chair in Berlin as his reward.

The young historian had first refused; but the Prussian victory soon dispelled his scruples. As always happens with apostates, this Saxon of Slav origin became the most Prussian among Prussians, and the most inflamed theorist of German unification by "Prussian conquest," not by

---

* A freedom which the Pope lost with the Lateran treaties of 1929.

free federation. He revived, but in more solemn and more
"scientific" form, the wanderings of Joseph de Maistre
on the marvels of war. "War," he wrote, "is the best
medicine for a people." Tens of thousands of students
went through the aula of the University of Berlin where
Treitschke pontificated for years.

In the crowd of students who drank the master's con-
victions, a young naval officer whom no one knew, a certain
Tirpitz, was always among the first, in the first rows.
After the lecture, the young officer feverishly followed
the "marvelous man," as he was to call him later, to the
bier-halle. The marvelous man being as deaf as a post,
the pupil endeavored to secure, on bits of paper, answers
mainly to questions about the possibilities of destroying
England. Treitschke had written in 1882: "A day will
come when not even a dog in Germany will accept a piece
of bread from an Englishman," and later on: "In England, even the children are bent on betraying Germany."

For, like all the nationalists, the good man combined
in himself two phenomena which would seem to exclude
each other: megalomania and persecution mania.

Tirpitz's letters of the days when he was inhaling
Treitschke's science include sentences like these:

"I hope to live long enough to see the end of England's
Freedom of the Seas" and "The young German Navy must
win its spurs by fighting against the power which holds the
Freedom of the Seas."

Prince von Bülow in his *Memoirs* has very bitter words
concerning Tirpitz who always stopped the Emperor from

listening to advice of discretion in his policy with England.
But he never thought of tracing, still less of blaming, the
intellectual causes of all this blindness in Germany. Worse
still, I heard him myself a hundred times in Rome, after
the war, blaming the errors of his country to a pretended
congenital incapacity of the Germans for political life.
It was too easy.

The truth is that, as Chancellor, he never rose against
the petty Treitschkes of his days, who with a *Sedanlacheln*
(Sedan smile) added traits to the master's preaching as
ridiculous as the naïve conviction of the right of the elected
people to take the place of the fallen Nations and States.

The unreal pedantry of the professors reached the sublime when, in Bülow's time, they charged the British Empire with being made at random through "illogical" generations whereas, thought they, an empire worthy of life
should arise only according to plans elaborated by pure
reason;* a way of preparing political thought, notes Croce
in his admirable *History of Europe*,† which reveals the
same defects as those so often noted in German art and
literature; that is to say, the theoretical formula preceding
fact: a danger grave in spiritual matters, but mortal in
politics.

As for Hitlerian Germany, it resembles one of those
volcanoes which rumble and fume and from which, even if
a certain amount of work may be carried out on their

---

* The French also are irritated, as by a lie, when the English say that
they have "stumbled into an empire," but they go no further; they do not
pretend to teach others how one should create an empire scientifically.

† Published in 1932.

slopes, a new eruption, a new earthquake may at any time endanger everything again. The aspect is sometimes dreadful. But even Nazi violence and stupidity will have been of some use if, through the break with all traditions which they seem to have fulfilled, we may hope some day, after sufferings and trials in plenty, to see the birth of something more alive, more real than the stifling period of William II, when the mixture of artificial pasteboard romanticism and of cold-blooded economic imperialism seemed to us so hateful.

With her history, bold in thought and timid in deed, with her dreams and her *caporalisme,* with her fits of humility and of sudden arrogance, and even with her Nazi and racial rabidness that poorly hides a persistent inferiority complex, Germany's every feature tells us that, despite Bismarck's amazing success, she is not yet one, as France is. She is not "the Germanies" in the old Westphalian sense of the French reactionaries; even less is she so since the downfall of her presumptuous and at the same time cowardly Marxist Socialism; not the "two Germanies," in the rather facile sense in which Briand used the words a little too often toward the close of his career. Germany is twenty, thirty Germanies which clash in harrowing birth pangs. It is impossible to foresee whether she will crystallize as France did or whether she will remain for a long time yet an alarming volcano.

One fact is certain: books have been written—cases of intellectual sadism—on a pretended downfall of the French people or on the fall, which was said to be inevitable, of the British Empire, but no one thinks of writing about the "decadence" of Germany. All one can say in defense of the Germans is, that what they do and undergo may be explained by a long history of servility and passive obedience.

But it is in nobody's power to foretell how the future European Germany will crystallize, in what equilibrium, under which common laws.

V

FRENCH ERRORS: THE RUHR; DISARMAMENT

BRIAND would have been very much astonished if, in the days when among friends, me included, he criticized the Ruhr policy as it was applied by Poincaré in 1923, anyone had reminded him that, two years earlier, he too had spoken of "collaring Germany," a figure of speech which, already at that time, signified the Ruhr.

Briand would probably have shrugged his shoulders, as when Jaurès tried one day to apply to him Saint-Simon's words about Lauzun:

"One would not dare dream as you have lived."

Jaurès had in mind the thousand contradictions in Briand's life. But the latter, in good faith, did not see them. All he had meant, when he had spoken of "collaring Germany," was to extract a vote from the notorious militarist Chamber elected in the still intoxicated days of 1919— a Chamber which did not trust him; it would have been his business later on to find a compromise. For compromise was the essence of his character; he saw in it the only possible method and sole finality of political life. What he disliked most in the narrow patriotism of the nationalists was the odor of intolerance and of religious infallibility it exhaled; whence, for that matter, his indifference to accusations of lukewarmness, of betrayal even.

75

I met Briand after the Ruhr, during the occupation of
Corfu on which the Fascists, feverishly seeking a success
of some kind, had inconsiderately decided. Briand, who
knew he could talk freely with me, made ironical comments
on certain Italian liberal papers and men who, although
they were opposed to Fascism, pretended, for fear of seeming "unpatriotic," to approve of an enterprise from which
Italy would manifestly come out badly.

"And you, during the Ruhr? What else did you do?"
I could not help flinging at him.

Briand, with his nonchalant loyalty, owned that he had
suppressed his apprehensions and his misgivings in public.
But he added: "All the same, it was different. Maybe
we had to go through with it; we had overplayed the
Ruhr threat at home: the bubble had to be pricked."

The Ruhr myth, in point of fact, was slow to arise in
France. Toward the end of 1918, the Rhine population
was cruelly short of coal. A temporary occupation of the
Ruhr might then have been passed off quite legally, as far
as form was concerned; it would have been enough to make
use of one of the monthly renewals of the Armistice.

But Clemenceau constantly rejected the numerous suggestions which were made to him on this point. One in-
dustrialist from Lorraine thought he had persuaded him
to go into the Ruhr when Clemenceau, suddenly rising to
dismiss him, said:

"No, no, do not believe I shall risk the life of a single
French soldier to procure coal for you rich industrialists."

It was probably the only case, after the war, in which Clemenceau agreed with Foch. I have said elsewhere* how suspicious Foch was of the idea of the Ruhr occupation, that "frightful hornets' nest" as he often termed it in his conversations with me. It seemed strange, during the Spa Conference for instance, to those Frenchmen who advocated a policy of violent pressure on Germany and thought they could rely on Foch to uphold them. Indeed, already in 1919, the latter had wished to reduce the psychological and financial difficulties of the Rhine occupation to a minimum. Had he not, during the Peace Conference, on May 6, 1919, declared: "It is objected that I am occupying a country; that is wholly inaccurate; I am occupying the Rhine passages, and this requires very small forces."

In good faith, Foch forgot that these occupations never remain limited to the plan originally conceived. They inevitably swell out, by a sort of unconscious conspiring of military interests, in the professional sense of the word.

This was well brought out again by what happened about the Ruhr.

Originally, a "mission of engineers" was to be sent, escorted by "the detachments necessary to their security"; this is how the French and Belgian Governments notified their action to the German Government on January 10, 1923. A few weeks later, a real army had been sent into the Ruhr—into the "hornets' nest," as Foch had foretold.

---

* In *Makers of Modern Europe.*

It began with the troops shooting in Dortmund on unarmed crowds singing the *Wacht am Rhein* in the Koenigsalle; it ended with the arrest and prosecution of the most highly respected citizens of the region, with mass expulsions of thousands of employees whose only sin had been that they remained true to orders. The wave of disgust and shame that rolled over the French and Belgian troops at the task imposed on them speaks in favor of the sense of justice of both peoples. French and Belgian officers have acknowledged it to me. Unfortunately, in Germany the vexatious incidents created by silly young officers only too glad to play at "invasion" and "war" were more widely known.

The gravity of the situation soon obliterated the juridical reasons which had prompted Poincaré to strike his great blow. The lack of all proportions between a semi-mobilization and a shortage of one and one-half per cent in the total of German reparations in kind became all too obvious. The general public in France still does not know on what fallacious grounds the Ruhr occupation was decided.

And yet, this episode has a large share in the German grudges against France; it should not be lost sight of, to understand certain German reactions, that injuries suffered after peace are more difficult to forget than the horrors of war and especially so when the war was, alas, waged in other peoples' lands.

That is the reason why I think it necessary to say all I know about the matter. On January 3, 1923, a few days before the occupation of the Ruhr, Bonar Law* had proposed to the Paris Conference a plan of revision of German Reparations which constituted an unhoped-for windfall for France and Italy. The plan meant official recognition of the interdependence of reparations and war debts; complete cancellation of French and Italian debts to Great Britain; and thereby a tremendous argument in favor of a generous settlement of French and Italian debts to the United States, who could hardly have shown themselves less generous than the British Government.

---

*Bonar Law is almost forgotten as a British statesman; a new proof of the injustice of history. A sturdy Canadian, a man without imagination, he was a strong moral character. I knew him intimately before and after he became British Prime Minister in 1922-23 and I may testify that the French *beaux esprits* were wrong, at least about him, when they launched, during the Peace Conference, à propos of the three main British statesmen at the time in Paris:

> Balfour knows but does not believe;
> Bonar Law believes but doesn't know;
> Lloyd George neither knows nor believes.

The story of Bonar Law's offer of a compromise with France and Italy, the two war debtors in Europe toward Great Britain, is most amazing, although half forgotten.

Probably, only the state of health of Bonar Law at the time accounts for the failure of his generous and far-seeing attempt to settle with France, Italy and Belgium the common German reparations problem and that of the war debts.

In fact, he came to Paris to offer his plan in January, 1923, and he died in London a few months later. The doctors had advised him against the journey; they had gone so far as to tell him that he might die under such a strain. The Scotch Canadian answered simply:

"This is no argument."

Bonar Law's plan was a generous initiative. Its acceptance would have made for European reconciliation. It is certain at least that the main ideas of his plan were taken up again, years later, in identical fashion, in the Dawes Plan.

No one did justice to the plan or to its author. Worse still, in the countries most generously favored by it, like Italy, a press muzzled by the

If all this was lost, and with it a unique opportunity to
hasten on European reconciliation, it was due to the myth
of violent measures in the Ruhr which haunted so many
political writers in France. I said writers, and not statesmen; for I can testify to the lack of all real intent to
occupy the Ruhr on the part of all the French leaders
with whom I negotiated at so many inter-Allied Councils,
from Millerand to Leygues and to Briand. They all
wanted to use the word "Ruhr" as a sword of Damocles
which would drive the Germans to "execute." They all,
more or less, felt that the word might work wonders as
a threat, and disasters in practice. English advice was
often irritating in form. Italian advice, possibly more

Fascist censorship, covered Bonar Law with sarcasms. In France they
were more polite, but the lack of comprehension appeared just as complete.

Bonar Law had offered France and Italy precious concessions: British
solidarity on the question, still burning at the time, of the German reparations, and an official recognition of the interdependence of reparations and
inter-Allied debts. For Italy especially, the British plan was such that
the Italians could with difficulty have offered a better one themselves. In
fact, it simply meant the cancellation of all the Italian war debts to
England. Mussolini's refusal can only be explained by the fact that,
hardly come in power, he was desirous of such spectacular coups as might
strike imaginations.

Poincaré, who was French Prime Minister and Minister for Foreign
Affairs, refused because he was already thinking of the occupation of the
Ruhr; I have told in *Makers of Modern Europe* how I had felt that the
idea was gradually taking hold of him; I had been Ambassador to France
until the very eve of Bonar Law's arrival in Paris, and I knew that
Poincaré hoped that through the occupation of the Ruhr he might solve
the problem of French reparations and even of French security, without
any protective help from Britain. This was probably the most serious
blunder of the long career of Poincaré as a statesman.

After three poor days of angry discussions at the Quai d'Orsay, Bonar
Law's offer was rejected by the French and Italian Governments under
the meanest of motives. Bonar Law was already a dying man and he

useful because more cordial and less showy, was not lacking to them, for that matter, either at Spa or at Boulogne,
or in London, between July, 1920, and May, 1921. During
the three conferences, I was head of the Italian delegation;
and in spite of my friendship for France, or rather because
of it, I always spoke very clearly.

The great Ruhr mistake would not have happened if
Poincaré, on coming back to power, had not felt himself
more or less bound by his chronicles in the *Revue des deux
Mondes;* and especially if Italy, in the hands of Fascism
for the past eight weeks, had not sinned against her most
essential duties and interests by urging the rejection of
the Bonar Law proposals, by voting, at the Reparations
Commission, the Pharisaic statement of the German de-

---

failed to make his language understood. It was one of the frequent cases
in post-war conferences when a moderating Italian influence might have
been precious. But unfortunately Rome was already on the side of
demagogy and rash schemes.

Three months after his failure in Paris, Bonar Law was seeking in
the calm of Aix-les-Bains, in Savoy, a relief for his dreadful sufferings.
As I happened to be the guest of French friends in a neighboring chateau,
he asked to see me. He wanted to learn from me the explanation, if
possible, of what was still a riddle to his clear honest mind: why his plan,
so useful to France, so precious to Italy, had been rejected with jeers
and sarcasms.

I told him, sitting two hours on the terrace of his room, with the Lake
of Bourget at our feet, and in the distance the charming Savoyard hills,
what I believed had been his psychological mistakes, and his advisers', in
the presentation of the plan; and where he and his officials had lacked
the necessary persuasive power.

After a long silence, and with a sad smile, Bonar Law answered me:
"I see. Had Lloyd George offered a third of what I brought them, they
would have knelt at his feet. . . ."

But there was no bitterness toward his more brilliant colleague, rather
a stoical expression of contempt for the touch of demagogic vulgarity
which so often appears to be a necessary element of success in public life.

faults, thereby furnishing Poincaré with the juridical implement he needed to start the occupation.

The French bitterly resented the comparison with Shylock and his pound of flesh which went the round of the newspapers of the whole world during the Ruhr polemics. The average Frenchman knew he had not wanted the war; his harsh exaction of "reparations" was mainly based on the old Roman and now arch-French feeling that a law must not be violated; it is typical of the provincial Frenchman that he prefers winning a lawsuit and losing the money, to recovering part of the cash and losing the suit.

The inconceivable opposition by which Poincaré and his sudden ally, Mussolini, wrecked the salutary Bonar Law Plan prepared the ground for the Ruhr stroke. But a legal pretext was necessary. It was sought in paragraphs 17 and 18 of Annex II to Part VIII of the Treaty of Versailles, paragraphs vague in form and not precise in aims, to which Poincaré had already referred every time he wanted to prove that the French Government would act. Under Poincaré's pressure, the Reparations Commission began by doing away quite arbitrarily with the distinction between simple non-execution as provided under paragraph 17, and "willful" non-execution as provided under paragraph 18; and proclaimed, on December 26, 1922, that both terms were equivalent; that any German default was "willful" and that, consequently, the "respective" governments were entirely free to proceed.

On the same day, the Reparations Commission rendered a further service to Poincaré. For the first time it officially registered a shortage in the German deliveries in timber.

Germany had to deliver to France before the end of 1922 fifty-five thousand cubic meters of timber boards and two hundred thousand cubic meters of telegraph poles. But on December 15, 1922, she had delivered only thirty-five thousand cubic meters of boards and sixty-five thousand cubic meters of telegraph poles.

Aside from the circumstance that it was premature to record a shortage before the final term of delivery had been reached, the German Government had substantiated the delay in a manner that had seemed both honest and true to most of the delegates of the Reparations Commission, before the problem took on a political aspect. The Belgian delegate Delacroix, an eminent jurist, who had been my colleague at the Spa Conference, was very definite to me on this point.

For, on receipt of the French orders which had only arrived in the spring, the Reich Government had immediately got in touch with those *Länder* who were also forest owners and, by way of additional precaution, had even signed contracts directly with timber merchants. But when the mark fell, the latter had contested the validity of the contracts; and the government had been obliged to pass new ones with them on the basis of the gold mark. To this first cause of loss of time two more were added: the difficulties made by the French agents who had refused large deliveries; and the unusual size of the telegraph poles. Furthermore the German Government, while showing it had done its best, asked that the term of delivery be extended till March 31, 1923, promising to furnish the missing quantities of timber by that date.

This was a manifest token of its good faith.

But Poincaré asked the Reparations Commission to have the shortage put on record, and the Commission yielded.

Immediately afterward he asked the Commission to register a shortage in the coal deliveries. The German experts were able to prove that the shortage amounted to only fifteen per cent (about eleven million instead of thirteen million tons) and called the attention of the Commission to the fact that the shortage did not exceed the limits normally allowed for. But the Commission, which should have been an independent juridical body, had agreed to obey, and decided on January 9, 1923, that the non-delivery by Germany of fifteen per cent of the coal she owed must constitute a new default.

At the Reparations Commission, the British delegate alone always voted against, the Italian voted with, his French colleague. It was the time when Mussolini, newly come to power, declared in his interviews that the vaults of the German Reichsbank overflowed with gold ingots and that the Allies only had "to go and take them." Belgian Government and delegate reasoned more seriously, but what could they do? Had Italy gone over to England's side, they would have been freer; but as the situation was in January, 1923, they could only go on Poincaré's side. Belgium had been occupied for four years; it was only too natural that average Belgian public opinion should declare itself in favor of a policy that—requital of Fate— would bring King Albert's soldiers on German soil.

On January 11, 1923, Poincaré, announcing to the Chambers that the Ruhr occupation was decided, declared, alluding to the shortage in the coal deliveries, that since Germany had not supplied the coal she owed, there was nothing left for France to do but go and take it on the spot.

It was one of those catchpenny phrases which, in all assemblies under the sun, are always certain to draw wild applause. And of course applause did not fail this time either.

A few months later, right in the thick of the occupation, the Paris weekly, *Rire,* published a caricature of a French general who, wrapped up in his fur-lined coat and shivering, was writing from the Ruhr to Paris: "Everything is in our hands here. The only thing we lack is coal. Send some immediately."

The French ended by realizing that the occupation of the Ruhr had been one of those mistakes that do more harm than a crime. Even those circles which, for reasons of home politics, maintain that "a strong hand has good points," cannot disguise any more the fact to themselves.

But the extent and gravity of the consequences of the occupation in Germany have never been made sufficiently well known in France.

Indeed, whatever the mental reservations of the German Government, whatever the obstinate grudges of the German nationalists, nothing prevented the anonymous collaboration of the average man—the man that counts most—in the pacifying policy of Locarno more than the remembrance of the Ruhr and of the separatist movements. There had been before, in Germany, upholders of an *Erfüllungspolitik* (fulfillment of the treaties). None was to be found afterward.

By its supreme mistake of isolated action, the French Government succeeded in concentrating on France alone the "patriotic" resentment of the Germans, who, when they were spared the sight of an Italian contingent, forgot that Mussolini had shared with Poincaré the responsibility of the occupation.

It is, after all, possible that resentment would not have died down in Germany, even without the Ruhr.

But it is unfortunate that France, led astray by a press campaign, and Italy, fallen in the hands of extemporizers, should have given the German nationalists a tremendous argument in support of their contention that all the talk of the Entente as to right, and justice, and respect of treaties, only amounted to war stratagems.

It may well be that Hitler and the whole Nazist adventure would never have counted for anything in the history of Germany had it not been for the gross error of the Ruhr.

The artificial brakes put on disarmament did not irritate the Germans so much. But it nevertheless constitutes a second serious mistake on the part of Germany's former enemies. From a judicial point of view, the disarmament problem was, after the war, absolutely self-evident.

"In order to render possible the initiation of a general limitation of the armaments of all nations, Germany under-

takes . . ." Thus begins the Preamble to Part V of
the Treaty of Versailles, concerning the military clauses
imposed on Germany.

And Article 8 declares that "the members of the League
recognize that the maintenance of peace requires the reduction of national armaments to the lowest point consistent
with safety. . . ."

Treaties are often interpreted in the light of the official
discussions held prior to them. What do we find in these?

The note sent by Clemenceau to the German delegation
on May 22, 1919, in the name of all the Allies, acknowledged "with satisfaction the fact that the German Government is in favor of disarmament" and assured the
Germans that their former enemies were preparing "plans
concerning international disarmament."

The answer of the German delegation confirmed that
the Reich was ready to disarm first, but "on condition
that it be the beginning of a general reduction of the
armaments of all the nations." The German note even
specified that it must be understood that "two years later,
after the conclusion of peace . . . the adversaries shall
proceed to limit their armaments and to repeal compulsory
military service."

The Allies' answer, on June sixteenth, stipulated no
reservations whatever. On the contrary, it confirmed that
"the allied and associate Powers recognize that Germany's
acceptance of the terms provided for her disarmament
will facilitate and hasten on the carrying out of a general
reduction of armaments . . ."; that this German disarmament "constitutes the first step towards this reduc-

tion and this general limitation of armaments . . . to be achieved as being one of the best means of preventing war."

"Preventing war": therefore, a source of security.

This was the period of sincerity. We were just out of the furnace; we had not yet forgotten, not yet consulted military experts.

At Geneva, the latter took the upper hand again. Most often, the technical discussions on disarmament were nothing but bargains for a mutual sacrifice of out-fashioned items, with a possibility of having more recent models substituted for them. The fact was probably bewailed that halberds and two-handed swords had already all been consigned to museums. One would willingly have started a negotiation in order to insure to the various peoples this novel advantage: the suppression of engines too old-fashioned and too simple to be a source of serious profit to the arms factories.

There is no doubt that the non-fulfillment of certain pledges of the Versailles Treaty has proffered arguments to those of the Germans who, before and after the advent of Nazism, said: "We have been waiting since 1919; either the victors of Versailles will keep their word, or we shall arm as they have done, better than they; if they have their security to safeguard, we have ours."

Whoever could have believed that a great people, placed in the center of Europe, would remain disarmed, surrounded by armed neighbors?

Even the Treaty of Versailles did not dare to contemplate that possibility; a treaty which had yet been so optimistic as to base the reparations system on this psychologically crazy principle: Germany will work for us for generations; and the more she will work, the more shall she pay.

Clemenceau, for that matter, willingly admitted that he had been a stranger to the economic and financial discussions of the treaty. Arguments of this type were abhorrent to his literary and philosophic mind. But well he knew the history of the relations between the two peoples. His own most painful personal recollections should have been sufficient, indeed, to teach him that if Germany in 1871 had inflicted on France conditions of disarmament similar to those of 1919—minus the promise of the consecutive disarmament of everyone—the immense majority of Frenchmen would have considered it a patriotic duty to evade them, to violate them.

He knew also that under the Treaty of Paris of 1856 Russia had been forbidden to have ships in the Black Sea, but that as soon as the French losses of 1870 had occurred, the Petersburg Cabinet merely had to take the trouble of signifying to London, Paris and Vienna that this clause had now become null and void, and that everybody agreed.

Fourteen months after Tilsit, on September 8, 1808, Napoleon imposed a disarmament convention on the King of Prussia.* Under this convention, the King of Prussia

---

* For fourteen months Napoleon, busy with his mad Spanish adventure, forgot the disarmament of Prussia: a further proof of the executive paralysis which dictators sometimes provoke around them, no one daring to take their place, no one daring to make suggestions that might look like blame intended for the "infallible."

"wishing to avoid anything that might give umbrage to France" undertook (Article I) "to maintain for ten years, as from January 1, 1809" forty-two thousand men only.

And Article 2 added: "The ten years over, H. M. the King of Prussia will once more be subject to common law and maintain the number of troops he shall think fit according to circumstances."

Prussia amounted to very little in 1808 as compared with the sixty-five million men of twentieth-century Germany. The French Empire was then the most formidable power in the world; and yet Napoleon dared to inflict only a ten years' disarmament on Prussia. The imperial Ambassador, Count di San Marzano, was, or believed he was, the master in Berlin; and the control exercised by San Marzano and the numerous French officers he had at his disposal never had any results. At the very moment when the Prussian plenipotentiaries signed the disarmament convention in Paris, Stein wrote to King Frederick William III that the treaty could not prevent him from "protecting himself by cunning against villainy and violence. . . . Will it be permitted to the Emperor Napoleon only," continued Stein, "to substitute arbitrariness for right, and his lies for truth?"

Such was the first French experience of disarmament in Germany.

San Marzano himself, when he had returned to his Turin after 1815 and had once more become a subject of the King of Sardinia, wrote that it was impossible to imagine it might have been otherwise.

Heine it is who told us that Germany had not yet for-
given the beheading of Conradin, but it is a Frenchman—
a Frenchman who always allied the most ardent patriotism
with a Hellenic serenity of mind—Jules Cambon, whom
I heard admit more than once that the harm done to
France by Louis XIV's prestige policy was not yet entirely
dispelled. . . .

The Treaty of Westphalia stabilized the "Germanies"
of which Maurice Barrès still dreamed and wrote from
1914 to the day of his death in 1923,* but probably less
than is generally believed; in reality the Westphalia Treaty
strengthened Prussia, thus causing the birth of a new center
of Germanic reorganization. But, for the time being, it
had left the German world bereft of the framework and
even of the semblance of a State; and ever since 1648,
this has been considered the masterpiece of French
diplomacy. Just as the 1815 Treaty of Vienna, with the
division of Italy, was Metternich's masterpiece.

Insecure triumphs, like everything begotten of pure
diplomacy and not of life.

It was Napoleon who unconsciously wrought the destruction of a century and a half of French diplomacy. It
looked like a crazy wager: populations which had been
left under a slow-moving and somnolent rule he threw
in the furnace of rising nationalism, while at the same
time he wounded this feeling in them by his every act.
Napoleon had found a phantom as sublime as it was vain:
the Holy Roman Empire. He threw the worm-eaten

---

* Or more precisely, pretended to dream. As I knew him, Barrès struck
me as the devotee of a single creed: Art.

edifice to the ground, failing to realize that a nation, a great living nation would one day take the place of the old toy on the world stage.

Who knows? Had the Germans ripened politically within the framework of a national régime all the while that the French Kings from Versailles rejoiced at their slumbering, they would perhaps today constitute less troublesome neighbors for France.

Déroulède* was inevitable in France under President Grévy.

The nationalist fever was just as incvitable in Hindenburg's Germany, whatever the form, Hitlerian or other, it took on. Especially seeing the pitiful failure of the Socialist party which alone could have set the country toward other feelings and other ideals.

Certain feverish, violent fits of ulcerated nationalism inevitably manifest themselves among the beaten people; if they also broke out in victorious Italy it was because the nationalist rhetoricians, unable to see the truth that lies beyond words, failed to understand how great, how fruitful the Italian victory might have been just because it had remained moderate.

If the fits seem so much more violent in Germany than they were in France after 1871 it is because the psychology of the German masses is far more unbalanced in its *Überschwenglichkeit* (sentimental redundancy). And also because France in 1871 was never afraid of dying; and Germany in 1919 was, at certain moments, quite panic-

---

* 1846-1914; founder of the *Ligue des Patriotes* after the 1870 war; author of the popular martial *Chants du Soldat*.

stricken; as when she thought she would lose the left bank of the Rhine.*

Charles Maurras, the head of the French nationalist writers, has written somewhere: "From 1871 to 1890, France was governed by Queen Revenge" (*la reine Revanche*).

Why till 1890 only? Not because the new generations had disowned the legacy of sad memories which their elders had transmitted to them. But the Russian alliance had given the French the feeling that they were no longer the victims of defeat, that they were no longer alone.

Ten years after the Treaty of Frankfort (1871), France was able to go to Tunisia. The German Government then—the era of bad copies of Bismarck had not yet dawned—favored not only the occupation of Tunisia, but the whole colonial policy of the Third Republic.

Who shall dare to deny peremptorily that the interest of France, ten years after the Treaty of Versailles, might have prompted her to a conduct just as tolerant, as far-seeing? . . .

One Frenchman only, an old man who had during the war personified the spirit of resistance, one day dared to stand up in Parliament and, in one of those fits of proud sincerity which atoned for so many dark faults of his, said to his compatriots the necessary words.

---

* In his book, *Les grands Problèmes du Rhin,* Maurice Barrès tells that Clemenceau one day said to him: "The Germans will not pay, and we shall stay on." It was the mad idea of the everlasting tribute; and Germany felt it only too well. It is strange that Barrès did not understand that disclosures of this nature were not useful to the policy he was following.

It was Georges Clemenceau, then still at the zenith of his power and his popularity. Other Frenchmen had sketched the point even in the presence of a stranger like myself: among them Bourgeois,* in a long conversation we had together at the Villa Borghese in Rome, during the Roman Session of the Council of the League of Nations in May, 1920; or, later on, Ribot† in Paris.

But they had kept silent in Parliament.

Here are the essential parts of the speech Clemenceau made in the Senate on November 11, 1919:

"We are the masters. However, if we desire a conciliation which shall be useful to our children and the future we shall, to insure its lasting, handle our mastery with sufficient and adequate moderation. . . . To those Italian diplomats who do not understand that they must make friends with the Serbs and the Slavs, failing which there can be no peace in Europe, I often say: 'Unite with them instead of making enemies of them.'

"I should almost say the same thing concerning the Germans."

What did he mean by "almost"? A reservation?

The man continued with honest frankness and owned that he had hated them too much, the Germans, that he still hated them too much to see straight.

"I will not go and fetch them; I do not feel for them as I should; I prefer not to see them."

But after this avowal, in which one can almost feel that

---

* One of the founders of the League of Nations; Nobel Peace prize, 1920; died, 1925.

† French Prime Minister, 1885 and 1917; died, 1923.

he still suffered from bearing the scars of 1870-71 and 1914-18, he went on:

"All the same, sixty million men in the center of Europe take up room, especially when the men are remarkably clever men, men of science, methodical men, who have shown first-rate qualities in the industrial field. Have we any interest in denying it? Is it not the truth?"

The speech had struck me, for I was one of those Italians who held—and, might I say? with no need of advice from abroad—that it was a supreme interest for Italy to make a lasting peace with the Yugoslavs. But when I began writing this book and tried to find Clemenceau's words, I vainly asked Frenchmen from the Ministry of Foreign Affairs for the date of the speech. By a strange phenomenon, everybody had forgotten it; a recollection of his warning might have troubled the consciences. . . .

May I add an historical recollection which is quite as well forgotten? It would not have been displeasing to Clemenceau whom his enemies so often called "the Englishman."

The countries which finally conquered France at Waterloo had all in turn been allies. All save one: England.

In no country was hatred of the Corsican as deep and as constant as in England. With the English, far more than with the Germans, this hatred was mingled with a feeling of haughty aversion for the people who had accepted the bloodstained dictatorship.

And yet, with the advent of peace, this came to pass: that selfish England alone spontaneously returned most of the territories she had conquered during the long

struggle. Réunion, Guadeloupe, Martinique, St. Pierre
and Miquelon, Senegal, Gambia were returned to France.
Spain recovered San Domingo, Denmark her West Indies,
and the Netherlands the very wealthy Sunda Islands.

Lord Castlereagh wrote, defending these decisions
against the annexationists in his country: "I firmly believe
that our reputation for strength, true power, loyalty, is
more important for us on the Continent than any doubtful
acquisitions we might keep."

At the same time, Bonaparte at St. Helena was dictat-
ing contemptuous remarks on the "extreme stupidity and
ignorance" of Lord Castlereagh. The ex-Emperor was
wondering in astonishment why the English had not kept
"Hamburg, Java, Sumatra and Martinique."

Bonaparte's surprise at St. Helena at this policy of
territorial generosity, says much for his utter incapacity to
understand the most elementary lessons of history—and of
his own history. This possibly helps to explain why all
Napoleon's military successes were nothing but obstacles
to a happy peace for France.

Just a century later, another soldier—whom, rightly or
wrongly, we considered for years the military genius of
Germany in arms—Ludendorf, displayed an identical
degree of misapprehension. On August 26, 1918, he
presented the Chancellor of the Reich with a peace draft
wherein the evacuation of Belgium was to be proffered
only in exchange for other guarantees on the enemy's part,
among them "England's renunciation of Calais."

It is the men endowed with this amount of moral
perspicacity who loaded Germany with the heavy historical

responsibility for the peace of Bucharest, and that of
Brest-Litowsk. Russians and Rumanians have forgotten
them. Nothing remains of them so far as they are concerned. But Frenchmen can quote them against Germany:
"And you, what would you have done, had you been
victorious? Bucharest and Brest-Litowsk can tell us."*

---

* Herr von Kühlmann was one of the makers of the peace of Brest-
Litowsk. In 1921 the French writer, Lucien Herr, asked him how a man
as far-sighted as he, Kühlmann, ever came to countenance such a useless
piece of work.

And Kühlmann said:

"I agree with you, but what could I do? And what could Czernin
do, who thought as I did? Berlin had given full powers to General
Hoffmann only; the General was the victor; he felt certain of the
wonderful results of his formula. . . ."

Quite so; but what had Herr von Kühlmann and so many others who
thought like him, ever done before to curtail in Germany the power of all
the Hoffmanns?

VI

GERMAN SUICIDES: SOCIALISTS, JÜNKER

IT WAS Bismarck who remarked one day:

"If a future generation of Germans ever becomes republican, it will be for lack of kings, certainly not of royalists."

The more one studies the sayings and doings of the Social-Democracy in Germany, the more one feels how appropriate the jest.

The heaviest responsibility of German Marxism toward social history will be that it paved the way—it matters little whether or not Marx wanted it—for an atmosphere of indifference to the conquests of liberty. The easy defeat of the Socialist parties in those countries where they had seemed so formidably organized—and where, in so many practical ways, they sometimes constituted very useful elements of economic and social progress—originated in this essential failure of the German Mother Church: its failure to comprehend the necessity of freedom.

From its very first footsteps, German Social-Democracy was imbued with adoration of the State, thanks to Ferdinand Lassalle, a tribune of the Hegelian school and of imperious temperament.* The hope of soon using, on

---

* The two main points of Lassalle's program were universal suffrage and State Socialism; but he regarded the latter as the more important; the former being for him only a means to an end.

behalf of the "Fourth Estate," the resources of a strong government implied intrinsic approval of the methods adopted by the Prussian monarchy, its unique tone of command included, the dignity of which was enhanced by assimilation to Kant's Categorical Imperative. The atmosphere of "victories and conquests" prevalent between 1864 and 1871 emphasized in all classes of German society an unreasoned admiration for force, for the "enlightened" despotism to which they felt they owed the then beginning prosperity; the Workmen's party, whose rapid rise was in proportion to the increasing comfort, could not remain entirely untouched by surroundings. Opposed to the very restricted number of democrats whom prolonged exile in London had really accustomed to knowledge and love of freedom—such as Wilhelm Liebknecht and, in the following generation, Edward Bernstein—were chiefs like August Bebel or Vollmar, men of very high moral standing and heroic probity, who yet never suspected one could be unhappy in (well-kept) barracks nor fail to thank fate for having been born a German and thereby been saved from the moral frivolity or lack of intellectual depth (*Gründlichkeit*) characteristic of all other peoples, especially the English, the French, the Italians.

Of course, they felt neither respect for, nor love of, William II and—still less—the *Junker* of the right bank of the Elbe; but they considered their duty fully done when they gave themselves up entirely to organizing the masses with a view to an increase in their material welfare and their technical capacities.

Unfortunately, if they reaped success in this field, where

the tireless methodical German mind, tenacious discipline
and sense of an accurate distribution of petty material
responsibilities could give their full measure, this success
in its turn inured the leaders of the Socialist party to
deprivation of political liberties. The "rights of man and
of citizen" faded into abstract "principles" all the more
sacred that they were less often touched upon. The leaders
soon came to dread all serious struggle in the field of pure
politics. Might it not turn the energies of the proletariat
away from the "constructive work" and endanger the
magnificent material results so laboriously acquired? Such
the reason they alleged to others and to themselves; a
true reason indeed, even if a certain unavowed fear of the
"high hand" of the government helped to confirm them
in their pendent doctrinal attitude.

The doctrine of historical materialism countenanced,
for that matter, a certain amount of contempt for "constitutional questions." The doctrine stilled the voice of
conscience; it was known—had Marx not said it?—that
the proletarian drive must needs succeed automatically;
"effective liberty" would therefore be established without
effort on the day the proletariat achieved a predominant
situation in the "play of productive forces."

Indeed, under cover of the Marxist formulas, considered
more revolutionary than any others, the German Social-
Democracy merely continued the special mentality of the
old German liberalism. Just like the liberals who preceded
them, the Socialists were so full of reverence for the
technical bounties of the State that they held any encroach-
ments on the personal rights of citizens to be bearable

annoyances. On the other hand, they apparently never suspected the incompatibility that lay between the policy of expansion practiced by imperial Germany and the European solidarity which, since the eighteenth-century thinkers, had become an essential ideal of democratic action.

Throughout the nineteenth century the solidarity between the democratic parties fighting, in the different countries of Europe, for the emancipation of the disinherited masses and of the oppressed nations, was ardently extolled and more than once sanctioned by examples of romantic heroism. But never, that I know of, in Germany.

During his fifty years of propaganda for the republican idea and European federation, Mazzini never found a German at his side. Chateaubriand came to Italy and discovered that, in spite of her shackles, she was "ripe for freedom." A Frenchman, Andryane, went one better still: conspiring with Pellico and Maroncelli, he got himself condemned by the Emperor of Austria to durance vile for life in the jails of the Spielberg. The French engineer Laviron fell defending Mazzini's republican Rome against Oudinot's troops, and said that he died for Italy and for France. One does not hear of Germans who, like the Italians Nullo and Bechi, died for freedom in the plains of Poland, resisting the Czar's troops. It is impossible to conceive of a German rival to Armand Carrel fighting with the Spanish liberals against the French expedition to Spain led by the Duc d'Angoulême.

At the Frankfort Parliament, which aimed at laying the foundations of a German democracy, vehement speeches

were made, by members who believed themselves warm
Freisiniggere (liberals), to reject, in the name of the
unwritten rights of the Teutonic Order, all Polish claims
toward Poznan, however modest they might be, just as
the equally feudal rights of the Holy Roman Empire
over the Bishopric of Trent were learnedly put forward
against Italian aspirations to unification.

This state of mind was inherited—unconsciously, but all
the more definitely—by most of the Socialists of Germany.
Never did the persecutions of the Alsatians, the Poles in
Poznan or the Danes in Slesvig cause among the Social
Democrats any movement comparable in the least to
Shelley's indignation at the English oppression of Ireland.

Marx himself never had anything but suspicious sarcasms
for the miracle of the Italian Risorgimento. They who
are so blind when others are concerned prepare a sterile
future for themselves.

On the eve of the European war, the Social-Democrat
party was nothing but a gigantic administrative organization: the body tremendous, but the soul very puny. Liebknecht, Vollmar and Bebel gone, the fierce and impractical
younger Liebknecht suspected even by his own for his
unbending freaks, the party at its congresses continued to
vote the revolutionary phrases of the past, but everybody
knew they constituted a mere matter of ritual formulas.
The idea of an unheaval of the State would have horrified
the party leaders; like the Socialists in Italy who voted
against Giolitti and prayed to God he might remain in
power forever. Happy in their success, proud of the
parliamentary respectability they had earned for them-

selves, their conscience at rest because of the development of Social Insurances, why should the Socialist leaders have wished for a change? Therefore, and for even pettier reasons than Bismarck—with Bismarck it was contempt for everybody; with them, suspicion of intelligence—an inverse selection resulted for all the party offices. Any ardent personality was set aside for fear he or she might not always bow down to the mardarins. Promotions, including nominations to the Reichstag, became exclusive rewards for exactitude, for formal discipline, for all the qualities required of a good lower middle-class employee.

The narrow distrust with which the Socialist party kept out Franz Mehring, the only brilliant writer German Socialism could boast of, remains as a manifest token of the real fear the Socialist leaders had of original brains and of iconoclasts. Had Mehring not dared to write a book—cruel and unjust, perhaps, but luscious—criticizing the work of His Majesty King Frederick II?

The bigwigs of the party, nodding their respectable heads with ever lessening indulgence, noted that the younger Liebknecht was always haunting Russian revolutionaries. It must have been due to these sorry companions that the young barrister insolently submitted to the congresses of the party plans of action entirely devoid of "caution"; and, in order to countenance "Karlchen's" extravagance, they had to remember that most of the old comrades had held him on their knee and that his father was, so to speak, canonized. As for Rosa Luxemburg, they only rallied from the terror her cutting irony and undaunted dialectics inspired by dint of repeating to themselves Heine's verse on alien trouble-makers: "*Auslander sind es, fremde Leute* (they are aliens, a foreign people)." There was no danger that good German comrades of either sex would be led astray by this Slav incendiary.

The "steadier" Socialists contributed to the *Socialistische Monatshefte,* the organ of the moderate or Right faction, whose influence was gaining sway over the managing boards of the party and the syndicates. Economic nationalism, stretching from high protective tariffs to dumping, might, after all, promote a rise of salaries as well as of profits. The development of sea-power, the exploitation of colonies and such grand schemes as the Bagdad Railway and the organization of a *Mitteleuropa* first awakened the keen curiosity of the specialists of the Socialist party, and finally captured their imagination, always ready to be attracted, as the only thing that mattered, by the technical problems bearing on the material progress of the German people.

In spite of their sincere aversion for perilous adventures, and although any perfidious intention of considering the *Internationale* covenant as a "scrap of paper" was entirely alien to them, the Socialist leaders, in July and August, 1914, were entirely incapable of withstanding the war fever and of refusing prompt adhesion to a "sacred union."

Although they admitted the inner struggle by which they were torn, between their desire to be loyal toward their common German fatherland and equally loyal to their Socialistic ideals, I do not think I am being unfair if I say that during the three crucial moments of the war they reacted as follows:

—at the declaration of war, a sign of satisfaction when the danger of Czarist invasion gave to some a reason, and to others an alibi, for not dissociating their dual feelings;

—during the Russian Revolution of 1917, cruel embarrassment which led them, much against their secret desire, to assume a more independent attitude toward the government and military command; but even then, they did not see far afield: all they came to was a formula of peace without annexations or war indemnities; and even so, they only followed in the wake of the Catholic Center, and relieved by the agreement and advice of a few clear-sighted and anguished high officials;

—at the end of the war, deepest surprise and terror on hearing of the first rebellions of the German soldiers and sailors and the flight to Holland of the War Lord.

It is in no way due to the conduct of its leaders, but only to the obdurate prejudices of the ruling cast, who did not understand that it was their interest to appoint Scheidemann or Noske or Ebert at the head of some Ministry during the war, that the Social-Democracy kept its prestige with the masses almost unimpaired until the end of 1918 and later saw it increase.

But quite reluctantly did the Socialist party, thunderstruck by the defeat of the imperial armies, let the discontented elements gather around the Red Flag it was compelled to unearth. And it must be added, to boot, that only a minority of the parliamentary group (Haase, etc.) consented to have dealings with the "seditious elements"—Berlin workmen, Kiel sailors, soldiers in a fair way of deserting; that these "independents" were blamed and disowned by most of the Socialist leaders; and that Kurt Eissner, who was head of the insurrection in Bavaria, was also a dissident.

All this shows very clearly what dread of responsibilities and what repugnance to any idea of "revolution" froze the soul of the poor German Social-Democracy when a supreme task fell to its lot after the flight of William II to Holland.

The very idea of having to assume the responsibilities of government horrified the Socialist leaders.

I have from a friend of Prince Max von Baden a report of the short conversation which took place between the Imperial Chancellor and Fritz Ebert who had become head of the Socialist party, after having, in honest and mediocre fashion, climbed all the rungs of the "career."

"I leave the Reich in your hands, Herr Ebert."

"I shall do my best, Your Highness. Have I not given the lives of my children to the Reich?"

Loyal, and even moving words. But was not this a regular transmission of powers in a continuous administration? Ebert and his men did not understand—or would not understand—that the disgraceful fall of the dynasty imposed new duties on Socialists and Germans. They did not even understand what should have been obvious to everyone in Germany, that a Socialist party breaking radically with the past might have hoped to wrest more favorable peace conditions for the Reich in Paris. But not at all. And Hermann Müller came to Paris to sign the Versailles Treaty with such a beaten soul as Count Brockdorff-Rantzau never would have shown.

The same was true in home politics. No sooner were
they in power than the Socialists behaved as if they had
but one single thought in mind: to win over, by dint of
moderation and humility, the masters of the imperial era.
Magistrates, high officials, dignitaries of the Lutheran
Church who had become so deeply enfeoffed to the dynasty,
they all expected destitutions, radical changes. They soon
perceived that the orders were: "Change things as little
as possible"; that the only plague-stricken were Liebknecht and Rosa Luxemburg, the heretics of the Socialist
party. The old officials began to breathe again. They
found a new courage. And the more the Republican Government treated them with infinite clemency, the more they
despised the new régime. The murderers of Liebknecht
and Rosa Luxemburg, whom everybody knew, were not
even prosecuted. The young Bavarian *Geborene* who had
assassinated Kurt Eissner was pardoned.*

The government's ridiculous tolerance of those officials
who had betrayed it during the Kapp *Putsch* (1920)†
made general, among magistrates and officials, the *sabotage*

---

* This leniency toward the assassins of "extremists" is also colored by
something like hatred between neighbors if one remembers that the Socialists
did succeed in having ten years' forced labor inflicted on the man who
attempted the life of Scheidemann, one of the official bonzes of the party.
Yet the story of this attempt is mainly reminiscent of the misadventures
of Monsieur de Pourceaugnac: the "murderer" had met Scheidemann while
he was taking a walk and pursued him brandishing . . . a syringe
(which, it was asserted later, contained prussic acid) till the former
Socialist Minister, untouched, fainted, but from fright only.

† Captain Pabst, then trusty lieutenant of the Socialist Noske, was one
of the promoters of the Kapp *Putsch*. Dismissed (but promoted to the
rank of commander) he organized the Austrian Heimwehren and also
had "business dealings" with Italian Fascism.

of a régime that trusted so little in its own power. Insults
to Ebert and the Republican régime became a most popular
game as soon as it was known that the judges let the
insulters off. This would never have happened had the
government dared to bring an action like that which
Azana (who, incidentally, had not spent his time in Spain
condemning the *bourgeois*) did not hesitate to bring against
General Sanjurjo. But the Socialist leaders did not even
dare to contemplate punishing the manifest complicity of
the *Jünker* by measures similar to the expropriation of the
Spanish Grandees ordered by the non-Socialist Government
of Madrid after the monarchist attempt of the summer
of 1932.

Instead of that, the Socialists in Berlin never put a
stop to their servility. A forgotten detail: they even
went so far as to authorize the detachment that had
shared in the Kapp *Putsch* to take their quarters, armed,
in the Rittergüter of Mecklemburg to protect the lands
of the feudal lords against the agrarian claims of the
landless peasants.

But, if all this is more or less known, the psychological
reasons are less known which explain and connect the
errors of judgment and of conduct committed by the
Socialist Government in foreign and military affairs, affairs
even more closely connected in post-war Germany than
elsewhere.

Sincerely devoted to peace, desirous of giving an example
of cruel sacrifice, too frightened over a hypothetical danger
of French sanctions, they never learned to negotiate, I
mean negotiate seriously. How could they, since they

felt so weak even at home? At Versailles, as I have said before, Hermann Müller certainly believed he was serving his country. But he never found the right accents which would have seemed so natural in the mouth of the representative of a party that might have said, like Goethe at Valmy: "Here begins a new history. We will it so." And it was nearly always thus—for instance, when the same Hermann Müller, replacing Stresemann who was ill, at Geneva in September, 1928, allowed Germany's position to be compromised in those international negotiations that later produced the unfortunate Young Plan.

Weaknesses of this kind were bad even for France, where they were entitled to think that, since Germany had finally given in, the few former petty tussles were nothing but the tricks of debtors who had tried not to pay up.

Feeling vaguely that others would have put up a better fight than they, the Socialists sought steadily a patriotic alibi in the incredible weakness they always showed toward the mysteries of the military budgets. Not only, so long as they were out of power, did they confine their efforts to platonic resolutions which the heads of the Reichswehr would not even condescend to notice; but, when they came back to the Chancellery in March, 1928, they adopted at once as their own the Reichswehr program as Hindenburg supported it. Odder still, the Socialists, for over ten years, had in their power a magnificent body of troops, the *Schupo,* with which they might have kept the high hand over the rebellious chiefs of the Reichswehr. They thought so little of using it to this end that, at the crucial moment, this "rampart of Republican institutions" went over to Schleicher without a moment's hesitation.

To get the Socialists' assent to a reduction of democracy to absurdity, the *Junker* only had to scare them by using the words "national interest" in a manner implying the formula so dear to the Prussian military: "And above all, don't try to understand."

In September, 1930, the masses, discouraged, began to vote for the Communists or for the Nazis. It spelled the beginning of the downfall, even numerically speaking, of the party which had been the strongest party in Germany.

Old Bebel, of yore, had had bitter words for the *Bedientenseele*—servile soul—of the Germans. And yet he had not witnessed anything approaching the cringing respect which the Socialists, when to all appearances they were masters of Germany, manifested for generals, industrialists, *Jünker,* with the result that the masses continued to pay for agrarian protectionism, for subsidies to the privileged classes, for uncontrolled military expenditure.

The following example is typical, and by no means the only one. The *Ostbank für Handel und Gewerbe* had been founded some seventy years back at Poznan for the political purpose of denationalizing this Polish province, and had been transferred to Berlin after the war. It found itself, in 1929, in a very critical condition owing to the somewhat dubious management of its directors, the president of whom was Hugenberg, head of the German National party and relentless enemy of the Socialist Müller Cabinet then in power. Müller granted the bank an unconditional state guarantee and thus saved his worse enemy from all financial and penal responsibility. By way of thanks, Hugenberg immediately organized the campaign for the plebiscite against the Young Plan, which the German Government had adopted.

Socialists in France and England endeavored, when the defeat came, to defend this policy on the plea that it was a proof of self-denial. Self-denial of this kind is very near suicide. The distance seems great between the French of the Revolution who shouted, "Perish our glory, if so our Republic may triumph," and the leaders of the German Social-Democracy who did not shout, but moaned, "Perish the Republic, if so our counts and barons may not get angry." Certainly the Prussian *Jünker* might not be reproached with ignorance of what they wanted, or with failure to will what they did want. Their ancient motto had at least the merit of being outspoken: *Sei der König absolut, dass er unser'n Willen tut* (Let the king be absolute so he may do as we desire).

The Teutonic Order settled along the Baltic in the thirteenth century, to help the Poles subdue the Prussians and Lithuanians who were given the choice between baptism or massacre. The same spirit of adventure that, in the East, characterized the Crusades, drove to the Order excellent recruits for its work. First powerful, then weakened by Polish hostility, the order was on the way to collapse when the last Grand Master had sufficient political talent to turn to Protestantism and declare himself (1525) a secular prince. Afterward, his territories amalgamated with Brandenburg which had become the Kingdom of Prussia in 1700.

Whereas the Prussian sovereigns—out of hatred of the German Emperor who sat in Vienna—most often pursued an anti-Germanic policy and promoted French invasions along the Rhine, the lords who now owned the landed property of Prussia had kept the instincts of their ancestors, the Teutonic knights. They still had the greed of colonizers and were as alien to what was becoming the popular soul of Prussia as their equals in Esthonia and Latvia were toward the humble Baltic populations which surrounded them.

Prussian annexations in the West, industrial development in old and new Prussia, rendered more and more unjustified the political predominance of a class whose ideas had not altered for centuries. But this class had qualities. It gave youngest sons to the king for the administration of the State. The system seemed solid. The day Bismarck declared it might be good to have the office of Prime Minister reserved by law exclusively to the *Junker,* it was not only his *Junker* blood speaking in him; it was his feeling that even a mediocre *Junker* became, in his time at least, a better official than the bourgeois who had matured in universities.

But if the *Jünker* kept their real or supposed superiority in Prussia it was due to the three-class electoral system which gave the franchise to a minute minority—themselves. In order to wage the Lybian war, Giolitti had provided universal suffrage in Italy; the Prussian waged the whole World War with an electoral law that even the conservatives unhesitatingly declared was scandalous. It disappeared only with the fall of the Hohenzollerns. And

the *Gutsbezirke* which, constituting as they did real administrative entities, turned each *Junker* into a small feudal
lord, lasted until 1925.

Needless to say, the *Jünker* had long since become past
masters in the art of playing the patriotic chord. Possibly
in good faith—it is so easy to believe what is convenient—
they finally identified the defense of their caste with the
safeguard of Prussia, of Germany. Were they not the
heirs of the pioneers of Germanism in the East, the keepers
of the borders against the Slav tide? This, however, did
not stop them from driving their German peasants to run
away from starvation wages and desert the sacred border;
after that, they used Poles instead and ceased hating them
as soon as they found them cheaper. The reconstitution
of the Polish Republic was a stroke of good fortune for
the *Jünker*—and even more so, both the imaginary and
the real dangers inherent in the Corridor—because, henceforth, any claim of the *Jünker* became State law.

Inflation had cleared all their debts—twenty-three billion
marks. But if stabilization found them debtless, it also
left them penniless. And they found it quite natural, and
the Republican Government with them, that the State
should give them money.

Immediately after the stabilization, as early as 1924,
the Rentenbank granted them a credit of eight hundred
seventy million marks; in 1925-27, the Rentenbank-
Creditenanstalt, four hundred forty millions; the Deutsche
Giro-Zentrale, eight hundred millions; the Golddiskontbank,
two hundred fifty millions; the Reichsbank, one hundred
millions, plus a series of special favors; the Prussian Gov-

ernment, one hundred thirty-two millions; the Reich
Government, one hundred twenty-five millions and guarantees for twenty millions; and the list is probably far from
complete.

The more money they received, the more they wanted.

Any pretext served to bring them, begging with threats,
to the Treasury door. Was the rye harvest too big, as
in 1924? In a free country, landowners would have had
the idea of changing their crops, of going in for crops
that paid better. These were shopkeepers' notions. The
Jünker simply requested new customs protection. And the
government gave in at once, with devastating results for
the bulk of the population.

Otto Braun, Socialist, President of the Prussian Cabinet
until 1932, has confessed that relief of every kind granted
to the *Jünker* of East Prussia alone, between 1924 and
1928, amounted in all to one billion marks. As these
figures are hardly to the credit of the Minister, one may
be allowed to believe them.

For twelve years, the State tried to save its face. The
State was bled for the *Jünker,* but still the laws pretended
to provide measures generally applicable. In 1931, even
those scruples were abandoned. One no longer talked of
the conversion of the debts (*Umschuldung*) of the *Jünker,*
but of their payment (*Entschuldung*) by the State, to the
tune of two and a quarter billion marks. The Reich and
Prussia supplied one billion and a quarter. The other
billion was contributed by the Bank of German Industrial
Obligations, instituted in 1924 under the Dawes Plan and
galvanized into life for the circumstance with fresh capital.

They therefore did not hesitate to keep alive one of those organs of foreign control which the *Jünker* had so violently attacked while the Dawes Plan lasted. They did provide limited means for a future repayment on the part of the *Jünker;* but the Reich Commissioner for East Prussia, Treviranus, candidly declared to a Reichstag Committee, on March 17, 1931, that never would the *Jünker* pay a pfennig.

Measures of this sort—these are only quoted by way of example—were not only immoral, since they favored an extremely small part of the population to the grave prejudice of the masses—they were also harmful for precisely those whom they were supposed to help. In fact, the only result of the *Entschuldung* was that the estates benefited by it could never become active concerns again.

The patriotic industry of defense against the "Polish danger," at which the *Jünker* of East Prussia had become past masters, soon awoke the envy of all the landowners of the provinces that, luckily for themselves, also bordered on Poland. Despite the desire of the feudals of East Prussia to remain the sole recognized defenders of Germanism, similar favors had finally to be bestowed on the *Jünker* of Pomerania and of the Grenzmark. It soon became grotesque: the *Jünker* from Oldenburg wished to be just as patriotic; was there not a Dutch danger? Those from Slesvig proved there existed a Danish threat. Nowhere, I think, did abuse of the "national" pretext to further class ends reach such scandalous proportions. It is true—one must add to be quite impartial—that the Conservative papers in France and England which so often veiled their faces at the squanderings perpetrated under the Social Insurances system in Germany, never found a word to stigmatize the crazy expenditure of the *Jünker,* an expenditure which might easily be proved to have constituted for the mass of the German population a burden double that of Reparations under the Young Plan; and this without taking into account the incalculable losses incurred by German economy through the striking decrease of exports, due mainly to the ultra-protectionist tariffs which the *Jünker* constantly compelled all the post-war German Governments to raise.

Both Socialist and Catholic Governments in Germany failed equally before the threats of the *Jünker* who, being patriots by definition, sometimes did not hesitate in East Prussia to use the menace of secession.

But the error of the Socialists was much heavier than that committed by the Catholic Center; first because the Socialists advocated a doctrine which was the direct opposite of the *Jünker* privileges; and chiefly because they were the masters at a time when they might have forged a new Germany; at a time when, the monarchic framework having tumbled down, the *Jünker,* cowering on their estates, awaited the end of the world. A vast and radical agrarian reform might have meant the real, the pacific revolution inaugurating a new era and a new order in Germany. The German Marxists never even dared think of it.

Brüning succeeded no better. But the head of the Center can at least boast he fell because he dared to propose to Hindenburg a vast scheme of internal colonization in East Prussia, with expropriation of the more hopelessly ruined estates.

It is more than likely that history will one day declare that the *Jünker's* absurd and desperate attempt, in Prussia and especially in East Prussia, to instill new life into the corpse of an agrarian Middle Age constituted one of the most efficient factors in the disorganization of Germany.

If France is today the country of Europe in which the dogma and love of private property seem bred into the very bones of her people, she also owes this, to a great extent, to the more or less spontaneous renunciation by the nobles of their ancient privileges at the beginning of the French Revolution.

Some of them thought they were being generous: they were being farsighted and careful.

The *Jünker* believed they were defending their interests, and they have probably prepared for themselves a tragic awakening. Already they have become wrecks of German life—even more than the Socialists. The Socialists lacked men who were worthy to lead, and courage; they may recover from that. The *Jünker* acted like the Bourbons in France and in Spain: they showed they had "forgotten nothing, learned nothing."

VII

BRITISH AND FRENCH

THE English have one really imperial trait in their make-up: when a British interest leads them to take a stand in international situations they are, in all good faith, convinced that their judgments are exclusively moral and disinterested. It is just by chance, they say, that the moral appreciation always favors the practical needs of the moment.

Under Leopold II of Belgium, English spinsters and clergymen launched a violent campaign against Belgian atrocities in the Congo. There is absolutely no doubt that they were honestly sincere. But the English miracle lies in this: the sentimental strife began only when it was discovered that one of the provinces of the Belgian Congo, the Katanga, contained gold.

The German Reich was the most threatening continental power during the decade preceding 1914; and Germany appeared to the English laden with all the sins of Israel.

After 1919, France seemed the strongest power on the Continent. And the English political instinct forthwith centered on "militarist" France most of its suspicions and dislikes.

One may even say that, in spite of a certain regard for appearances—due to the remembrance of four years of

war waged in common—things went almost worse than
with Germany before the war. In those days there had,
at least, always been men like Morley and Haldane, who
insisted that the intellectual bonds with Germany should
not be broken; who several times advocated political
alliances. There was nothing like this with France; it
looked as if the centuries-old dislike had joyfully come
uppermost again.

Yet, if the English only would take the trouble to do
so, they might easily, and better than any other people,
realize the anxieties of a large part of French public
opinion.

A moment of introspection would suffice.

What the army means today to so many Frenchmen,
even to the least militaristic Frenchmen, the navy has
always meant to England. When the German naval con-
structions, a few hours away from British ports, threatened
British supremacy at sea, London experienced the same
shiver of anxiety as in the days of Bonaparte. The fact
is not devoid of significance that, whereas Waterloo is
only an episode of British military history, as glorious an
episode as you please, the very word Trafalgar has become
sacred.

Those Italians who, true to Mazzini's tradition, wished
to build up, with me, an atmosphere of peace and trusting
collaboration with the Yugoslav nation—and that in spite
of the grudges and misapprehensions left behind by the
war—are probably the only people in any way entitled to
make remarks about certain misgivings and fears which,

after the war, always checked the most generous and far-reaching impulses in France. But they know that nothing is more useless than sermons from abroad and they realize that Italian generosity toward a younger nation was both easier and more natural.

If, at the end of the war, there was among the belligerents one case of complete and absolute misunderstanding of the most essential interests of a nation, with never a voice to warn the country, it was in England.

It occurred—I have alluded to it in a preceding chapter—with the rejection of the Freedom of the Seas formula that Wilson had wanted to make the second of his Fourteen Points. The full text of it ran as follows: "Absolute freedom of navigation upon the seas, outside territorial waters, alike in peace and war, except as the seas may be closed in whole or in part by international action for the enforcement of covenants."

The enforcement of this principle might have signified for Great Britain that her importation of foodstuffs and raw materials would at all times be safe; and that the vast British mercantile marine would have nothing to fear from submarine or other attacks in any sea.

As soon as this point became known, Lloyd George, from whom French and Italians were accustomed to learn how grand and generous he would have been in their place, showed himself a victim of the most anachronistic English memories; so much behind the times as a poor Frenchman awakening from a sleep that had lasted since the Treaties of Westphalia.

Lloyd George and the other English leaders were possibly influenced by the fact that the blockade had been one of the most important factors in the war against Germany. But they forgot that it was not so certain that, in another war, Great Britain would be the blockading power.

In vain did Wilson endeavor to take up the discussion again with Lloyd George and make him understand— Colonel House has told me so more than once—that the second of the Fourteen Points would, in the future, constitute only an advantage for Great Britain, since the growing power of America meant the indeterminate possibility of development of the United States fleet, and since the juridical bonds and guarantees to be written into the Covenant might give the British a complete moral security.

Nothing could shake the traditional British ideas. And Lloyd George for once thought and felt like the most stubborn of those old admirals we find caricatured in *Punch*.

If Lloyd George considered the rejection of the Wilsonian formula as a triumph which might one day become a source of force for Great Britain, it is not to be wondered at that, when Stresemann communicated to the British Foreign Office, in February, 1925, the draft of the plan which later became the Locarno Pact, Sir Austin Chamberlain discarded it as of no importance and informed Stresemann that he thought his idea "unwise and premature"; which did not, a little later, stop his being awarded the

Garter as one of the promoters of Locarno. So wags the world!

Herriot, who had received Stresemann's overtures at the same time as his English colleague, took an opposite course. Although he was immediately won over to the German statesman's idea, he made no haste to answer. He did not even bring the question before the Cabinet at once—often a token of the extreme importance a Prime Minister attaches to an idea. He discussed Stresemann's plan with a few colleagues only and with them under the seal of silence.

But Chamberlain being due in Paris on March seventh, Herriot, out of national and personal dignity, wished to avoid looking as if he had waited for foreign advice on a question so vital to the progress of real peace. He declared to the German representative in Paris that he considered Stresemann's plan to be an excellent foundation for wide and fruitful negotiations.

Chamberlain was dumfounded when he learned from Herriot himself that Paris in no way shared his suspicious and pessimistic impression.

There have been both a Locarno illusion and a Locarno mistake, but the British Foreign Secretary perceived neither, far from it.

The Locarno mistake consisted in this: the English and the Italian guarantees were one-sided. If one adds to this that they happened prematurely, or at least unexpectedly, one will understand why the French masses did not appreciate their value more.

During the Locarno days, the public men in France who were hostile to, or suspicious of, Briand's policy, showed their self-control by forbearance from underlining the fact that France, throughout her history, had not been in the habit of having herself protected. True or false, the argument might have had a not-to-be-neglected demagogical influence. Poincaré, for instance, did not insist on the point in the many speeches he made at the time; but he remarked on it bitterly more than once in private conversations with me. Herriot had shown the same feeling as Poincaré, but as he was above all devoted to the cause of peace, he had buried the feeling even deeper.

But if it be untrue that one-sided pledges of the Locarno type risk engendering, in those who voluntarily assume them and receive nothing in return, a consciousness or attitude of superiority, the fact remains—however paradoxical it may seem—that such pledges do not continue so keenly alive in the hearts of those supposed to benefit by them. Things paid for are valued most.

The Italian guarantee, for instance, would have had far greater moral and material weight if the promise regarding peace on the Rhine had found a counterpart in some specifically Italian interest. An Anglo-French-German guarantee for Italian interests, for example, in the South-Tyrol Alps, would have been an exclusively Italian asset in appearance only. It might have constituted a reason for similar French and German pledges on behalf of British interests which would have added enormous strength to the Locarno Pact. When Hitler destroyed it in 1936, it was comparatively easy for him to do so, because only a French direct interest seemed to be at stake.

But it was impossible for the Fascist Government to defend Italian interests intelligently at Locarno. Governments of this type have their personal concerns which do not always tally with those of the country they rule over. The interest of the Fascist régime lay in making the Italians believe that the peace of Europe was highly unstable, that a bold government with plenty of elbow-room would be able to seize on the moment of inevitable scramble to wring rich spoils for Italy from a rotten Europe. The Fascist Government, therefore, did everything in its power to wreck the Locarno agreements. When, in spite of its efforts, these agreements came near conclusion, there was nothing left for it to do but to rush to the little Swiss town and add its signature, for fear of losing all its prestige if it stayed out. But, because of its previous maneuvers, the Fascist Government went to Locarno without either strength or authority.

A few weeks after Locarno, Briand wanted to see me. I was on my way through Paris and we had lunch together. He asked my opinion on the potential force of the new Pact. I told him: "It may be that a pacific Europe will rise out of it, but on condition that you capitalize the latent possibilities of the new atmosphere at once; for miracles last only for a day."

"Which means that . . . ?"

"Which means, for instance, that you should evacuate the Rhineland while you can still make it look like a spontaneous movement on your part. When it is forced on you, it will be too late. Only seeming rashness may constitute a wary policy for France."

Briand remained silent for a few minutes, watching the smoke of his cigarette. I felt he thought I was right. And then, in that chaffing way of his which hid only too well the real sincerity of his intentions, he said:

"One can see you are in opposition and enjoy it."

For this is the terrible difficulty which lay in the way of a constructive peace policy such as Briand desired in the last years of his life: whereas in England public opinion is decidedly pacifist, whatever party (with a few exceptions) an Englishman may belong to, in France the idea, not of peace, but of pacifist propaganda, is often suspected of being the token of a "dangerous" trend in home politics.

English pacifism has its roots in the very history of Great Britain, in her religious and liberal traditions.* To accuse it of being a veil to British imperialism is just as futile

---

* It was in January, 1935, that the English League of Nations' Union, under Lord Cecil, started a straw vote with the following questionnaire:

"Should Britain remain a member of the League? Are you in favor of an all-round reduction of armament by an international agreement? Are you in favor of all-round abolition of national military and naval aircraft by international agreement? Should the manufacture and sale of armaments for private profit be prohibited? If one nation attacks another, should other nations compel it to desist by: 1. Economic non-military measures? 2. Military measures if necessary?"

The voters numbered 11,628,000, ten millions of whom were for economic sanctions. This important result was reached long before Mussolini declared war on Abyssinia. The reaction of British public opinion against the compromise which Sir Samuel Hoare and Monsieur Laval tried to impose on the League in 1935 was due to the moral force represented by this straw vote.

as to talk of the "perfidy of Albion." But it is true that, as I said at the beginning of this chapter, England has reached a degree of unconscious skill which nearly always succeeds in making ideals and interests go hand in hand.

Why does England pursue a League of Nations policy? Not only because, she hopes, the League may help to ward off war, but also because London hopes League action may make it unnecessary to go into excessive military expenditure for the protection of British interests throughout the world; and again because London has realized that Geneva is proving a precious ground on which to shape, without effort or friction, a common policy with the Dominions.*

French ideology and the French material position differ from the British in almost every respect.

Great Britain feels that she is free to choose her policy. France is bound to any policy which may bring her allies in case of a new German aggression. The elasticity and freedom of British policy is often resented in France as a disregard of the interests the two countries possess in common. The press and writers of both capitals add to the feeling of estrangement. The London press, on the whole, faithfully reflects the pacifist trends of the people; and so do the major writers. In France, on the contrary, the greater part of the Paris press presents to the world a public opinion whose verbal violence apparently has no other basis than a vague inferiority complex toward

---

* This point will be treated more fully in the next chapter.

Germany and also toward England.* The pagan-catholic writers in fashion in Paris add to the impression, in striking contrast with the more generous, more humane, more Christian views of their British colleagues.

Never before, as now in post-war France, has it been so clearly proved that, in order to serve one's country usefully abroad one should above all avoid giving the impression of being, night and day, mobilized in her service.

Like all the other virtues, patriotism needs to be well mantled in discretion.

---

* This is certainly not true of many important newspapers of the French provinces, like, for instance, the *Dépêche de Toulouse*. It is a pity, for France's reputation abroad, that such papers are not so well known in foreign countries as the Paris press.

VIII

GREAT BRITAIN AND THE DOMINIONS

THE British Empire, tacitly but radically, was transformed under our very eyes into the British Commonwealth of Nations. This title was officially used for the first time in the Irish Treaty of 1921. It was not invented by an Englishman, not even by an Irishman; but by a Dutchman from South Africa, General Smuts, who had popularized it in a series of powerful war speeches between 1914 and 1918.

No Englishman ever gave a definition of the formula. The best we have is from a Canadian, Sir Robert Borden:* "Our Commonwealth," he wrote, "may be regarded as a League of Nations owing a single allegiance and possessing international relations that are still in a state of development."

What is the distant origin of the idea which, slowly but surely, and against the opinion of English officialdom, brought the Dominions to their present freedom? It may be found in the strong will of the New Englanders to impose on the London Government the rights and privileges of their assemblies. When, after the American Revolution, the Americans who had remained Tories emigrated

---

* Conservative leader, sometime Premier of Canada.

to Canada, their first care was to set up a Canadian Parliament, a thing never dreamed of by the something like sixty thousand Frenchmen who had settled along the St. Lawrence and had become subjects of the English Crown. Peasants mostly, and coming from a country where the kings had successfully fought against the rights of parliaments, the French had not thought of asserting rights of autonomy; they had merely remained good subjects. It was thanks to the American newcomers only that the Constitutional Act of 1791 instituted two representative assemblies, one for the French-speaking Canadians and one for the Americans who had settled in Upper Canada.

All that followed, everywhere, was only a tardy imitation of the Canadian initiative.

Progress, subsequent to the Canadian turning-point of 1791, was slow, nearly always opposed by London, often by means of sanguinary military repressions, sometimes in one colony, sometimes in another; but every success achieved by the Dominions on their way to independence was won thanks again to a Canadian initiative.

It was in 1859 that a Finance Minister of Canada,* Sir Alexander Galt, incorporated in the budget protective duties even on goods imported from Great Britain. England protested most violently, but Galt answered that Canadian self-government would be annihilated if the Canadian people did not have the right to choose the sources of their revenue for themselves, and London had

---

* Upper and Lower Canada had become united by then.

to give in, thus acknowledging a new step toward the independence of the Dominions—the establishment of their complete fiscal autonomy.

Among the subsequent constitutional developments, the most spectacular occurred during the World War: the admission of the Dominion leaders into the Imperial War Cabinet. But an Imperial Conference held in London simultaneously with the first meetings of the War Cabinet had even more important results. For the final resolution proclaimed that, regarding constitutional relations, "any readjustment . . . while thoroughly preserving all existing powers of self-government and complete control of domestic affairs, should be based upon a full recognition of the Dominions as autonomous nations of an Imperial Commonwealth, and of India as an important portion of the same; should recognize the right of the Dominions and of India to an adequate voice in foreign policy and in foreign relations; and should provide effective arrangements for continuous consultation in all important matters of common imperial concern, and for such necessary concerted action, founded on consultation, as the several governments may determine."

But, in England more than elsewhere, the final token of any radical change is furnished by a fact, rather than by a text. And the dramatic fact occurred in September, 1922, when the Turks of Kemal Pasha, having pursued a routed Hellenic army right up to the Dardanelles, found, at the port of Chanak, a British detachment under orders to hold them up. It might have spelled war. Lloyd George, then

Prime Minister, even seemed to want it.*   He was angry
with the Italians and the French who had refused to join
him and, I may add, had a personal grievance against me,
for I had made the mistake of foretelling the victory of
the Turks from the very beginning of the crazy enterprise.
Turning his back on our peace advice, he appealed to the
Dominions for their immediate military co-operation.   He
never doubted it would be given.   Had it not, up to 1914,
been assumed that when Great Britain was at war all
the Dominions were at war by her side?   But the Canadian
Prime Minister bluntly refused.   Canada had not been consulted as to British policy in Turkey.   The matter, therefore, was exclusively British.   It belonged to the Canadian
Parliament alone, he declared, "to determine whether the
country should participate in wars in which other nations or
other parts of the British Empire might be involved."

It was a hard lesson; but it had its result.   So much so
that when I met Lord Curzon a few months later and
asked him whether he thought Lloyd George could come
back to power, he answered unhesitatingly: "No; his terrible mistake with Canada during the Chanak affair has
rendered his return impossible for ever."

There dislike of his former chief led Lord Curzon to
exaggerate; for there is no mistake, except dying, that
makes it impossible for a politician to return to power.

---

* Lloyd George through the Foreign Office sent a note to Kemal announcing that the British Dominions, Yugoslavia and Rumania had been asked
to promise military support against the Turks.   This announcement incited
Kemal to immediate action by its threatening tone.   France and Italy had,
on the contrary, withdrawn their contingents from the Straits.

The relations between England and the Dominions carry two lessons of humility that every statesman should learn.

The first concerns the results which Canada's proud fight for independence might engender for the good of the world and of the British Empire. If the British Empire has one chance of escaping the lot of all empires—Spain for example—it lies in the fact that it was compelled to change into a free federation. Only realistic rulers, *real-politiker* of the militarist and Fascist type, may smile at an organization based on reciprocal free-will. It may quite well be that the Canadian statesman was right who, after the achievements I have just described, wrote: "Three-quarters of a century ago political prophets declared that responsible government in the British colonies would shatter the fabric of the Empire. Today there are short-sighted men who sincerely believe that the national states which the Dominions have attained will have the like result. On the contrary, I am convinced that the status which we gained . . . will result, not in weakening, but in strengthening the real ties that bind together the nations of the British Commonwealth."

The English people, with their generous and natural idealism, have finally, thanks mainly to the admirable campaign led by men like Lord Cecil and Gilbert Murray, declared for a general peace policy based on the League of Nations. But the professional diplomats of the Foreign Office would probably have impeded this national conception to the best of their ability, blinded as they frequently were by immediate interests, had they not grasped that the

League of Nations was providing them with a marvelous instrument with which to deal with the most dangerous problem in store for the Nations of the British Commonwealth: Who is to decide about war?

For the Dominions who would refuse to obey London are ready to obey Geneva and its Covenant. Under the Covenant they know that they are bound to go hand in hand with all the other members of the League in case of a breach of the Covenant. This is more than enough for England who, satisfied with her lot, is quite determined not to risk other wars of aggression.

The second lesson lies in the mistake England made for a long time in believing that, in the interest of the State, the French Canadians should be annihilated. Few readings are more useful, morally and politically, than the passage which Lord Durham, so perspicacious in other matters, devoted to the French Canadians in the final report he submitted to his government in 1839 after his short but fruitful mission to Canada:

"The French Canadians . . . are but the remains of an ancient colonization, and are and ever must be isolated in the midst of an Anglo-Saxon world. Whatever may happen, whatever government shall be established over them, British or American, they can see no hope for their nationality. . . .

"It is but a question of time and mode; it is but to determine whether the small number of French who now inhabit Lower Canada shall be made English, under a government which can protect them, or whether the process shall be delayed until a much larger number shall have to undergo, at the rude hands of its uncontrolled rivals, the extinction of a nationality strengthened and embittered by continuance.

"And is this French Canadian nationality one which, for the good merely of that people, we ought to strive to perpetuate, even if it were possible? I know of no national distinctions marking and continuing a more hopeless inferiority. The language, the laws, the character of the North American Continent are English; and every race but the English (I apply this to all who speak the English language) appears there in a condition of inferiority. It is to elevate them from that inferiority that I desire to give the Canadians our English character. . . ."

A century after this report,* Britain's main concern regarding Canada lies in the fear that the attractive power of the United States may become too great. Already the dollar in Canada is American, and industry is Americanized though in a softer mold. And those very French Canadians, who Lord Durham said "can see no hope for their nationality," having increased in number from sixty thousand to over three millions and, constituting thirty per cent of the whole Canadian population, have become the most effective break in the Americanization of Canada. This is due to their fidelity to the Roman Church, but even more to their invincible individualism which causes their pro-

---

* A similar case of unconscious British complacency of the Victorian type is offered by Lord Macaulay when he declared that the local languages should be superseded by English in India since the culture of India was "bound in time to become English."

found suspicion of what they call American standardization.

But all Canadians, whether of English or of French origin,* desire the maintenance of close and trusting relations with the United States, with whom they share a frontier—the only one in the world—which has not a fort or a gun. Here again, they have, being now independent, rendered a precious service to England by confirming her in the pursuance of a policy which has almost become a dogma with the British Dominions: no dangerous divergence of opinion between London and Washington.

---

* In fact, there is also a good leaven of Scots, to say nothing of a good many Germans, Italians and Scandinavians.

IX

FRENCH AND ITALIANS

THERE is one rather frequent psychological mistake of the French which consists in a somewhat too schematic use of certain phrases like "indissoluble historical bonds," "fraternity of race," "identity of culture." Franco-American relations would probably have been none the worse if the French had quoted Lafayette a little less often in their toasts.

This holds good also of relations between French and Italians. At least, that is how I have always felt personally. There are statesmen and diplomats in France who know how much I had it at heart to promote a thorough understanding between their country and mine. Yet more than once they could hardly hide their surprise at the cool welcome I gave—as Foreign Minister in Rome or Ambassador in Paris—to suggestions of theirs for banquets, for celebrations of anniversaries of wars ranging from 1859 to 1918, for Franco-Italian meetings. . . . I am not so sure they ended by understanding that I intended to serve more safely and with greater dignity the cause we defended with equal earnestness.

The differences in temperament and psychology between the Italians and the French, far deeper than is generally supposed, stand revealed even in our two literatures, at least to the few who know both well. Corneille and Racine are sealed books to Italians. Of the great Italian writers of the nineteenth century, one only—one of the greatest, it is true—shows deep love and knowledge of the French mind—Manzoni. But he is himself practically unknown in France. When I was quite a young man, I once spoke of him to Zola. Despite his Italian blood, all the French novelist remembered of the *Promessi Sposi* was the scene of the bolting horse in the Lazzaretto of Milan. The knowledge of Italian, so frequent in France throughout the eighteenth century from Voltaire to the belles of Versailles, has decreased enormously, except in certain very interesting Italianistic centers. On the other hand, French language and literature are mastered in Italy far less than the display, in the shopwindows of Milanese or Roman booksellers, of the latest *"novelties"* of the French literary output might lead the French to suppose. If one were to be so rash as to state which masterpieces are most appreciated by the Italian intellectual élite, I believe one would have to place Shakespeare and Cervantes far ahead of Molière, LaFontaine or Voltaire.

The psychological differences between French and Italians manifest themselves constantly in their respective manner of reasoning, of appraising facts, of facing the future. The powerful Cartesian light of French rationalism is, for the Italians, like a beacon in the night: an excess of light which ignores the value of shade.

It is no indifferent fact to note that the golden age of Italo-French relations was not the time of their common fate during the war, but the days of the Triple Alliance in its post-1902 form.

French historians have not always been fair to the loyalty that inspired Italian policy during the Triple Alliance period; they can quote one name in excuse—Crispi. But, after all, the real fault of the Sicilian patriot lay in the fact that he was of an essentially emotional temperament. Intellectual maturity alone—and he always lacked that—might have persuaded his ardent love for his country that Italy could not spring, all armed and complete like Pallas Athené, from four centuries of foreign and papal rule. From this misapprehension arose his feverish agitation, his everlasting quest of immediate success, his naïve satisfaction over the first flattering words Bismarck addressed to him. Crispi had always blamed men like Minghetti and Visconti Venosta, whose haughty moral dignity he could not even understand, for having been too "French." Just as he always failed to see that his predecessor as Foreign Minister, Count di Robilant, had safeguarded national dignity more by his silent action than he by his over-excited sayings. Robilant had signed the Triple Alliance; but Bismarck would say of him: "What a hard man to deal with." For Crispi, a Sicilian, the occupation of Tunisia in 1881 had been a tough blow, something like what he must have felt in 1866, at the outcome of our second unfortunate war with Austria. He was perpetually on the alert, afterward. More than once as old men do, Giolitti, in his patriarchal home at Cavour, told me the story how, when he was, in 1889-90,* Treasury Minister

---

* The first time he was Cabinet Minister. He was Prime Minister 1892-93, 1903-05, 1906-09, 1911-14, 1920-21. He died in 1928. His *Memoirs*

under Crispi, the latter, to his great surprise, had summoned him urgently one day and told him that France was preparing a coup on the Spezia; that he had "proofs" at hand. All Giolitti's efforts to demonstrate to him that the thing was impossible were futile. The good man who, contrary to Giolitti's advice, had immediately had an English squadron dispatched to the port of Genoa, believed he had saved his country from a terrible danger. When Giolitti, in his turn, became Prime Minister, he decided to find out how Crispi could have been misled to such an extent and discovered, so he told me toward the end of his life, that the origin of the fantastic story lay in a secret report sent to him by Vatican agents whom Crispi was paying to be informers.

It must not be thought that Crispi's policy constituted a precedent for the Fascist episode. The old Risorgimento conspirator really believed he was serving Italy, the ideal of his life. To make use of Italy for personal ends, to deafen the ears of a throttled nation with nationalistic slogans—like the Fascists who speculated upon his name forty years after his death—would have seemed to him worse than blasphemy. Respectful of Parliament, he believed in liberty. There is, therefore, nothing in common between him and the Fascist phenomenon. At most was there a slight resemblance between his characteristic intellectual limitations and all those honest and naïve elements (lower middle classes of classical and "Roman" training,

---

have been translated into English and bring out well the great economic progress Italy made in Giolitti's time.

ex-service men, etc.) who flocked to Fascism at the beginning, to that dubious stream in which so many appetites and passions mingled without ever melting together.

But, aside from the Crispi period, the Triple Alliance was used by Italian statesmen as a guaranty of peace—with Austria-Hungary especially, with whom we were obliged either to be friend or foe—and of our territorial integrity; nothing more.

I said, territorial integrity. The opening of the imperial Austrian archives, which the first Republican Austrian Government had the rare merit of making as complete as possible, gave us an opportunity to know of Pope Leo XIII's overtures to Franz Joseph concerning "a crusade of Christian Princes against Italy."

Unlike most diplomatic documents, which lose their flavor quickly because they are based on surmises, one dispatch of general instructions sent by Visconti Venosta from the Consulta, a few years before the conclusion of the Triple Alliance, to Count di Robilant, then Italy's representative in Vienna, is still so full of life that its essential part is worth reproducing:

"If a war were to break out through the folly or rashness of France, or if it were to break out on the clerical question, our position would be clear, and we should have a direct interest in common with Germany. But if a war were to break out through Germany's deliberate will to attack France, Italy could not come into the war on Germany's side. She would look, not like an ally, but like a hired assassin who is about to be paid his price. Indeed, the result of a war between France and Germany would always be harmful to Italy. If Germany were to crush France again, she would wish to dismember her and would, wrongly, consider the dismemberment as final: one of those excessive, artificial, and so short-lived, arrangements of the type Napoleon used in making and unmaking his peaces. Now Italy would have neither strength nor future in a Europe whose balance was broken."

Except for the allusion to the dangers of an eventual clerical majority in France—a danger which soon disappeared—this page from Visconti Venosta describes not only his state of mind, but that of all the statesmen worthy of the name who succeeded him through many years.

The treaty of the Triple Alliance faithfully reproduced the intentions of the Italian Government only in the form it assumed when it was renewed in 1902. The treaty was signed on June twentieth; but on July third, before its ratification on the eighth—and the ratification alone is valid—the Italian Foreign Minister, Prinetti, declared to Paris and to London that the treaty contained "no stipulation obliging Italy to share in an aggression." Prinetti authorized his two colleagues, Delcassé and Lord Lansdowne, to impart his declaration to their respective Parliaments; which was done in the Palais Bourbon and in the House of Commons on July third. The statement read by Delcassé, every word of which has its import, was as follows:

"After the declarations made to us by the Italian Government, we stand convinced that the policy of Italy, consequent on her alliances, is, neither directly nor indirectly, aimed against France; that in no case could it entail a menace for us, and that in no case, nor in any manner, could Italy become either the instrument of, or accessory to, an aggression against our country."

The German Ambassador imparted to Berlin the impression of relief that these words, listened to in deep silence, had produced. Prinetti in Rome fully confirmed them to the German representative. The ratification of the treaty not having taken place, as I have said, until a few days later, on July eighth, it is evident that Berlin and Vienna had acknowledged the spirit in which Italy had adhered to the renewal of the Triple Alliance.

Prince Bülow, in his day, described these acts of Italian diplomacy rather contemptuously as *"tours de valse"*; just as, once the war had broken out, showers of *"Deutsche Treue"* (Germanic fidelity) were thrown at the Latin ex-ally from Berlin and Vienna.

In point of fact, our conduct, even considering, or rather especially considering, the extreme measures of pacific prudence taken in 1902, might have constituted a lesson in loyalty for everybody, Hohenzollern Germany, to begin with. Italy notified her neutrality to France and Great Britain in case of a war of aggression against them, and informed her allies of it; whereas Bismarck had concluded his famous counter-insurance treaty with Russia at a time when an Austro-Russian war seemed possible (this made the act all the more disloyal), and kept his treaty secret, although he was definitely bound, under one of the articles of the Triple Alliance, to communicate conventions of this kind to Rome and to Vienna. But it is an admitted fact that Italy alone is "Machiavellic." And may I wonder— it explains a good many misunderstandings between French and Italians—how many French writers have thought of the preceding facts, and thought of bringing them out, to enlighten French public opinion?

It is futile to wonder at the frictions which occurred between France and Italy after the World War. It is the same old story; the fruits, that, in all times, have ripened on the trees of coalitions.

If, a century earlier, France came out more than honorably from the difficult trial of the Congress of Vienna, it was mainly because Talleyrand succeeded in making his country champion an idea, which is always stronger than a material interest; but especially because France had to deal with a coalition of Powers who hated one another far more than they hated their enemy of yesterday.

Over and above the inevitable disputes between allies, there were, during the World War, special reasons, I shall not say of friction, but of misunderstanding between France and Italy. The main enemy for France was Germany; for Italy, Austria-Hungary.

We have here a striking example of how empty shadows can bring forth mutual misapprehension and distrust.

Having declared war on Austria, did Italy delay for a few months to declare war on Germany? The Elysée and the Quai d'Orsay knew what to think of the matter. They knew quite well that one could tax the Italian Foreign

Minister Sonnino with everything else—we Italians objected especially to his lack of comprehension and imagination—but that his loyalty was above all suspicion. But in
how many "well-informed" *salons* of Paris did those "in
the know" shake their heads at this new token of the
legendary Italian Machiavellism.

In Italy, on the other hand, nerves were irritated by
the fear of the Austrophile elements who continued their
work in France, particularly in the aristocratic and diplomatic circles. With all their ardent but misinformed
patriotism, these friends of Vienna* did not know how
much their dreams and their regrets went counter to the
permanent interests of France. It is still not known in
France, nor in Italy, that the London Agreement (April,
1915), which bound France, Great Britain, Russia and
Italy for the duration of the whole war, was morally, if
not juridically, already achieved when the Russian Foreign
Minister Sazonow proposed to the French Ambassador in
Petersburg a separate peace with Austria-Hungary; and
that, if the suggestion was finally rejected by Poincaré and
his government, it had not been rejected from the beginning
—far from it—by several French agents, of whom it may
be supposed that they kept in their hearts the feeling that
the French President and the French Cabinet had been
better advised to act otherwise.

The Paris peace negotiations were much as everybody
knows. Mistakes in methods were probably equal on both

---

* For instance, my old friend, the Marquis de Castellane.

sides, French and Italian. But the mistakes of the plenipotentiaries from Rome were only psychological mistakes with their own people. Indeed, not one other nation had achieved her aims in the war to the same extent as Italy had; not France who, in a Europe far from pacified, would always have a tremendous neighbor to fear beyond the Rhine; nor Great Britain who had definitely lost her secular naval supremacy. Italy, on the contrary, had gained one advantage only, perhaps, but a priceless one: the disappearance of imperial Austria, a fact which at one stroke eliminated her great tragic dilemma whether to be ally or foe of the Hapsburg Monarchy; and gave her full diplomatic freedom of action for the future. Instead of making all the Italian nation conscious of this magnificent result, the narrow policy of Orlando and Sonnino in Paris rendered the lower middle classes in Italy—who later constituted the sincere element of Fascism—fascinated by only one fact: their plenipotentiaries had been isolated in Paris and "fooled" at least once, when Wilson, Lloyd George and Clemenceau seized on the occasion of Orlando's and Sonnino's independent departure for Rome* to give Smyrna to Greece—a fatal present.

Wilson, Clemenceau and Lloyd George probably never deserved the gratitude of the Italian people as much as on the day they thought they had done Italy a bad turn. But it was nothing odd if many Italians, belonging in the main to those middle classes that are everywhere more sensitive

---

* When, after a long and bitter discussion, they had not succeeded in bringing Wilson to approve their claims to Fiume and Dalmatia.

to national chauvinist prestige, considered that victory had been "mutilated." Was anything more natural than that public opinion, ill-informed and ignorant of the fact that the overwhelming majority of the Dalmatians were Slavs and wished to remain Slavs, should find it difficult to stand the idea—after a victory that had cost so much blood—of losing the ancient possessions of Venice? And this, it was said, on behalf of those Croatian and Slovene neighbors of whom Paris was making so much—half of whom had fought against us under the flags of Austria-Hungary.

From the Macedonian front during the war and as Foreign Minister later, I opposed a sterile anti-Slav policy which would have deprived us of the essential results of our victory, since it would have necessitated our maintaining a system of police compression of the imperial Austria we had destroyed. Yet I own I often felt how insincere those counsels of "broad-mindedness" sounded which Paris lavished on us. Not that the advice was bad— on the contrary—but it was bestowed by preachers who would probably have turned annexationists against the real interests of their country had they been in a position analogous to ours. However much one must allow for the ways of adventurers and mischief-mongers, one cannot wonder at all that the middle classes, who had lost thousands of their children on the battlefields of the Carso, should have been irritated by this avalanche of friendly advice, however sound in itself.*

---

* See the chapter on Sonnino in my *Makers of Modern Europe*.

After the war, the relations between the French and Italian Governments underwent a series of rather marked ups and downs. Public opinion in Italy soon realized that, if lasting peace were to be established in Europe, relations should be reinstated with Germany, based on something a bit more normal than the crazy formulas of everlasting reparations and unilateral disarmament. This was resented in official France as an attempt to weaken a common front, which by then existed only in the illusions of the Quai d'Orsay. Official France, have I said? In reality, even in 1919, the French masses notwithstanding the shows staged in Paris by the politicians, were deeply desirous of a true and lasting peace. Nowhere in the world, save perhaps in Italy, had the cry "the war to end war" been so sincerely felt as among the peasants who, on election day, are the real masters of France. But even the Frenchmen most desiring a true peace thought friendly the attitude of the few foreign leaders who, like myself, refused to join with Lloyd George and others in attempting, at the various Supreme Councils of the time, to force on France a too rapid revision of her judicial position.

Those among my successors—the Fascists included— who inaugurated a system of lecturing France with the vulgar slogan of "Revision of Treaties," contributed much less than I with my confidential attitude and action looking to the said revision. On the contrary, they rendered revision more difficult by increasing the misgivings of even such Frenchmen as were most inclined to question the perfection of the Versailles Treaty.

There were other points that, from time to time, provoked sour discussions between French and Italians after the war. For instance, the discussion of the colonial compensations France owed to Italy, and the debate over the status of the Italians in Tunisia.

Both these questions were officially settled under the Roman Agreements concluded in January, 1935, by the two Prime Ministers, Laval and Mussolini, from which sprang the campaign against Ethiopia.

I shall say nothing here of the first question. When I was Minister for Foreign Affairs, I was satisfied to keep it alive, as my duty commanded, without urging an immediate solution. My knowledge of the Mohammedan state of mind* and of the situation brewing in Asia— where Soviet intrigues were and remain only a futile contribution to far deeper causes of unrest—led me to consider a formula which today still seems to me much safer and more useful. I shall explain my thought on this point in one of the final chapters of this book.†

But, in spite of the Roman Agreements of 1935, there is a possibility that the question of the Italians of Tunisia may prove stronger than rash and hasty formulas; that is why I think it may be useful, if only from an historical point of view, to state in what the question consists.

French diplomacy was not particularly happy when, at the end of the World War in 1918, it denounced the Italo-

---

* I was in China at the beginning of the World War, and in Turkey as High Commissioner immediately after the Armistice.

† See Chapter XVIII.

French conventions concerning Tunisia. These conventions, concluded in Paris in 1896, were among the first tokens of the *rapprochement* between the two countries after the Crispi period. They constituted, on the part of Italy, a compromise and concession of her rights and privileges as guaranteed by the Italo-Tunisian Treaty of 1868. Possibly the best method of terminating them, after a long war waged together, did not exactly lie in informing the Roman Cabinet by a note from the French Embassy that, "with a view to adapting the commercial régime freely to the new situations brought about by the war," the 1896 conventions were hereby denounced. Especially as it soon became clear that the motives which had prompted the decision were political rather than simply commercial.

Indeed, the seriousness of this action was felt to such an extent even in Paris that it was suggested, simultaneously with the denunciation, that the old agreements should be tacitly renewed every three months until new ones were concluded.

All those who have tasted the joys of power know how such things happen. The agents in foreign lands, and the offices which, in the capital, receive their reports, are all sincerely convinced that the safety of the mother country rests on the solution of some one of those problems they lovingly study, cultivate and sometimes embitter. They are certain that by clamoring for its solution they serve the most vital concerns of patriotism. When I complained once to Balfour, in a friendly conversation, of a certain irritating and meddlesome insistence on Italo-Afghan relations with which Curzon had been pestering me for months—I had given the Italian relations with Afghanistan a full diplomatic form—the charming old man said to me: "Why are you surprised? George Curzon belongs to the terrible breed of those who have been there." And Balfour meant that having been "there," they hold that everything that counts is "there."

The French agents who spend their time saving France from pretended dangers of infiltration in Tunisia or Morocco, frequently succeed in creating embarrassments to their country. At all events they create the impression that, for all their chauvinistic talk, they have a very mean idea of her power of absorption.

But let us hope all this is ancient history. Haunted by the fear of coalitions, Bismarck said to the British Ambassador to Germany in 1881, immediately after the occupation of Tunisia by the French: "I am well pleased. The French in Tunis—that means any understanding between French and Italians is, henceforth impossible." The Italo-French fraternity in war from 1914 to 1918 gave Bismarck the lie.

The situation of the French and of the Italians in the world still tells us, after so many gross mistakes and so much wasted time, that the reasons for union are far deeper, more essential, more European, than the old nationalistic causes of jealousies and misapprehensions.

The two peoples are ready to understand each other. When will they find leaders worthy of them?

X

ITALIAN LEGENDS

WHILE he was Ambassador of the United States to Rome, Henry White was selected by Roosevelt to represent his country at the Algeciras Conference in 1906. I was there myself, a young and unimportant diplomat, as head of the secretariat of the Italian delegation. White had been my patient golf teacher in Rome. He had a liking for me, as old men frequently have for beginners in their own field. He paid great deference to my chief, the Marquis Visconti Venosta. So it happened that, in spite of our difference in years, we became intimate. Algeciras, indeed, sealed real bonds between all those who lived through the three long months of the conclave at the Hotel Reina Cristina. Had we not, we youngsters who had always refused to believe in it, seen the shadow of war—worse still, the shadow of a war of prestige?

But on a later day while I was on leave in Rome, I asked White if we had not exaggerated the Algeciras nightmare; if a war on account of Morocco, or on account of prestige in Morocco, was not impossible.

By way of answer, White took out of a drawer the minutes of a conversation he had had with Arthur Balfour, whom he had known intimately during his long years as Counselor to the American Embassy in London.

Balfour's words, which he read to me, were quite recent and, added the arch-scrupulous and arch-anglomaniac White, reproduced word for word:

"What fools we are not to wage war on Germany before her fleet and her trade increase any further!"

And White replied: "You, a man with your principles, you a great philosopher, to say that! If you want to overcome German trade, you should work more."

"But, my dear White, that would lower our standard of living. And would it not be simpler to go to war? It may be the only way to maintain our supremacy. . . ."

White, as if he regretted the confidence he had given, made me promise to keep it, to forget it. I kept silence, but I did not forget. It was only ten years later, when I came to know Lord Balfour well, who doubted everything and admitted everything, that I realized his talk had probably been nothing more than an exercise in dialectics.

But other Englishmen, less skeptical than Balfour, had sometimes spoken, and in public. Suffice it to quote Lee, Civil Lord of the Admiralty, who in a speech made at Eastleigh, on February 2, 1905, had expressed his opinion hypothetical, it must be said, that the English fleet could attack the German fleet by surprise and annihilate it.

A similar suggestion was, indeed, offered in another country, six years later.

While all the Italian forces were engaged in the war with Turkey in 1911, the head of the Austro-Hungarian General Staff, Conrad, used all the influence he had at

Vienna to wrench from the old Emperor his consent to a "preventive war" against Italy. Aehrenthal unhesitatingly qualified Conrad's plans as "a policy of highway robbery" and Franz Joseph sided with his Minister for Foreign Affairs. Conrad resigned, but continued to preach his great plan in intimate circles. It must indeed, at one time— Conrad having very soon been reinstated at the head of the General Staff—have seemed very near to becoming an accomplished fact. Late in 1911 the German Ambassador to Italy was instructed to impart the following extraordinary notice to the Italian Foreign Minister, the Marquis di San Giuliano: that it was understood that, in case of war between Austria-Hungary and Italy, Germany would remain neutral, the Triple Alliance Treaty being silent on this hypothesis.

During the short period he had remained out of office, Conrad, in his recriminations, had even gone so far as to declare that Austria-Hungary had been wrong not to seize in 1908 the opportunity offered her by the Messina earthquake and not to declare war on Italy on that occasion.

Do we want a proof of the persistence of all the myths that flatter the vanity of a nation? These facts, historically certain, did not prevent sentimental German writers from continuing to doubt the loyalty of Italy during the period of the Triple Alliance. The truth is that the most critical study of the diplomatic documents of the time only serves to demonstrate the fact that if—in the wary *mariage de raison* represented by the alliance between Austria and

Italy—there were thoughts and acts of dubious loyalty, they are always to be found on the side of imperial Germany and Austria-Hungary. The fact becomes clear if one bears in mind that, as regards Italy, the treaty became imperative not for positive ends, but for reasons of a negative character. Italy had realized she could not live under the constant threats of a neighbor who hated her by tradition and of necessity. Did not united Italy embody the principle of nationality so abhorred in Vienna? Moreover, Italy felt in her very flesh, with the Trentino thorn, the menace of this powerful and unfriendly neighbor. No safeguard was to be found in international law in the anarchic Europe of that time. There was nothing left for Italy to do but agree to an alliance. She would at least derive from it a neutralization of all temporal drives emanating from the Vatican, which might have become dangerous in the event of the reactionary parties in France returning to power.

But Bismarck, from the beginning, demanded a freedom which he denied his allies. He periodically reproached the Italian Ambassador with every normal attempt made by Italy to set up tolerable relations with France, as evidence of disloyalty; and this at a time when he was himself doing his best to flirt with Paris.

When Italy occupied Massaoua in 1885, the first step toward the creation of Italian Eritrea, Bismarck protested in the name of the integrity of the Ottoman Empire, though at the very moment, in his private conversations with other European statesmen, he was launching with them the idea of a final partition of Turkey. In fact, Bismarck had been annoyed only because the occupation of Massaoua had taken place in consequence of a direct agreement between London and Rome. And he wished Rome to be on bad terms with London, especially because he was himself, at the time, indulging in bitter-sweet discussions with the British Government on colonial questions.

The first notion of an Italian occupation of Massaoua arose out of a conversation between the Italian Diplomatic Agent to Egypt, De Martino, and his English colleague, Sir E. Baring (afterward Lord Cromer). The Englishman led De Martino to suggest the occupation of Massaoua to the Consulta. He feared France might go there herself—and the Entente Cordiale was, in those days, still very far off.

This did not stop Lord Cromer, when he wrote his *Modern Egypt,* from expressing his pious regret that Italy had not used her strength on an exploitation of Sicily and Calabria instead. As we have seen, Lord Cromer was the last man entitled to express such a view.

Machiavellism, in the wretched sense attributed to the word in the centuries of the Counter-Reformation, was to be found far more on the side of Berlin and Vienna than on the side of Rome.

During the Congress of Berlin in 1878, Bismarck categorically offered Tunisia to Italy through the Italian Foreign Minister, Count Corti. But the offer was only formulated to him after it had been made to France, in agreement with Lord Salisbury, and once the eventual

acceptance of the Quai d'Orsay had been secured.* To
set Italy and France at variance, in order to benefit by their
quarrel, is anything more Machiavellian?

As for Austria, the serious point of friction with Italy
was first Albania; later on, Albania and Macedonia. Count
Nigra, the Italian Ambassador to Vienna, had succeeded
in making an agreement with the Ballplatz based on the
most absolute mutual disinterestedness, an agreement later
confirmed between Tittoni and Goluchowski, Foreign Ministers of the two countries. But, in practice, what happened? My personal recollections as a young diplomat in
Constantinople might suffice to show. From the very
day after the agreement, from 1901 till 1904, at every
audience after the Friday Selamlik, the Austro-Hungarian
Ambassador, Baron Calice, succeeded in extracting from
the Sultan semi-promises on behalf of Catholic Albanians
and even of Albanians as such against the Greeks from
Albanian Epirus. . . . All this was known at once
at the Italian Embassy, so desirous was the Sublime Porte
of finding some support against the ever more encroaching
Austrian demands. The Italian Embassy immediately protested at Yildiz Kiosk and drove the Consulta to protest
and bring Vienna back to the observance of the Nigra
agreement. But Vienna—while unable to cite similar
intrigues on the Italian side—thought each time she saved

---

* More prudent than Bismarck—or more careful of "respectability"?—
Salisbury who, probably in agreement with his German colleague, made
similar overtures to the Italians, merely said to the second Italian plenipotentiary at the Berlin Congress, Count de Launay, that Italy "should
occupy something in Northern Africa."

her face by endless tirades against the spirit of distrust manifested by the Italians, whose anticlerical liberalism failed to understand why His Imperial and Apostolic Majesty owed it to Austrian traditions to protect Catholicism in the East.

For ill-informed Germans, victims still of the necessarily poisoned war-time polemics, the fact remains that, on the day of trial, Italy broke a pact which had lasted since 1882. In the preceding chapter I have described the meaning of the renewal of the Triple Alliance in 1902. It will be enough to add only a few remarks.

On the eve of the declaration of war, at the end of July, 1914, the Vienna leaders may have believed—and public opinion in both the Central Empires did sincerely believe—that the case was one for defense.

Article VII of the Treaty of the Triple Alliance bound Italy and Austria, in case one or the other should desire to alter the *status quo* in the Balkans "by a temporary or a permanent occupation, first to come to an agreement with the ally based on the principle of mutual compensation for each advantage, territorial or otherwise, that either of the two Powers might gain over and above its present position."*

It was Austria that, ignoring this article, deliberately violated the treaty with Italy.

It is interesting to disclose that Kalnoky† the Austria-

---

* See the chapters on Pachich and Sonnino in my *Makers of Modern Europe.*

† Count Kalnoky was the all-powerful Minister of Franz Joseph from

Hungarian Foreign Minister, had strenuously objected, in 1887, at the time of the renewal of the Triple Alliance, to the inclusion of a similar formula required by Robilant, which later became Article VII of the Treaty. Bismarck persuaded Kalnoky to give in, calling his attention to the fact that it would be easy, when the time came, to elude the obligations provided under Article VII.

It is regrettable that the German document containing Bismarck's advice was not included in the large official collection of diplomatic documents on the *Grosse Politik* published in Berlin after the World War.

The perfect loyalty of Italy to the Triple Alliance had, I am ready to admit, a profound realistic basis as regards Austria. The thought which all those who were responsible for Italy's foreign policy had in common was this: no conquest of *irredente* lands is worth a war; if the Italians continue to progress as they do, in a general peace, whereas Austria will more and more be driven into a corner by insoluble problems consequent on the awakening of the nationalities she harbors, Italy will inevitably reap the harvest of historical evolution on the day the Hapsburg power falls. The Italian statesmen of the Triple-Alliance period were sufficiently intelligent to realize that the problems at stake were of such scope as to render senseless— all considerations of loyalty set aside—any attempts to

---

1881 to 1895. A conservative unimaginative Hungarian, he once caused friction with Italy by stating in a speech to the Austro-Hungarian Delegations (1891, Triple-Alliance time) that the question of the temporal power of the Pope was still unsettled.

hasten their solution through dangerous diplomatic intrigues.

Had there, in the troublous times that began at Algeciras and ended with the Austrian declaration of war on Serbia, been no other Machiavellism than that of the Italian diplomacy, the history of Europe might have been less bloodstained and less beastly.

With the Italians who rule the Roman Church the difference is one of ideals, not one of temperament.

We do not change the subject, therefore, if we study a few foreign legends regarding the action of the Vatican during the World War.

In spite of the profound discipline which more and more characterizes the attitude of all Catholics toward papal authority even in questions that do not concern faith, it is still being murmured in Belgian and French Catholic circles that the action of the Vatican was, during the war, unduly pro-German. Another token of the tenacity of legends which, born in the fever of war, withstand, after years, the most evident proofs of their falseness.

The truth is that in 1914 it was only for essentially religious reasons that the Vatican first inclined toward a victory of the Central Empires.

The lack of sympathy of the Vatican toward Protestant England, anticlerical France, liberal Italy, has been exaggerated. Traditions are long-lived at the Vatican; and what mainly scared the Roman Curia, in the make-up of the Entente, was Russia. For indeed one could hope for pro-Catholic movements of opinion in France, in Italy, even in the English High Church where symptoms of this nature were already to be detected. But Russian orthodoxy, under the leadership of Czarism, was an unshakable rock. The victory of Russia implied for the Vatican in 1914 the disappearance or, at least, humiliation of imperial Austria, the only great nation where the Catholic religion still enjoyed unequaled external prestige;* an ever stronger hold of Russia on Catholic Poland; Russia, mistress of Constantinople where she would have breathed new life into the Ecumenical Patriarchate, whose suspicion of the Bishop of Rome had been unabated since the fifteenth century; the foregoing of all hope of a union of the independent Churches in the Balkans; a loss of prestige of the Catholic missions in the Levant and possibly even in China, where the pressure of a victorious Russia would have been tremendous; finally, the loss of the privileges which, in the Holy Land, had remained in the hands of the Latins but were already seriously threatened by the orthodox monks.

Such, at the time, was the stock of dangers implied, in the mind of the Head of the Catholic Church, in a victory of the Entente.†

---

* External, for all vital religious life had disappeared from official Austria. When the Archduke Franz Ferdinand compelled the Emperor to appoint Conrad head of the General Staff, he knew the latter was no believer, but he requested him "to go to mass." Conrad himself tells the story in his *Memoirs*.

† See in my *Makers of Modern Europe* (chapter on Pius X and Benedict XV) documents proving that at the end of July, 1914, the Vatican wished the ruin of Serbia. The official organ of Catholicism in France, *La Croix,* expressed the same idea on the eve of the war. In its numbers of July

At the Vatican, a victory of Russia came to be considered a disaster even more serious than the Reformation. As this assertion may seem excessive, I shall adduce evidence. After Russia had withdrawn from the Entente, in April, 1918, Guglielmo Ferrero paid a visit to Cardinal Gasparri at the Vatican. The Secretary of State having spoken with the greatest warmth of the Entente countries, and especially of France, and the famous Italian historian having shown some astonishment at this, Gasparri replied with some heat (and Ferrero repeated it to me verbatim) :

"But how could we favor the Entente as long as Russia belonged to it? You know very well the manner in which Catholics were treated in Czarist Russia. The victory of Russia, to whom France and England had made so many promises, would have constituted for the Vatican a disaster even greater than the Reformation."

The Roman Church knew that the Belgian and French Catholics would always remain Catholic; she could sympathize with them in their trials, help them where she could; and she did. But her most essential interests were vested in Austria, just as her hopes of aggrandizement lay in the East. She could not desire that a new danger should threaten her precisely in that field where, since Leo XIII, she had multiplied her efforts of penetration.

This feeling endured even after the war. I have an accurate recollection of several cases which came to my

---

26-27, 1914, it said with violent irony to the French rulers: "The moment is well-chosen, gentlemen, to tell Austria she oversteps her rights. Faced with the manifest right of Austria . . ."

knowledge when I was Foreign Minister and which proved
to me that the Vatican viewed Bolshevism at the beginning
as undoubtedly a horrible evil, but also as a necessary evil
which might possibly have salutary consequences. Which,
from a strictly Catholic point of view, was no mistake.
The structure of the Orthodox Church would never have
given way so long as Czarism, its official protector, lasted.
Among the ruins accumulated by Bolshevism, there was
room for everything; even for a religious revival in which
the influence of the Roman Church might make itself felt.
The manifold conversions to Catholicism of White Russians who emigrated to France and Italy are perhaps no
proof; but, during my post-war travels in Russia, I personally have more than once, in the course of confidential conversations with Russians religiously disposed, detected the
acknowledgment that their old Church was dead, dead for
ever; and that they would perhaps one day have to find
grounds of agreement with Catholicism.

It is equally untrue—and here we deal with a legend that
was spread in Italy only in war-time—that Benedict XV
entertained feelings of hostility toward his country. Had
he not been a creature of Leo XIII who, bred on the
literature of Italian, Spanish and French legitimists of the
Donoso Cortes type, saw nothing in the unity of Italy but
"the works of the sects"?

Benedict XV was of a mind far more serene and ripe.
And he probably remained, in his attitude toward Italy,
what he had been from childhood up: a Genoese patrician,
proud of the glories of his old republic, harboring still—

a relic of the speeches he had heard as a child—a kind of
rancor against the Savoy family who had annexed the
state of Genoa to Piedmont in 1815. But, if he did not
like the monarchical Italy of the Risorgimento, he deeply
loved the Italians, even when they did not call themselves
sons of the Church. How often did the friend of his
childhood, Baron Monti, who as director general of Cult
Affairs at the Ministry of Justice often served for secret
agent between the Pope and the Italian Government when
I was Foreign Minister, repeat to me Benedict's words at
times when agreement on some litigious point seemed difficult to achieve: "Between ourselves we must agree."
And his nationalistic "between ourselves" would prove the
right word.

As regards the independence of the Holy See, Benedict
relied essentially on the feelings of an Italian democracy
which, he admitted, was patriotic and unitarian, but which
he hoped would be more and more Christian;* evidence
is not lacking in support. The artificial formulas of
sovereignty over palaces—so dear to his successor, Pius
XI—possessed for Benedict only the value of a diplomatic
position which he considered it his duty not to discard but
to which his realistic mind never attached any serious importance.

---

* Hence the support granted to the constitution of a Popular party
(Christian Democratic party), the destruction of which by the Fascists was
viewed with pleasure by Benedict's successor, Pius XI. The founder of
the Popular party, Don Sturzo, was obliged to leave Italy with the advent
of Fascism into power.

XI

ITALIANS AND YUGOSLAVS

THERE are two types of men that follow each other uninterruptedly in Italy throughout the long history of my country. Between the two types, the opposition is only apparent. The one is the man of realistic thought, who derives his philosophy from the cold observation of social life. Of this type are Machiavelli who opens up in Italy the era of modern thinking—Machiavelli whose true character is so different from the Machiavellism of manner invented by superficial strangers; Cavour, the most complete statesman of the nineteenth century; and, of yesterday, Giolitti with his somewhat pragmatic simplicity, his hatred of all rhetoric. The other type is that of the human saint, like Saint Francis of Assisi, Saint Filippo Neri, Mazzini, the Bandiera brothers shot by the Hapsburgs and the Bourbons, Mameli, the young hero-poet killed by a French bullet during the siege of Rome in 1849, Garibaldi, Battisti, the pure Trentino hero.

It is worth while to note that both the great classical types of Italian genius harbored, during the nineteenth century, the same ideas and the same hopes concerning what then constituted the problem of the Southern Slavs.

Our eastern neighbors in the first half of that century

164

were undergoing the first conscious aspirations of their national awakening. And Mazzini's *Lettere Slave* constituted the first and most eloquent defense of the Yugoslav people's reasons for life. Spread in France, in England, they put the Yugoslav problem in the minds of the thinkers of liberal Europe. All the Yugoslavs know—or should know—these pages which are still so much alive today. The Italians all knew them, or at least did until Mazzini's ideas were repudiated by a régime that censured and suppressed books as never Austria had dared to do under Francis I. (It is probably because of the numerous extracts from the *Lettere Slave* which it contained that a little book on Mazzini which I had published at Milan in 1925 was, by order of the Fascist Government, suppressed even in the catalogues of the firm who brought it out.)

The fact is less well known that Count Cavour, an Italian of a type directly opposed to Mazzini's, wrote—a few years after Mazzini—pages inspired by just the same sympathy for the independence of the Yugoslav people.

The Italian war against Radetsky's Austria was in full swing. The Croatian troops were fighting for the Austrian Emperor in the plains of Lombardy with a dynastic loyalty which their Kaiser a little later rewarded with the characteristic Hapsburg ingratitude "that astonished the world," even the world of the other sovereigns—and that is saying a great deal.

And Cavour, in his newspaper, was saying from Turin to the Italians: "It is futile for you to hate the Croats.

They are, like yourselves, the victims of a selfish power that sets its subjects, with their eleven languages, against one another. These Croats must one day become, with their brothers, the other Southern Slavs, the best friends and allies of Italy. . . ."

The memory is still fresh within me of one of the long war-time walks I used to take in Corfu with Prince Alexander, the future king of Yugoslavia. We were at the end of the old Venetian road of the *Cannone,* in a pine wood facing the island of Ulysses. I quoted to him the articles written by Cavour in 1848 on the Slavs. He knew Mazzini's *Lettere Slave,* but not Cavour's writings. He asked me for them. And as I did not have them at Corfu—although the house I lived in possessed a very beautiful collection of Italian books—I had them sent from Rome to Alexander at Salonica where he had gone in the meantime. He wrote me the following letter in response:

"My dear Count,

"I thank you very sincerely for the books you sent me and the words that went with them.

"Cavour's thought must some day become reality.

"My regards to the Countess Sforza. I hope your children stand the privations of Corfu well.

"Believe me," etc.

I am still certain today, as I was then, that his words about Cavour were much more than a compliment to me, though he knew how deeply convinced I was of the need for our two people to come to a fruitful understanding after the fall of the Hapsburg monarchy—a fall I never doubted for an instant, even during the most critical junctures of the war. I met Alexander Karageorgevich so often—in moments when there was no room for diplomatic attitudes—that, as I'll say later on, I can well assert he never ceased to wish for a real understanding between our two countries, as being the only means of insuring final security for his country.

How did it come to pass that so many Italians failed to agree, after the war, on the policy toward Yugoslavia which Mazzini and Cavour had advocated, the only policy, to my thinking, that would guarantee the security and the prosperity of our people?

It is historically interesting to make out the causes which have, in Italy, excited such wide differences of opinion even among men who all equally desired the good of their country. But I was myself the promoter of a decisive turn in Italo-Yugoslav relations; and as I wish to avoid the risk of seeming to exaggerate a personal contribution, I shall limit myself to stating facts, rigorously established facts.

Everybody knows that, when the war broke out in Europe in 1914, Italy could do nothing but proclaim her neutrality. I have explained in the preceding chapter that Vienna, having prepared the ultimatum to Serbia without informing Italy, had thereby violated the most essential clauses of the Triple Alliance.

But when, in September, 1914, Marquis di San Giuliano began to study the aims and conditions that would justify

Italy's entrance into the war on the side of the Entente, I found his views much clearer than his dilettante skepticism had led me* to expect from him. It is true that death was watching for him, that he knew it, and continued nevertheless to work stoically for his country—and that conditions of this nature are apt to purify a mind capable of holding up under the stress.

His ideas—as I was able to make out later from his correspondence and notes—may be synthetized thus:

To make sure that the Entente, who would be inclined to consider Germany the sole enemy, would not be tempted to spare Austria, the direct cause of the crisis;

To enter the war at the same time as Rumania;

To acquire the national Alpine frontier everywhere, as well as some Dalmatian islands, but to refraim from territorial conquests in Dalmatia, an essentially Slav province;

To wage the war in complete political agreement with Serbia, who also had a vital interest in the disappearance of the Hapsburg monarchy;

After the war, to continue a policy of collaboration with Belgrade, with a view to insuring Italian political influence in the East.

When San Giuliano died, on October 16, 1914, his ideas and plans had not yet taken definite shape. His successor was Baron Sonnino, the only one among first-rate Italian public men who had considered the possibility,

---

*I had been the Councilor to his London Embassy in 1909 and his *Chef de Cabinet* in 1910 when he became Foreign Minister.

when the World War broke out, of Italy taking part on the side of the Central Empires.*

It happened with Sonnino as it often does with honest but narrow minds. They can realize only immediate possibilities and have no vision of the future. Worse still, those well-meaning minds are suspicious of anything that seems to them "idealistic" or "sentimental" and feel safe only on the solid ground of "realities"; which simply proves that they are not sufficiently broad-minded to see all the "realities."

San Giuliano may have been right, or he may have been wrong, in the practical means he contemplated. But at least he had perceived that an old world was falling to pieces and that something new would take its place.

As for Sonnino, he saw nothing in our situation toward Austria but a juridical problem to solve. He never faced the assumption that Austria might disappear as a Great Power, and the new National States arise which Mazzini, with his prophetic insight, had foreseen.

Sonnino brushed aside his predecessor's comprehensive views as so many intellectual acrobatics. He gave his mind to the Treaty of Alliance. Article 7 of the Treaty —as we have seen already—bound Austria-Hungary and Italy, if they should change the *status quo* in the Balkans "by a temporary or a permanent occupation," to come to an understanding by preliminary agreement "on the principle of mutual compensation for each advantage, territorial or otherwise, that either might win."

---

* One party only, the Nationalist party—which later joined Fascism— shared Sonnino's opinion.

On this point he started discussion with Count Berchtold who answered from Vienna with pitiable distinctions between "temporary" and "momentary" occupation. The two men seemed to have one idea in common: that the life of the Austro-Hungarian monarchy was not really at stake.

Thus it came about that Sonnino, his legitimate demands for compensation having been rejected, came to sign his Treaty of London with the Entente powers,* by which he secured for Italy a portion of Dalmatia. This latter fact alone should have made Sonnino—had his mind been wont to see far ahead—forego any thought of a lasting agreement with Belgrade such as San Giuliano had wished; on the contrary, Serbia became for him a potential adversary.

Facts, indeed, took good care not to give him the lie. From the day the war began, General Cadorna, who had not been in favor of Dalmatian annexations, had to admit that collaboration with the Serbian Army, which he had wanted to be close and unceasing, did not materialize.

When I discussed this phase of the war later on with Pachich in Corfu during our walks to the *Cannone,* or with Serbian generals, my comments on their military passivity elicited nothing but specious apologies. Except one which, I had to admit, carried a certain weight:

---

* Signed April 28, 1915, by Sir Edward Grey and the Ambassador of Italy, Imperiali, the Ambassador of France, Paul Cambon, and the Ambassador of Russia, Benckendorff.

"The Treaty of London as Sonnino had wanted it," said Pachich, and several Serbian generals corroborated the statement, "became in the hands of the Austro-Hungarian High Command a tremendous argument with which to persuade their Slav troops that by fighting for the monarchy they avoided Italian imperialism, which had already acquired a right to a part of Dalmatia where over ninety per cent of the population was Slav."

If, in the spring of 1915, Serbian passivity, amounting almost to desertion, could be largely imputed to the grievances of the Belgrade politicians who had emigrated to Corfu, Sonnino alone was responsible for preventing, a few months later, a military collaboration that had by then become possible. The Italian and French General Headquarters were agreed to send an Inter-Allied military expedition to the Serbian front. Cadorna, on his side, counted on it to make a serious advance on the impervious Carso front, from which the Austrians would have been obliged to withdraw troops. The French had unhesitatingly admitted that the commander-in-chief of the expedition should be an Italian general. As was meet for republicans, the French had even gone so far as to suggest that the Duke of Aosta, first cousin to the King and Commander of the Third Army, should be chosen. But at the last moment, Sonnino refused.

I have said that the responsibility for Serbian passivity in 1915 lay mainly with the Belgrade politicians. The exiled Croatian leaders showed themselves, at least for a certain time, more reasonable and less suspicious. Having been appointed Minister to the King of Serbia, but having first been sent to Switzerland on a confidential mission for a few months, I found there that the Croatians were far more open than the Serbians to my suggestions of censure.

"You are afraid of the Treaty of London," I said to them. "But how can you fail to understand that, the more efficient the Serbian military action, the more you will be entitled to a reasonable revision of the London Treaty?"

Naturally, I repeated my conversations word for word to Sonnino whenever I rushed back to Rome. And the man whose straightforwardness I admired as much as I dreaded his mental short-sightedness, used to answer:

"Just go on doing as you think best; but don't tell me about it."

Being honest, he felt my action was necessary; but, shut up within his poor juridical frame of mind, he feared any breath of air that might upset his house of cards.

When it became evident in 1918 that the supreme ruler of the peace negotiations would be Wilson, I wrote to Sonnino asking him again to allow me to come to a complete understanding with Prince Alexander and Pachich. "If," I wrote, "we come to the Peace Conference with our Oriental problem settled, we'll be able to look for a much greater influence on world affairs. Otherwise we risk spending all our forces in a sterile struggle with the Yugoslavs."

Sonnino, who knew what I meant by an honest com-

plete agreement (more or less what I accomplished at
Rapallo) wired me that he authorized my conversations
with Pachich. But a few days later he wired again,
instructing me to suspend all conversations and await "final
instructions" which never arrived.

When I saw him again and told him that his way of
considering the problem struck me as rash, he answered
simply, somewhat embarrassed, since he knew how deeply
I felt that the method I urged was the only one that
could guarantee the interests of our country:

"You know, I am like the Tuscan peasants. I prefer
to lower the price of my cattle during the last hour of
the market. . . ."

The leaders of a war in which Europeans died by the
million were often like that—on both sides of the trenches.

The later manifestations of Sonnino's objection to any
sort of military understanding with his Eastern allies
came to look very much like mental obsession. Italy had,
on the Macedonian front, a body of troops which often
exceeded seventy thousand men. Officers and men always
entertained the most cordial relations with their Serbian
companions in arms. But this contingent, so important
and highly appreciated, was officially called only the 35th
division. As names count in foreign politics, I had
insisted several times that the name, in this case as important as the thing, should be an Army Corps. Probably
without precedent in the history of the war, Sonnino
always vetoed the suggestion. He was quite willing to
help Serbia, but he did not want it to be known.

Sonnino had always contemplated a short war, and his Treaty of London, with Allied loans that would hardly cover a few weeks of hostilities, proves it.   He had imagined a war ending without the destruction of Austria, and he had never resigned himself to the fact that history might evolve along lines different from those he had imagined.

At the end of the war, Italy would have been entitled to tell herself that six hundred thousand of her children had not died in vain.   Not only had she reconquered her natural frontiers, but the downfall of imperial Austria had given her back full diplomatic liberty; for before the war, as I have already said, Italy had been bound by an ever-present dilemma: whether to be friend or foe to Austria.   Whence, with Austria-Hungary gone, resulted an increase in the international influence of Italy, now entirely free in her decisions.   Even the gropings and contradictions of Fascist diplomacy have not succeeded in obliterating this influence, at least not in Central Europe and the Balkans, where I was sure, when I was in charge of the foreign policy of my country, that it should become preponderant—in the interest of the organization of peace.

But Sonnino was in peace-time just as he had been during the war: convinced that Italy would have fought in vain if the letter of his London Treaty was not fulfilled. Like all those who cannot imagine victory otherwise than as armed and threatening someone, he considered in good faith that Italy would lose the fruits of her victory if, like a new Austria, she did not settle in Dalmatia.

Everybody remembers the endless and sterile discussions at the Peace Conference over Dalmatia and Fiume, between Sonnino and Wilson, Sonnino and Clemenceau.

Is anything more natural than that an important part of Italian public opinion should imagine that victory had been "mutilated" and that the fault lay with those Slav neighbors, half of whom had fought fiercely against us under the Austrian colors?

Besides, plausible explanations could be added to these fallacious feelings. The conquest of Dalmatia, as it had been imagined by Sonnino and his nationalists, was only a sign of weakness, or, at least, of suspicion—a barbed wire against a neighbor far weaker than ourselves; whereas I, after Sonnino, convinced as I was of the reasons for Italian superiority, wished to open up the East to Italian influence. But Dalmatia was full of towns, of monuments, of all kinds of relics of ancient Italian glories. Nothing strange, therefore—as I have said in the preceding chapter—if public opinion disliked the idea of giving up the ancient possessions of Venice.

Nothing unnatural also, alas, that after the violence and the sufferings engendered by four years of war, the generous and prophetic words of Mazzini should be forgotten—Mazzini who had preached the European need of, and Italy's interest in, the resurrection of the nationalities subject to imperial Austria. Few generous thoughts withstand the atmosphere of war—and of victory. The childish and aggravating exaggerations of the young Yugoslav nationalism, for that matter, helped to perfec-

tion the propaganda for anti-Slav hatred that the Italian
nationalists were carrying on in Italy. It is just the same
in Italy and in Yugoslavia as in France and in Germany:
rival nationalisms are necessary to each other, are precious
auxiliaries to each other, with the mentality, the fixed
ideas they have in common—megalomania and the persecution mania.

When I became Minister for Foreign Affairs in June,
1920, my personal situation toward my two predecessors,
Tittoni and Scialoja, might seem paradoxical. But only
in appearance. Tittoni had not rejected the offer of a
borderline a few kilometers from Trieste which Lloyd
George had suggested to him at Clairfontaine in the
autumn of 1919. Scialoja had been ready to break the
geographical unity of Istria by accepting a frontier that
cut it in two.* As for me, I considered that, after four
years of war and with more than half a million dead, Italy
—so often invaded in the course of her history—should
stretch to her most perfect natural frontier, the Alps and,
as Dante has said, "Quarnaro's bay, which shuts in Italy
and bathes her strands."† But, on the other hand, I was

---

* Ambassador in Paris in 1915 during the negotiations of the London
Treaty, Tittoni had been definitely opposed to Sonnino's views on Dalmatia;
and he did not hide from Sonnino, in his dispatches, that he thought it
dangerous to render future Italo-Yugoslav relations difficult. His accurate
appreciation of Italy's interests at that time should have made Tittoni more
uncompromising on the question of the natural frontier in 1919; for he
could have proved to Wilson and to the latter's representatives that he
had been in favor of a policy of friendship with the Slavs long before
Wilson himself had been.

† *Inferno,* IX.

ready, for the supreme interests of my country, to face an
unpopularity which, as I have just explained, would not
have been entirely artificial.

A few days after the constitution of the Giolitti Cabinet,
in which I had taken the portfolio of Foreign Affairs, I
was given an opportunity, during the Spa Conference
(July, 1920) to probe the real intentions of the Belgrade
Government, and to notify them of my own views. This
I did with Trumbich, Minister for Foreign Affairs of the
neighboring kingdom, whom I had met during the war
at the conclusion of the Corfu pact between Serbs and
Croats. At the same time I made it clear to my Spa
colleagues, Millerand, Lloyd George and Curzon, that I
was determined to have very soon a final settlement, if
possible in full agreement with Belgrade, but if necessary
quite independent of Belgrade as well as of London and
Paris.* Millerand and Lloyd George understood. Indeed
it was at Spa that the atmosphere was built up out of
which, five months later, arose the Treaty of Rapallo.

As soon as Europe had become convinced that the dis-
orders, which were then sporadically breaking out in Italy,
were only a transitory result of post-war neurasthenia, and
that the clever legend of Bolshevist danger (kept up later
by Fascism for publicity's sake) had vanished from all
clear-thinking minds—thanks to the sober but firm meas-

---

* My idea was, in case of Yugoslav opposition: formal unilateral annexation of all the regions—and those only—which later on the Treaty of Rapallo
acknowledged as Italian; and the simple continuation, under some sort
of autonomous rule, of military occupation in Dalmatia, waiting for
Yugoslav repentance and conversion to the advantages of Italian friendship.

ures taken by Giolitti—I summoned the Yugoslav plenipotentiaries to Rapallo to settle the Adriatic question at
last.

The American historian Shotwell has recounted a few
dramatic details of these negotiations.*   The Treaty of

---

* From Shotwell's study, *A Diplomat in Exile:*
". . . Count Sforza refused to place the negotiation on the basis of
ordinary diplomatic bargaining.   It was to be an honest conciliation of
the national aspirations of two peoples which should finally result in an
entente between them.   He offered therefore to meet the claims of the
Yugoslavs with a single sweeping concession of all Dalmatia (excepting
Zara), but on the north he stood firm for the natural frontier of the
Eastern Alps.   This the Yugoslav ministers were not prepared to grant.
Count Sforza's final ultimatum was an appeal that they should face the
unpopularities of the settlement—for any settlement would be unpopular
—with a courage equal to his own, for he was prepared to carry through
the policy of peace in the Adriatic at the cost even of his exile or death;
then turning on his heel he abruptly left them as though the rupture had
actually come.   Next morning the Yugoslav delegation accepted the Italian
program and two days later the Treaty of Rapallo was signed. . . .
In this episode Count Sforza's character stands revealed.   Orthodox diplomacy was thrown aside.   Dramatic and decisive speech violated all the conventions, but it spoke to the conscience of responsible statesmen as man
to man.
"It was not merely by the Treaty of Rapallo that Count Sforza laid
the lines of a sound Italian policy in the Adriatic.   He evacuated Albania
while guarding the island of Sasseno to watch over Valona.   It is small
wonder that he should attack the adventurous policy of Mussolini in
Albania and the pin-prick policy with reference to Yugoslavia.   Sforza
saw clearly that the supreme need of Italy in Balkan politics was a
consistent and generous attitude toward any movement of pacification,
even if it envisaged the creation of a single Balkan State; he saw that
order and prosperity in the Near East were more to Italy's advantage
than anarchy, and that the best way to diminish the exuberance of Serbian
nationalism was to increase the wealth of the people and add to the
responsibilities of the government of Belgrade.
"This is far-seeing statesmanship, and one can understand Count
Sforza's impatience with the short-sightedness of Mussolini's substitute for
it in the interference in Albania, in diplomatic coquetry . . . with

Rapallo (November 12, 1920) secured for Italy Alpine frontiers more perfect even than those attributed to Italy under the Roman Empire, the whole of Istria, the islands of Lussin and of Cherso, privileges for the Italians in Dalmatia, the sovereignty over Zara and the independence of Fiume. Fiume, after a long struggle, was recognized as an Italian free city, directly united to the territory of the Kingdom of Italy—that is to say, she was to be Italian in everything, but to keep the autonomy which was the very essence of her history and necessary if she was to assume the function of common center for both Yugoslav and Italian trade—a need that the downfall of Fiume, under the artificial régime imposed on the unfortunate town by Fascism, has definitely proved.

But the moral value of the Rapallo Treaty consisted mainly in this: that it constituted the first post-war treaty to be concluded not only freely, but also with the joint active will of both countries to collaborate in the future. The anti-Hapsburg convention we signed on the same day was the first proof of this, reinforced by the adhesion to it of the Czechoslovakian and Rumanian Governments, given to me with a broad understanding of the higher interests of the successor States of Austria, which Benes had been the first to formulate clearly.*

---

the reactionary elements in Hungary. The foreign policy of Mussolini in the Near East is the exact antithesis of that followed by County Sforza . . . and one does not have to wait for history to form a judgment of their relative wisdom."

* A disciple of Masaryk, Eduard Benes has been at the head of the Czechoslovakia foreign policy since the creation of the State. On December 18, 1935, he succeeded Masaryk as President of the Republic.

Twelve days later in Parliament, in answer to a member who maintained from the nationalist benches that I might have asked for more, I said:

"Is it wise to build a Chinese wall where we want free and fertile outlets to the East? Mr. Federzoni says that, had we gauged the international situation more accurately, we could have asked for more. No, we knew the situation quite well; but had it been a hundred times more favorable to us, I should still have considered that I was betraying the future destinies of Italy by asking for more. And you know quite well, Mr. Federzoni, that my opinion has never varied on this point."

Fifteen months after the resignation of the Giolitti Cabinet, toward the end of 1922, chance would have it that the semblance of power, not power itself, fell to the lot of a rabbit-hearted politician by the name of Facta, who, half unconscious and half a traitor, opened the gates of Rome to Fascism.

Fascism had only one program: to remain where a miraculous stroke of luck had brought it. It therefore indifferently turned every color in foreign politics. It began by proposing to go and "fetch the reparations gold in Berlin" and ended by defending all the German revisionistic theories. It first helped Poincaré to go to the Ruhr, and later on dictated a campaign of hatred against France. It seriously suggested a continental entente against England, and a while after entered Chamberlain's service to threaten Turkey with invasion, until Mustafa Kemal gave in to the British Foreign Office on the gasoline question—

Italy, in the bargain, getting nothing but calls from Chamberlain on Mussolini and the said Chamberlain's praises of Fascism. The same thing occurred with Yugoslavia. Fascism began by pursuing a friendly policy with Belgrade, so much so that a member named Giunta was found who, in a House as domesticated as the Fascist Parliament, exclaimed one day:

"But it is Sforza's policy that is being continued!"

For a long time, Fascism, among other grievances, reproached France for her alliance with Yugoslavia. It saw in this a danger of encirclement: so true is it that personal régimes all end by repeating themselves with monotonous similarity. As in Germany under the last of the Hohenzollerns, Italy witnessed the re-birth of "dry cannon-powder," "encirclement." . . .

Indeed, I cannot possibly see, in this particular case, what the wrongs committed by the French Government might be. The first idea and first proposal of a three-party treaty between France, Italy and Yugoslavia, came from Rome in 1923, when Fascism was already in power. The suggestion did not materialize. It was taken up again in 1925, on the initiative, this time, of the Minister for Foreign Affairs at Belgrade, Ninchich. This loyal Serb, full of insight, with whom I had shared in Corfu the monotonous pastimes of Austrian bombardment, was a warm partisan in his country of the policy of understanding and diplomatic collaboration which I initiated in 1920 and '21 with the Treaty of Rapallo and the anti-Hapsburg convention. This time the proposals came from Paris to

Rome, but the Fascist Government, apparently not hostile to them at first sight, ended by raising numerous objections and by asking Belgrade for a formal alliance exclusive of any other power. The result was such as could easily have been foreseen. Belgrade, fearing isolation, began negotiating simultaneously with Paris and with Rome. These negotiations, on the point of conclusion in Paris, were delayed through Briand's courteous wish to await the issue on the Italian side. As the Italian treaty seemed imminent, Briand was satisfied merely to initial the Franco-Yugoslav draft, out of regard for Italy and to enable the Fascist Government to conclude and sign first. This flourish of the pen was renewed three times during 1926 and 1927, in order to let the Roman Cabinet smooth the ceaselessly recurring difficulties that prevented the understanding with Belgrade. And when Briand proceeded at last to sign the treaty on November 11, 1927, he had six weeks before informed the Roman Cabinet of the forthcoming signature and of the conditions under which the treaty had been negotiated.

Had a free press been able to give honest information to my country, there is no doubt public opinion would have recognized that Briand did all he could to allow Italy to keep the rank and state to which she is entitled in the East; a right Briand was ready to acknowledge in the most formal manner. He told me so more than once.

But questions of prestige and show have, with personal governments, an importance that is often detrimental to the real interests of a country.

It seems obvious that a three-party treaty, with a loyal admission on the part of France of Italy's special interests, would, better than any two-party treaty, have insured greater advantages to Italy—and made for peace. For my part, faced with a proposal of this sort, I should have been afraid only of the opposition of those who, in France, believe in their turn that their country is diminished if she does not enjoy an exclusive position everywhere.

It is not admitted by everybody, either in France or in Italy, that the prosperity and independence of the successor States of Austria-Hungary are supremely important for both countries. For as long as Italy shall desire to maintain the victory that brought about the destruction of this European anachronism—a big dynastic State whose chiefs had as sole watchword their secular and hateful *divide et impera;* for as long as Italy shall desire that the sacrifice of six hundred thousand of her children shall not have been in vain; for so long must she will the independent life of those National States which Mazzini had invoked in 1850 as a consequence of the liberation of the Italian fatherland and as condition of its true independence. Far be it from me to deny that the new States, freed of the long Germano-Magyar hegemony that saw nothing in them but human herds born to serve,* committed many errors and excesses; but this only proves that violence calls for violence. The essential remains; and if I secured at

---

* *Tot ember, nem ember* (the Czechoslovak is no man); how often did I hear this proverb on haughty Magyar lips in the picturesque Tatra Mountains.

Rapallo the cordial and willing recognition by the Belgrade Government of the fact that half a million Slavs must become Italians since they lived on our side of the Alps, it was only due to the fact that I succeeded in making it understand that a common danger still existed from the Hapsburgs, and that the friendship and good will of a great power like Italy deserved some sacrifices.

A little while afterward, the unfortunate Charles of Hapsburg's attempt to recover his throne proved how far I was right. As honest as a weak man can be* and certainly well-meaning, the last of the Emperors of Vienna —an innocent victim of the nemesis of his family—soon learned that no action, no sympathy from old French circles, no vague promise, could help where the common will of Italy and the successor States manifested itself. The immediate decision with which Benes, from Prague, and I, from Rome, thwarted the danger proved, as facts alone can, the usefulness of the understanding I had set up between Rome, Prague and Belgrade.

In spite of all their mistakes, and the much more serious and less excusable errors we, the Great Powers, committed at their birth, the new nations which have taken the place

---

* Having retired to Switzerland, Charles had given his word of honor to the Federal Council that he would not foment any plots against his former States from the Helvetian territory. Having learned that, in spite of his given word, he was busy preparing a raid, I immediately advised the government in Berne. These republicans—men of sound judgment—wondered that I should question the word of a Hapsburg to such an extent. Certain archælogical phenomena were beyond them: of what value could that promise be, for the heir of so many emperors, which Swiss churls had extorted from him?

of old artificial Austria are living entities. They are the permanent material out of which a new organized Europe may one day be built.

European history has more than one example to show of great States whose diplomacy axiomatically considered that their interest lay in having small neighbors only. But Italy, sure of her strength and of her vitality, can witness only with satisfaction the old animosities between Serbs and Croats, and even more between Serbs and Bulgarians, give way to an intimacy that may one day become the kernel of a free union between all the Southern Slavs* in which none shall pretend to the part of guide or umpire.

There again, the magnificent story of the Italian Risorgimento could be studied with profit by our neighbors. If the unity of Italy was sealed so quickly, it was thanks to the abnegation of Piedmont which, having risked and given everything, stoically coalesced with the other regions of Italy, losing all its ancient privileges.

Indeed, if there are two peoples whose interest lies in agreeing with each other, they are the Italian and the Yugoslav. I should still say today what I said in the Italian Parliament at a time when the air was full of quarrels and grievances:

"The two peoples must agree. If they do not agree out of love, they shall one day agree out of necessity and interest."

---

* Yugoslavia, indeed, means only Southern Slavia.

XII

THE LITTLE ENTENTE

LORD SALISBURY used to say that the Anglo-Russian relations were imperiled by only one fact: the small size of geographic maps giving the impression that the Russian bear was just round the corner, ready to hurl himself on poor disarmed India.

A like simplicity of conception has helped to create a certain nostalgia for old imperial Austria-Hungary. The vast unicolored blot stretching from Bohemia to Sarajevo was more reassuring than all these Balkan stains of color out of which had come, during the nineteenth century, too many rumors of wars, plots, uprisings.

The Roman Church has helped a great deal to form all over Europe a sort of posthumous benevolence toward old Austria-Hungary. At the Vatican they knew well enough how little true Christianity lay behind the outworn pietism of the Hapsburg monarchy, a fact I have alluded to in a previous chapter. But Austria-Hungary was the single great State where the sovereign followed, every year, bareheaded, the solemn procession of Corpus Christi, hour after hour. Well they knew at the Vatican the price they frequently had to pay for such external homages: servility in Albania, painful compromises in the

Levant. . . . But all that occurred in secret, just
vaguely guessed by the French and Italian Embassies in
Vienna and Constantinople, equally jealous of any attempt
on the rights of their political protectorates over Catholic
missions in Turkey.

In Paris also—if not in France, so much more sensible
than Paris—a strong Austrian tradition had long existed,
especially in aristocratic salons and diplomatic circles.
Traditional French groups too often pay the penalty
for an almost too finished historical and political culture.

When I was Ambassador in Paris how frequently I fan-
cied that each pigeonhole at the Quai d'Orsay contained a
copy of the Treaty of Westphalia, the ideas of which, inspired as they were by the end of the Thirty Years' War,
still seem to direct the political notions in fashion with the
Académie Française and other equally stuffed bodies. I
once said something of the kind to Briand, and he replied:
"*Oui, oui* . . . the Peace of Westphalia"—and I
immediately felt that he was not so sure about dates and
ideas; then after a smile—"Yes, these gentlemen around
me know many dead things and very little of life. . . ."

The Westphalia idea was to break up the Germanic
nation into fragments. After the World War, the French
traditionalistic idea was to use an Austrian monarchy to
divide again the German nation at least in two.

England also had her lot of Austrophiles and Hungaro-
philes; society people who had friends among the great
landowners of the Austrian aristocracy, newly created

lords who had become easy victims to the exquisite charm
of the Magyar leading families. . . .

The ex-Emperor Charles was still living then, in Switzerland, a claimant to the Hungarian throne.

It was natural, therefore, that the successor States of
destroyed Austria-Hungary should have become conscious
of common ties which soon developed into the Little
Entente, thanks to the action of Eduard Benes.

The first diplomatic act marking the union was the
Czecho-Yugoslav Convention signed in Belgrade on
August 4, 1920, by Benes, then Czechoslovak Minister
for Foreign Affairs, and Ninchich, then in charge of the
Yugoslav Ministry for Foreign Affairs in the absence of
its titular head, Ante Trumbich. Three men they were
who had suffered personally too long under Austria not
to agree quickly on a common defensive action in the event
of a common danger. The Convention envisaged only
an unprovoked Hungarian attack, but the future President
of Czechoslovakia well knew that the link forged in
Belgrade was only a first step toward a wider diplomatic
outcome.

A few weeks before, at the Spa Conference, I had
spoken to the Yugoslav Foreign Minister Trumbich in
terms novel in the dreary and sterile series of polemics
over the Adriatic question. I had known Trumbich in
Corfu during the war and I talked to him with complete
frankness. The Serbians are braver fighting an enemy in
war than face to face with political responsibilities. That
is why I told him that I was prepared, for my part, to

brave any unpopularity in the lasting interests of Italy; that the Government of Belgrade was confronted, in the Giolitti-Sforza Cabinet, with a strong government ready to act and assume heavy responsibilities, but that I could not accept the mean territorial compromises agreed to by my predecessors, Tittoni and Scialoja;* that I would be inflexible for the complete Alpine frontier, including Mount Nevoso; but that, on the other hand, I should treat with Belgrade in a spirit of fecund union; to show which I offered them an Anti-Hapsburg Convention.

They accepted, tempted mainly by this Convention, which was signed on the same day as the Treaty of Rapallo.

The three following are the essential articles of the Anti-Hapsburg Convention:

1. The two Governments pledge themselves jointly to take all political measures calculated to prevent the restoration of the House of Hapsburg either to the throne of Austria or to that of Hungary;

2. The two Governments pledge themselves to afford, each to the other, such diplomatic assistance as is most suitable to attain the above aim;

3. The two Governments pledge themselves to mark all activities against their reciprocal safety, whether coming from Austrian or from Hungarian territory, and to that end they will maintain the closest possible contact with each other.

Another article added that the Italian Government,

---

* They had accepted a frontier line within ten kilometers of Trieste. Both became later on supporters of Fascism.

which had learned with deep satisfaction the agreement reached between the Yugoslav Government and the Czechoslovak Government, would bring the Convention to the knowledge of the Prague Government.

The Convention drafted by me did not provide for the hypothesis of a war, which had been envisaged by the Benes-Ninchich Convention; for all the rest, the spirit was identical. From the moment Italy entered the lists, an hypothesis of war had become a practical impossibility; Hungary would never have ventured upon war.

Three months later, in February, 1921, Benes came to Rome on an official visit. We confirmed on this occasion the perfect identity of our views.* In dealing with Benes, I came to feel how deserved the praise was which Masaryk

---

* We exchanged the following letters:

"Rome, February 8, 1921.

"To the Czechoslovak Minister for Foreign Affairs.

"Sir,

"I am happy to have had the opportunity of ascertaining, in the course of the conversation I had with Your Excellency, the absolute identity between the views and guiding lines of both our countries in their foreign policies, an identity which results from the interests our two peoples have in common and which is even more manifest in questions pertaining to the enforcement of peace treaties and to the policy which should be followed toward the successor States of the Austro-Hungarian monarchy, because the goals we aim at in the interest of the security and prosperity of our peoples are perfectly concordant.

"I am glad of this fact, all the more because it guarantees the agreement and political collaboration of both States even more efficaciously than the special provisions of a Convention could do.

"But in consideration of the fact that the Italian frontiers were fixed under the Treaty of Rapallo concluded between Italy and the State of the Serbs, Croats and Slovenes and that a special Convention of a political nature was drawn up on this occasion, it is natural that the communication made to the Czechoslovak Government of the grounds of Article 4 of the

once bestowed on him in a pithy sentence: "As fast as events evolve, so fast does Benes grow."

After the visit of Benes to Rome, ex-Emperor Charles tried the move of his Hungarian restoration which I mentioned in the preceding chapter. But my agreements were ready, were perfect—and annihilated in a few days an adventure which, had it succeeded, would have destroyed all the results of the World War; for the full sense of the latter will be grasped only when it is called by its true name: the War of the Austrian Succession.

Shortly afterward, a conference of the successor States of Austria-Hungary met in Rome at the Chigi Palace, under my presidency, and in a spirit of trust and collaboration. We had to discuss economic questions existing between our respective countries. "We will prove to all Europe," I declared in my opening address, "and prove it with the matchless eloquence of facts, that in our existing society it is impossible to conceive an economic state

---

said Convention acquire the significance that the agreements and pledges thereunder provided shall be valid also for Italy and Czechoslovakia.

"Believe me," etc.

(Signed) "Sforza."

To which Benes answered:

"Rome, February 8, 1921.

"To the Italian Minister for Foreign Affairs.

"Sir,

"I have the honor to acknowledge receipt of your note, the context of which follows:

[Here follows reproduction of preceding letter.]

"I am glad to be able to communicate to Your Excellency that my Government fully agrees with the contents of the note above, and I beg Your Excellency to believe me," etc.

(Signed) "Edward Benes."

of real well-being not indissolubly joined to the well-being of our neighbors."

Evident truths for any serene student of world affairs, they were nevertheless bitterly criticized in Italy by the nationalist group and in France—where the memories of the war were still too fresh—by almost everybody. I cannot say that even today they have become over-obvious.

A new link in the Little Entente was forged later on by two treaties which, in the same spirit as their forerunners, allied Rumania with Czechoslovakia and Yugoslavia. Before he definitely started on the negotiations which led to the signature of the two treaties, the Rumanian Prime Minister, Take Jonescu, had asked my advice and my assent. I answered with a long private letter, the essential parts of which ran as follows: "The States born of the destruction of Austria-Hungary or aggrandized in consequence of this destruction, may have faults and make mistakes; but as they arose in opposition to purely dynastic interests, purified by their national vitality, they will be useful to Europe tomorrow if they show that they are capable of inter-organizing themselves instead of shutting themselves up in exclusive nationalisms. Europe yesterday was artificial. You are the sound material from which an organized Europe may spring tomorrow. Show that you are capable of understanding each other, of uniting with each other."

It matters little if men change. Instead of Take Jonescu, Rumania has in Titulesco one of the keenest minds of contemporary Europe. What was the greatest danger in pre-war Europe? That the Balkan States might become cat's-paws for the secret quarrels and jealousies which the Great Powers did not openly dare to avow.

One may point to many faults still in the States that make up the Little Entente. But at least they are living entities. They are, as I wrote Take Jonescu, the healthy permanent material out of which a new peaceful organized Europe may some day emerge.

Those who regret pre-war Europe forget that with the old selfish, militaristic and bureaucratic empires, like Austria, Germany and Russia, it would have been useless to hope for a Europe which could bow to a higher moral law. The sterile oligarchies of courtiers, bureaucrats and generals which governed these empires, with their dangerous material force and sterile moral life, were even incapable of realizing that the need was imperative to put a stop to the anarchy of Europe.

But today, at least, the problem challenges the conscience of all the peoples of our new Europe.

XIII

THE BALKANS: THE POLITICAL ATMOSPHERE

NOTHING is pettier, and at the same time more pompous, than the distant manner in which the Great Powers are wont to talk of political life in the Balkans.

As a young diplomat, I went practically everywhere in the Balkans. Later, I spent three of the four years of the war with the Serbians at Corfu and in Macedonia. After that, when I became responsible for the foreign policy of my country, I had, with Balkan statesmen, discussions sometimes bitter, and relations always interesting. Shall I say that I never noticed that Balkan political life had produced any very different types from those of the West? Pachich was as silent as an old Turkish Sultan, but no more so than Sonnino. Stambuliski was whimsical and spontaneous, but no more so than Churchill. . . .

After the 1919 treaties, a saying enjoyed a certain vogue, "Europe has been Balkanized. . . ."

Never has there been a more thoughtless and unjust saying: first, because the most serious Balkan faults and mistakes nearly always find their origin in the instigations and intrigues of some Western cabinet; but especially for this moral reason, which we, in our pharisaic pride, too often forget in the West—that the somber and tormented

194

history of the Balkan nations often constitutes an excuse
for a good many of their errors and sins and for their
backwardness and always explains them.

Let us reflect for a moment. Italy also has known
centuries of servitude and bondage. But even in the
darkest days, its language and its marvelous literature
always shone like a beacon light in the hearts of Italians.
In the Balkans, fate would have it that Greek should at
first be the language of culture and trade among the
Christians, whereas the Slav and Latin accents of the
poor were contemned as barbaric jargons.

With the rise of national independences during the nineteenth century, another evil hindered the progress of
public life: the over-hasty and factitious creation of a
class of pseudo-bourgeois politicians who substituted for
the sound virtues of the peasants, the artificial vices of
the West, omitting all its solid virtues.

Anyone well acquainted with the ancient public life of
Turkey knows that the legend of Eastern corruption arises
partly out of a Western misconception. In the old Turkey
of the four or five last Sultans—the Turkey whose flag
still flew from Belgrade right into Moldavia—the pashas
rarely drew their emoluments, and by way of compensation, had to ransom those under their jurisdiction; but
the latter, in their turn, paid for corrupting officials only
what they saved by not paying their taxes. Deplorable
customs, indeed; mainly because of the lowering of moral
standards they entailed by making lying a necessary implement of daily life. But what did we learn in the West

after the World War? That as soon as rifts occur within our rigid old administrations, as soon as some bold *coup d'état* succeeds in getting hold of power, the immediately consequential public and private scandals are such as to neutralize decades of scrupulously clean management. To cite one Fascist régime only, suffice it to remember that the Weimar Republic fell mainly because the swindling and thieving of the noble feudal lords of the Ost-Elbe had to be covered up. How shocked would Berlin and Vienna have been, had one-tenth of these misdeeds happened along the banks of the Danube!

Political life in the Balkans is not, after all, from the moral standpoint, worse than in the West. I should even go so far as to say that, despite certain appearances, it is, in a sense, almost better, because it is a little more human, a little less mechanical, and consequently less cruel.

On the other hand, an essential trait of public life in the Balkans seems to be a lack of courage in face of sudden decisions, and a certain tendency to tergiversation in the whole administrative life. There is the same difference between the Balkans and the West—as regards speed— as between Latin and North America. But as for that I have just returned from the United States, where I lectured before three universities through several long months, and I am not so certain that the dogma and the myth of speed have brought about more happiness from Texas to Chicago than the nonchalant Castilian laziness has created in South America.

A member of the Italian Parliament, and having inti-

mately known two other Western parliaments, I have
rarely seen, at Montecitorio, at the Palais Bourbon, or
at Westminster, a spectacle that, in its rugged peasant
simplicity, ever moved me to greater respect than the
sittings of the Serbian members stranded at Corfu during
the war: no brilliant oratory, no daring schemes, but
simply meeting to assert without bombast their unshakable
determination to resist, their faith in the life of old and
democratic Serbia, where each of the exiles owned a patch
of land for which he felt home-sick.

I said above that I often had to discuss, to negotiate, to
treat with Balkan statesmen. Our discussions were sometimes friendly, sometimes thorny. And as I had to negotiate also with the Lloyd Georges, Poincarés, Curzons,
Briands, I must confess in so many words that I did not
find the Balkan men decidedly different. The same emotions and the same motives led both: so rich in wisdom
and understanding is that old Italian proverb, "All the
world's one country." At most, if I had to bring out a
difference, I should say that Westerners are quicker to
decide, whereas hesitation seems congenital with Balkan
statesmen—save perhaps with Venizelos, and the blue-
eyed Cretan is essentially a Mediterranean. On the other
hand, and this is perhaps the greatest moral praise one
may bestow, the Balkan statesmen struck me as being far
freer from a terrible fault which mars a good many of
the Western: an unceasing concern not to admit anything
which may one day constitute an advantage for yesterday's
forerunner or tomorrow's successor. This concern is some-

times carried so far as almost to go, unconsciously, against
the interests of the country, and I cited for example certain
dictators' fear of being charged with copying or following
ideas of their democratic predecessors. The Balkan statesmen's thought of serving their country has always seemed
to me pure of any dross of this kind.

What I should deplore, rather, in the public life of the
Balkans is this: that even the best servants and most
enlightened leaders of the State have always been content
to do themselves what they considered useful for the
country; but they have nearly always failed in another,
less apparent but higher and more difficult duty: to create
a political tradition, to bring the younger men to follow
willingly the path which is being traced under their very
eyes. Such was the supreme thought of the most pregnant
political mind of the nineteenth century, Cavour. Such
was the constant preoccupation of one I knew intimately
and respected profoundly, King Albert of Belgium. For
the rare men of this type, to create a tradition amounts to
suppressing chance, to warding off dangerous and wayward
slips. Thus it is that Italy owed her best servants to
Cavour's development and tradition, from Visconti Venosta
and Robilant down to yesterday. I have found no trace
in the Balkans of this moral force with its historical and
permanent results. But was it to be found in Bonaparte or
Bismarck, who yet had some sort of genius? It may possibly be difficult to pretend that it should exist in statesmen of
countries where everything was to be done, where so many
urgent problems pressed hard on one another.

What one may assert, without fear of exaggeration, is that the vast mass of the people of the Balkan nations would have grasped, better than the neo-bourgeois minorities, the efforts of a statesman who had considered the future as much as the present, the moral and social progress of the race as much as his own immediate political satisfactions. Of the Balkan populations, the groups with which I came into closest contact are those of the small landowning Serbian peasants of Chumadia and—so different in origin and language, so similar in moral dignity—of the semi-feudal shepherds of the Wallachian communities scattered from Epirus to the Vardar's banks. To find moral dignity as proud and political judgment as straight, one must go to those magnificent Piedmontese peasants among whom an innate love of order and discipline goes hand in hand with a haughty distrust of the aristocrats of yore, of the demagogues of today; or to those English farmers who, on Saturday evenings, gather to discuss the merits of the bills that are being passed by the House of Commons.

If I had to say which, to me, seem the weakest and most sterile elements of public life in the Balkan nations, I could point only to certain types of pseudo-bourgeois who have come back home after cursory studies in some French or Swiss University and who lack the wealth of inner life which is needed not to lose touch with the admirable rustic virtues of their parents and grandparents. Fortunately, however, this type tends to disappear more and more, thanks mainly to the beneficial action of Balkan

universities that will henceforth constitute precious and
immediate sources of national culture.

The town, the *civitas,* is the very essence of Italian
civilization. Party strifes, often gruesome in the towns,
have made the grandeur and glory of the communes of
Lombardy and Tuscany. I think I made this clear in my
book *L'Ame italienne:* every time the struggles inherent to
free life became dormant in Italy, there followed, immediately after, a period of moral slumber and of intellectual
laziness.

In the Balkans, the secular traditions live in the popular
songs celebrating the stand made against the invader,
expressing a mournful and constant aspiration toward a
true Christian peace. The Balkan generations from which
the élite of tomorrow will spring, should seek inspiration
in this patriotism, at once generous and broad. And it
will be all the better if this national genius shall be Serbian
here, there Bulgarian, and again, Albanian, Rumanian.
. . . Emulation among numerous and varied centers
will keep it more alive. But the Balkans of the future
will have squandered with their own hands their best assets
for life and progress, if they succeed only in accentuating
the differences between neighbors, instead of remembering
every moment that true patriotism, the kind that never
dies, needs only the continuity of secular emotions. These,
in the Balkans, were never village hatreds, but bravery
and undaunted resistance to the foreign invader or exploiter
—of old, the Turk from Asia, and but yesterday, the
Hapsburg feudal lords who paid so dearly for their con-

tempt and misunderstanding of neighbors with essential qualities much more important than faults due to centuries of bondage and oppression.

A life of freedom—even with all the inconveniences that freedom entails—may bring about among the Balkan peoples, in the more or less near future, a political atmosphere that will find nothing to envy in the enslavement wrought by dictatorships which threaten to wreck the civilization of the old and glorious West.

XIV

BALKAN AND WESTERN LEADERSHIPS:
A PARALLEL

IT IS agreed that the best definition of politics is the art of possibilities.

But agreement is not general as to the definition of a statesman. Ability, talent, immediate success itself, are in no way sufficient, in my opinion, to make a statesman. Bismarck had all these assets, and yet was far from being a statesman, for he put too. much useless violence in his work and, above all, if he pursued a great policy, he always neglected to create what counts even more, a political tradition. This became manifest when his Reich fell into the hands of his weak successors.

To create a political tradition amounts to suppressing hazard as far as possible. To my mind, this is the highest duty of a statesman—of him who, being no demagogue, has no need at all to be feverishly in quest of rapid and well advertised successes.

Of the three post-war European sovereigns I have known most intimately, the two who have died faced this supreme duty in opposite manner. And yet both of them, Alexander, King of Yugoslavia, and Albert, King of the Belgians, were endowed with first-rate moral and intellect-

202

ual qualities. If Alexander Karageorgevich was much less aware of this duty than the Belgian King, it was the price he paid for the historical atmosphere from which he issued.

Writers who speak of kings know generally so little about them that it would perhaps not be useless for me to delineate here the character of the two men, as I perceived it in my intimate intercourse with them. They respectively embody the best one can hope from a young country of the Balkan peninsula, tormented still by urgent problems, and from an old Western soil which can boast at least of one of the most beautiful municipal experiences of Europe.

It was during the World War, from 1915 to 1918, that I constantly saw Alexander Karageorgevich, either in Corfu or on the Macedonian front. He was at the time Regent of the Kingdom of Serbia. His old father, King Peter, who was still alive then, had voluntarily renounced power, because he felt that his physical strength was waning steadily after the terrible ordeal of the occupation of his whole country by the Austrians and his retreat, with his heroic army, across the mountains of Albania to the sea, where Italian and French ships brought them safely to Corfu.

Leaning out of the window of his studio at the Hotel Bella Venezia at Corfu—before us lay the Hellenic seas which had carried the Italian galleys of Lepanto, the French frigates of Navarino, and now were dominated by the Austro-German submarines—how often Alexander of Serbia discussed with me his anxieties and his hopes! And

every time I went home after these long hours of confidential talk, I said to myself: "Really, everything Austrians and Germans will try on this young chief to make
him understand 'the interests of his House' will be in
vain."

He really was the most loyal, the best, of allies. And
in this it is all the more to his credit that he was far
from optimistic by temperament during the dark years
I spent at his side.

How often, whether at Corfu, a besieged city with all
the psychological failings that this implies, or in the
trenches of Macedonia, when we were discussing together
some bad news from the Western fronts—and bad news
came often then—would Alexander finally exclaim, after
a silence full of the agonies of the responsible head of a
nation: "Well, we shall perish all together, that is all!"

When I met him after the war, I asked him if, in those
days, my optimistic assurances had not seemed official
language on my part.

With the simplicity and absolute lack of charlatanism
that made him unique in the theatrical line of post-war
"dictators," he answered quite frankly:

"Afterward, when I saw you do in peace-time what you
spoke of to me during the war, I had to admit you had
felt sure of the future. As for me, all I wanted to be
sure of was that the name of Serbia should remain spot-
less."

The moral merit lay all on his side.

Stating his highest quality, I have simultaneously implied his greatest failing: valiant, hard-working, always convinced he was serving duty only, he lacked imagination.

And his mistakes in home politics were the fatal consequences of this lack of imagination. A century behind us, an Italian exile, Mazzini, had foretold the downfall of imperial Austria and the return to freedom of the Czechs, the Yugoslavs, the Rumanians. But Mazzini was one of the richest spirits in all Europe. He, Alexander, could not conceive such certainties. On the one hand, he had seen his old Prime Minister Pachich, who had never grasped the broader style of Yugoslav patriotism. To him the Yugoslavia idea had been only an invention of the Croats, false or impractical men, and he accepted the formula during the war as a strategical necessity, and after it, as a diplomatic instrument.

On the other hand, Alexander had heard the Croat masses, irritated by excessive Serbian centralization, after the enthusiasm and the honeymoon of 1918-20, express their anti-Serbianism and their suspicions of Belgrade more and more noisily.

There were nothing but inevitable spasms to be got over somehow. What a pity Alexander was not given to reading the dogmatic stuff of "well-thinking" writers in France, Belgium and Austria, between 1860 and 1870, on the ruin, always guaranteed to be due "tomorrow," of the "artifical construction" of Italian unity!

But Italy, happily, was Cavour's. All she put up against grudges at home and ill will abroad, was freedom. And she won.

Alexander, in good faith, believed he could preserve unity only by suppressing liberty; and he made up his mind to do it. But at least, in this also, he wanted to avoid all bluff. Speaking to a mutual American friend, H. F. Armstrong,* a little while before the *coup d'état* of January, 1929, he said to him: "If, by ill luck, I should have to resort to dictatorship, it will at least be my dictatorship. I shall take all the responsibilities on myself."

For, contrary to what has often been said, Alexander was not a prisoner of his generals. They shared in his dictatorial responsibilities in this sense that, in their incurable military candor, they were convinced Italy had become stronger under a dictatorship than under a rule of freedom though the latter had led her to victory after the fiercest of wars; and that setting up a dictatorship in Yugoslavia signified making her stronger against her big and dangerous neighbor.

At one of the darkest moments of the whole war, after the battle of Caporetto, I came back to Alexander after I had been up to the edge of the invaded regions where I had seen the tragic stream of refugees go by, as they had gone by in France and in Belgium. But on the new front I had felt immediately that Italy had won. Did we not witness a miracle there, possibly unique in history—a whole people in arms suddenly regaining possession of itself by its own efforts and beginning—much before the arrival of Franco-British contingents—the stand on the Piave; be-

---

* The editor of *Foreign Affairs.*

ginning it, even before any Italian general had ordered. (One of my brothers, arriving on the Piave, saw some detachments digging hasty trenches. "Who told you to do this?" he asked. And a subaltern answered: "Captain, we really can't go as far as Naples. . . ." Heroism, then, did not lie in words.)

I failed in making Alexander share my optimism. Per· haps I was asking too much. And yet, when I arrived in Constantinople as High Commissioner two years later* I learned that, during those same days when I was trying to convince Alexander, the Austro-Germans had demanded forces from Talaat Pasha, to take part in the "imminent" occupation of Venice, and the Grand Vizir had told them: "This is our worse defeat since the Marne. If the Italians have succeeded in holding after such a reverse, it means they think they can have their revenge. They then are the victors."

But is it not more heartrending still to think that two people as full of life as Italy and Yugoslavia are being crazily poisoned against each other by newspapers, blind with misunderstanding and hatred and hurling as though they were insults memories that should be sacred. Truly, the nearer the radio brings the voices of the peoples, the further their souls seem to withdraw and shut themselves up within the intellectual and moral mediocrity that futile "patriotic" words cannot conceal.

King Alexander, as I can testify, never ceased fcr one

---

* November 12, 1918.

instant to think that a loyal understanding between his country and Italy was an absolute necessity; and that this understanding was as indispensable to the safety of his people as the tradition of friendship with France.

When I negotiated with our Yugoslav neighbors the first post-war treaty which excluded all forceful pressure, I said one day to the Belgrade plenipotentiaries who seemed aghast at certain sacrifices I was demanding of them: "Istria, the Julian Alps? But do you not understand that your very life is at stake here; and that the future will teach us all that we shall have to defend the Adriatic together against the common dangers of Germanic hegemony?"

King Alexander shared this opinion from the first, and continued in it even after years of polemics as spiteful as they were futile whichever side they came from.

To create a political tradition is perhaps, as I began by saying, the highest duty and the highest merit of the leader of a people.

All things considered, it was the essential merit of Albert I as statesman. No matter what problem he was faced with, he never considered what press or public, necessarily concerned with momentary sentiments and resentments, would say. He thought only of future consequences, justifying in this—in the only telling manner— his part as hereditary chief. More than this: he never wanted to enforce his opinion, but only to persuade—in short, to create tradition. Hence, by the way, the joy he felt at seeing his son and heir freely share his ideas and motives; opposed in this to so many sovereigns who insisted on keeping their heirs out of the national problems.*

Merits of this kind are of the rarest. In the nineteenth century I can only see one statesman who possessed a sense of the future to a supreme degree. I mean of course Cavour who, when he lay dying and delirious, was haunted not by the recollection of his epic battles with Austria, but by problems of which no one, in 1860, perceived the importance, such as the economic revival of Southern Italy.

Albert I will probably remain the highest and most accomplished type of statesman in the first quarter of the twentieth century. The conventional apologists of "crowned heads" have repeated the usual phrases about him—which wearied him so. They have called him the hero-king, the chivalrous king, the king *"sans peur et sans reproche."* And he was all this undoubtedly. But this was almost nothing in comparison with his true essence, which he hid so jealously behind defenses built of modesty and pride. A stoic who expected little of men and nothing of glory—so Albert I struck me in those years when I make bold to say he spoke to me most freely; but a stoic for whom duty, his whole duty, constituted the only rule of conduct. Furthermore, this stoic was endowed with two gifts which, along with his Marcus-Aurelius temperament, made of him that very rare thing, a statesman as clear-sighted as he was generous.

---

* As Queen Victoria did in England with her son and heir, the future Edward VII.

First, he had, to a degree I have rarely seen excelled, what I shall call the sense of history. By this I mean an instinctive perception of the political or moral effects such and such a fact will have left after a few years. In 1914, from a military standpoint it would have been better for him to leave the last morsel of Belgian soil that remained free. But he instantly perceived how very much stronger Belgium would be, even toward her allies, on the far-off day of peace, if he could cling to the last strip of Belgian land. He immediately made it his deepest point of honor. On the morrow after the war, when the Belgian troops went into Rhineland for a long occupation, his unceasing concern, his most pressing recommendations, were to warn the Belgians against all bravado, against all trace of reprisals. He had few illusions as to quick possibilities of understanding with the Germans, but precisely for that reason he felt how imperative it was that Belgium should remain synonymous with right and equity. And this is one of the motives from which, in his heart, he was far from approving certain gestures of Poincaré's policy that the world, rightly or wrongly, interpreted as fruitless manifestations of aggressive rancor. On the other hand, he hailed with joy the dawn of the Locarno policy—the failure of which in no way proves it vain, because, really, a Locarno policy was formulated rather than carried out.

I have said that another trait of King Albert's character contributed to perfect his statesmanship. Beside his moral purity, which might, of old, have made a Saint Louis of him, there lay another personality in no way contradicting

the former: the collective Coburg type, ironical, knowing
the value of men's phrases, bows and cringes, especially the
sychophancy of men who most loudly proclaim themselves
"the loyal servants of the monarchy" in order to have their
own material interests served by the monarchial institution. It was from King Albert that I learned the saying
of the old Prussian feudalists: Let the King be absolute so
he may do as we desire,* which I have quoted in discussing
the *Junker*.

It is from this gift of irony—which, when it dominates,
does away with all generosity as in Frederick II or Bismarck, but which enlightens the spirit when it is allied to
the nobility of soul of an Albert I—that he derived his
swiftness of judgment. He hid this swiftness carefully,
indeed, so greatly was he set on inducing consent, on setting up a tradition of collective political thought, rather
than imposing a point of view. Nothing seemed to him
worse in taste or more factitious than a dictatorial attitude.
And when he heard about his slowness of decision, his disillusioned sarcasm enjoyed it. Now many people have been
misled by his air of juvenile embarrassment, or by his drawl
when he sought the opinion of his Belgian or foreign interlocutors.†

I know of no statesman of our times endowed with so
clear and complete a realism as Albert I. He was one
of the very rare—the too rare—spirits who never forgot
that the idealistic reasons for a national policy constitute

---

* See Chapter VI.
† See my *Makers of Modern Europe,* Chapter XXIV.

essential elements of reality. The demagogues who take
up so much room in post-war Europe believe, in their elementary naïveté, that they show manifest superiority by
playing exclusively at *real-politik*. And, from this come
most of the dangers that lie in wait for the old world,
should some sudden diplomatic crisis spring up, full of
hatred.

Albert I died suddenly on February 17, 1934. He fell
from a rock along the banks of the Meuse near Namur,
while he was training alone for his annual climbs in the
Italian Dolemites. Mountain climbing was the solitary
relaxation of his life—the monarchical formality of which
he endured only because it was his duty.

King Albert gone, Masaryk gone, George V gone, fast
diminishing is the number of the great European leaders
who held the secret of undisputed personal authority; who
knew that Authority, Order, are the necessary bases of any
wholesome State, of any viable human society; and who
knew that, precisely for this reason, they should not be
invoked at any and all times as the sole remedies for our
ailments. Cavour never mentioned authority; it radiated
from him almost in spite of himself. In Czechoslovakia,
and in a certain sense in Europe, the authority of a
Masaryk was supreme, unquestioned; but he never spoke
of his authority, or of authority in the abstract. The moral
values of a State, like those of individuals, need to be
wrapped up in some reserve, said Benes to me one day,
and he was Masaryk's favorite disciple and has become his
worthy successor.

George V possessed this feeling of modesty, of simplicity, to such a very high degree that it makes his name worthy to rank beside those of Albert I and Masaryk. "Knowing how difficult it is to be a limited monarch, I thank heaven every day that I was spared being an absolute king," George V said to Ambassador Page, who reported the phrase to me.

George V, like his cousin King Albert, was one of the few men of our photogenic epoch to grasp this very safe truth, that leaders who want their leadership to last should not be spectacular; for if stage successes may endure for years, it is none the less certain that they always end by doing great harm to the nation who produced them.

The demagogues talk big all around, raised on trestles like mountebank miracle workers. Alas, the only miracle which happens in history is the secure and dignified maturity a people may achieve solely through long generations of free struggles.* That is why Alexander of Yugoslavia erred in good faith when he believed that he could hasten by force the union—eventually inevitable—of the Yugoslav peoples. That is why Albert of Belgium was right when, on returning to his capital at the end of the World War, he declared that since all the Belgians had fought for the freedom of their country, they should all have the right to cast their vote to shape its destinies.

---

* Asquith, who deeply loved George V, has told me that several times, on hearing of Irish outbursts of anti-English hatred, the King had said to him: "We there pay the penalty for too long a spell of iron-handed policy."

XV

THE AUSTRIAN PROBLEM

FROM now on the union of Germany and Austria means nothing more than the coupling of two great historical names. Until the end of the war the two names covered—excluding the temporary conquests of their armies—656,418 square miles. Today their common surface barely amounts to 323,624 square miles. Until 1918, Germany and Austria numbered together 120,000,000 inhabitants. Today, united, the figures would not exceed 70,000,000.

It is true that the *Anschluss*—the union of Austria with the German Reich—would slightly increase their potential strength. But, for that matter, the union is already an accomplished fact in the judicial, cultural and scholastic fields—despite the different flags.

On the other hand, it is by no means certain that increase in territory necessarily means for a country increase in power and singleness of action, as the nationalists pretend it does. The extension of the British Empire has certainly not always contributed to its strengthening. In 1935, Malta, indefensible, rendered Great Britain's position more delicate in the Mediterranean than if she had not possessed this little group of Italian islands. And 1917 rent the veil that hid from us the weakness of a too vast Russia. . . .

I wonder, indeed, if there are not many Germans who see in the *Anschluss* the conquest of forbidden fruit but who, could they but rid themselves of this obsession, would say:

"The union is put off to another day."

One cannot imagine Vienna, the capital of the Germanic Empire for centuries, suddenly becoming a provincial town in which the ancient, august echoes would resound no longer. . . .

I know, for my own part, that, in a similar question, I scandalized a good many traditional diplomats at the time, but I still consider that I served the interests of Italy and of peace—they cannot be severed—when I answered those who warned me against certain tendencies of the Bulgarians to unite with the Serbo-Croatian-Slovene State:

"Are you Hapsburgers, that you can consider the part of Italy in the Balkans only from a *divide et impera* angle? The more the Yugoslavs accomplish union with their brothers and the more seaboard they have at their disposal, the more we shall gain in security and influence and the safer will be our understanding with them."

As I see it, the most serious danger from Germany in the event of a formal conclusion of the *Anschluss* would be for Vienna and the Danube to become a temptation to "improve and organize" the Balkans, or a spring-board to do it from. For a diplomatic realization of such a *Mittel-*

europa as Naumann proposed during the war would not be accomplished without grave risks for everybody.*

But in France, and everywhere, it should be realized that there is only one way of avoiding the *Mitteleuropa*, and that is to work toward organizing Europe.

And what do the Italian people think of the *Anschluss* and of the whole Austrian problem?

The continuous concern of those Italians who, after the war, had to study the problem mainly in connection with the new Italian provinces of Trentino and Upper Adige, was this: by a policy of generous autonomies and material and moral advantages to bring the German-speaking population of the Upper Adige to rally loyally to the new order. It was thought at the time that our forbearance had gone a little too far. As for me, I should in no way alter the advice I gave then. The bourgeois of Bolzano (Bozen) had presented to the Italian High Commissioner, Credaro, a pile of written grievances on the most varied subjects. The complaints were sometimes justified, sometimes fantastic. What did the Italian Government do? It published them, translated in Italian, in a book that was widely

---

*Naumann in no way conceived his *Mitteleuropa* as a means of European union. His book, published in 1915, was necessarily a war-book inspired by war ideas.

This soon became obvious, especially to the Austrians. The Austrian Social-Democrat Rudolf Hilferding wrote in the Austrian magazine, *Der Kampf,* in December, 1915: "(Naumann's) Central Europe is designed to be nothing but an organism of which all the component nations would become the political and economic vassals of the German nation; whereas the German nation itself would be only the political instrument of the ruling castes in Germany."

circulated. It wanted the Italians to know that the problem
was not easy and that it was not enough to glorify in
patriotic speeches the conquest of the Alps frontier. Not
one of the German-speaking subjects was prosecuted for
newspaper articles or speeches—and sometimes they were
very violent—in the days of the democratic governments.
Now and then, indeed, when a speech-maker became a
little too annoying, he was offered a German-language
chair in some high school in the south; he accepted, he
went, he married there—and his children now probably fly
into a rage if other children playfully call them sons of a
German. In this policy our colleague for Education, Croce,
in perfect agreement with Giolitti and myself, showed us
how a philosophical intellect can quickly acquire a masterly
control over the game of daily politics.*

Convinced that our patient system was the best way

---

* In one of my first conversations with Giolitti on the Upper Adige
questions, I told him: "The key to the situation lies in the hands of our
colleague Croce; he must ask us for dozens of German teachers especially
for our schools in the South; no German resists Naples' sun and a
Neapolitan wife."

Croce, present at the conversation, laughed, agreed and acted accordingly.

The Germans from the Upper Adige whom Fascism drove into exile,
were not so far wrong when they wrote in their pamphlets printed in
Munich and Vienna: "The democratic rulers of Italy put our consciences
to sleep. Fascist violence has given new life to our instinct of national
preservation."

In the same vein, intense Slovene nationalists spoke of me at a Lubliana
meeting as "the worst enemy of Yugoslav nationality in Italy." They
were right from their point of view, unable, as they were, to understand
that I was thinking of a better Europe and especially of relations between
our respective countries so improved that frontiers would lose a great
deal of their importance.

to accomplish, though of course with no miraculous swiftness, a loyal assimilation of our new fellow citizens, the
heads of the Italian democracy had this thought on the
Austrian question: that it was better for the Austrian
Republic to go on living, honorably and noiselessly, as
long as Italy's wise and silent work was on foot. After
that, one would see. Italy was not opposed in principle
to a union of Austria with the German Reich, if the
Austrians should still desire it.

In one case only would Italy have preferred the
Anschluss, even an immediate *Anschluss,* in spite of the
problems which the neighborhood of a turbulent nation
would occasion—a threat of Hapsburg restoration in
Vienna, or even in Budapest.* The leaders of Czechoslovak politics, Masaryk and Benes, wholly shared our
views.

The successor States of Austria must indeed prefer anything to the risk of a restoration of the Hapsburg monarchy
which, having usefully served Europe and Latin civilization
for centuries, had outlived its usefulness, and persisted in

---

* The few French dowagers whose salons continue to bewail the disappearance of imperial Austria and still do not understand that the 1914
policy of Vienna and Budapest was suicidal, should read the documents
and revelations collected by the Director of the Archives of Prague,
J. Opocenski, in his *Umsturz in Mitteleuropa.* They will read there that
during the dramatic interview held on November 2, 1918, between the
members of the German-Austrian Council and Emperor Charles, when
the latter protested that "he had not wanted that" and a Socialist leader
seemed to approve, the old Christian-Socialist Mayer got up and declared
with dignity: "Let us be honest. We all wanted the war. The people
wanted it. You have only to remember the universal enthusiasm in the
summer of 1914."

an atmosphere where its peoples were promoted to the courtesan rank of "good folks" only if they hated one another.

This is one of the numerous cases where Italy's direct interests are identical with the moral progress of Europe.

XVI

POLES

THAT Prince Radziwill who bought a whole block of Paris houses so his envoy might carry his notes to the Regent without having to cross streets, was probably one of the first of the Poles to be called *"Français du Nord."*

The noble deeds of the "armed confederations" that lived on Louis XVI's grants, the cavaliers slashed to death in the passes of Portugal, or throwing themselves in the Niemen under Napoleon's impassive gaze, Poniatowski drowning himself in the Elster—an imperishable Epinal picture—all these were typical gestures of the *Français du Nord.* The interests of their Polish fatherland counted for nothing in their sacrifice.

French sympathy for the *"pauvre Polonais,"* heroic and improvident, more guileless than any untutored savage, began to crystallize in the Romantic period—a time when every child of France and of England wept over Silvio Pellico's *My Prisons,* the book that "hurt Austria more than a battle lost." It was the golden age of exiles. Adam Mickiewicz, the "Polish pilgrim," inspired Lamennais' *Paroles d'un Croyant* and Michelet's *Bible de l'Humanité.* At the fall of Warsaw in 1831, Parisians went into mourning, like Athens at the fall of Miletus. On May 15, 1848,

the crowd invaded the Palais Bourbon shouting "Long
live Poland."

This period did not last long. The Poles might have
repeated the words: "God is too high above us, and
France too far away."

Young Floquet, who shouted, *"Vive la Pologne, Monsieur!"* when Czar Alexander II drove through Paris, was
only a belated specimen of a defunct age.*

By then France's Slav sympathies had turned to Russia.
The discovery of the great Russian novelists, Turgenev,
Tolstoi, Dostoevski, caused a greater sensation than any
Pole had ever created. One had to go back to the epoch
of the "Italianisants" to find a similar enthusiasm. Slo-
wacki, who died in Paris in 1849, was one of the truest
lyrical poets of the nineteenth century. His rhythm was
perfect. But compared with the Russians, he remained
almost unknown.

It is a less known fact that something analogous happened in Poland about the same time. Not that France
and French literature ceased to be popular. But the con-
spiracy style ceased to be popular as a fighting method.
It suddenly became clear that Russia could not be overcome by plots. The new watchword became: "Let us
have engineers. Let us build up a national industry. Let
us at last give our peasants a little comfort and some

---

* It is not generally known that Floquet, appointed to the Presidency
of the Cabinet in 1888, accepted the appointment only after he had been
assured by Baron Mohrenheim, the Russian Ambassador, that Alexander III
bore no grudge for the words he had shouted at his father. The agreements with Russia were already in the air.

education." And necessarily these things were learned in the school of Germans, either of the Reich or of Austria.

European opinion was completely ignorant of this slow and patient regeneration. And yet these obscure sacrifices, these persevering labors and endeavors—so opposed to the old selfish laziness of the eighteenth-century Polish nobles—were almost as useful in 1918 and 1919 as the long legend of heroes à la Kosciusko. The effort was all the more to be admired as the official atmosphere in which it unfolded tended to annihilate it.

The new classes and the new *élite,* molded along modern lines and in spite of the police-ridden atmosphere of Warsaw and the antiquated and priest-ridden atmosphere of Austrian Galicia, in their turn considered their grandparents' outbursts of love for France as touching but far-off recollections.

The new Polish middle classes, industrious and careful, who had made room for themselves in the old nation of magnates and lesser nobility, were unknown in France, where also—even among the Socialists—the new set of small landowning Polish peasants and intelligent workers, organized under the guidance of Socialism, were unknown.

The railroad from Warsaw to Vienna had been planned by Polish capitalists and executed by Polish skilled labor. Lodz, loud with machinery and trade, as Ladislas Reymont showed us in his *Promised Land,* was henceforth to be reckoned a great center on the Stock Exchanges.

But all this was better known in Berlin and in Vienna than in Paris.

In the same way, new and serious-minded Poland was less familiar with post-1870 France, with the magnificent revival in French scientific research, philosophy and art, than with the German universities, the art coteries of Munich and Vienna, Bebel's Marxism and Ketteler's Social Catholicism. Not to mention the fact that Waldeck-Rousseau's republic and the *affaire Dreyfus* were somewhat obnoxious to nobles for whom Catholicism often meant mainly a weapon of greed and hatred for use especially against the Jews; and that France of the Russian alliance had wounded patriots like Pilsudski too deeply.

The miraculous resurrection of Poland came about in 1918 thanks to a series of catastrophes—self-contradictory, like the collapse of Russia in the midst of Entente victory —and, all of them, paradoxically complementary to one another. "Providence blesses only the mad!" cries the hero at the end of a Polish novel brimming with luscious simplicity, when, having outfaced a thousand dangers, he has finally succeeded in coming home from Siberia to Poland and cannot get over the fact that he suddenly finds Poland freed, at a single stroke, of her three old imperial masters.

But the event that astonished, in such sincere and disarming fashion, the hero of Sieroszewski's novel, should not make us forget that even those Polish men and political groups who had continued to hope for the reconstitution of their people into a single—and at least "autonomous" —State, were also accustomed to consider that France was too far away. Roman Dmowski, in a book published in 1912, endeavored to find in an understanding with Rus-

sia the realistic means of reconstituting Poland; whereas
Daszynski and Pilsudski turned their eyes toward Vienna
and, in a certain sense, toward Berlin.

The same phenomenon had occurred with the best of
the Czech politicians. But the latter were quicker than
the Polish to see through the veil that hid the future.
They grasped the great truth of the war—that Austria-
Hungary was destined to perish. Whence their clearly
defined line of action—Masaryk's in the United States,
Masaryk's and Benes's in France and Italy.

In Poland, on the other hand, it was only at the last
moment the provisional government substituted the Wilsonian creation for the embryonic Polish State which Pilsudski's
legions and the good pleasure of the Central Empires had
brought into the world on November 5, 1916.

Poland's re-entry into the "orbit of French influence"
was therefore something sudden and somewhat artificial.
Begun in 1919, it came to a stop on Hitler's advent to
power in Germany and Pilsudski's unexpected understanding with him. The abrupt reinstatement of French influence was, for that matter, mainly due to the equally abrupt
eclipse of Wilson and Wilsonism, for, had it not been
for this eclipse, the old-style policy of alliances would not
have been thought of. Germany also contributed to it by
the hopeless candor with which every German of any party
showed, not so much his hatred—hatred can be forgotten
—but his "superior nation's" contempt.

German Socialists who had come to Rome to defend the
cause of their diplomatic action in Upper Silesia, first

initiated me, in a scientific manner of course, into the
pretended incapacity of the Poles for self-government.

The Treaty of Versailles formally provided, under
Article 88, for the division of Upper Silesia according
to the ratio of the plebiscite votes. Undoubtedly the
German arguments, based on the economic unity of the
territory, were tremendous.

But Italy had built herself up on plebiscites and the
nationality principle. To ask an Italian Minister to attach
greater weight to the unity of a system of mines than to
the vote of half a million Silesians who had expressly
declared that they wanted to become Polish citizens*
amounted to asking him to admit that Trent and Trieste
had more to gain by being under Austria. Quite likely;
but Battisti had consented to be hanged that Trent might
become Italian, even although he knew that the apples
from his orchard sold better on the Austrian markets.

The line which was called the "Sforza line" and which
the League of Nations was compelled to accept, after
several months of study, as that which came nearest to the
results of the plebiscite, had no other aim but to conciliate,
as far as possible, the respect of nationalities as the votes

---

* The results of the plebiscite were exactly: for Germany, 707,348 votes;
for Poland, 479,747 votes; per commune: 664 for Germany, 597 for Poland.

Section 88 of the Treaty of Versailles distinctly provided that Germany
should renounce in favor of Poland all her rights on "the *portion* of
Upper Silesia . . . according to the results of the plebiscite"; the idea
was further corroborated by the contents of paragraph 5 of the schedule
to the said Article, where it provided "a frontier-line to be traced *through*
Upper Silesia."

had revealed them, and the economic interests of the region.*

To those public men of Poland who expressed to me a gratitude I did not in the least deserve, I strongly advised one thing: to acquire the respectful admiration of Europe by pursuing a policy of industrial and financial solidarity with the Germans of Upper Silesia. That, I said to them, would be the only safe consecration of their success. They promised; they were sincere; they did very little of the sort. The fault, as always, probably lay with both parties.

France fiercely defended the Polish point of view during the Upper-Silesia plebiscite. But, having witnessed the whole episode, I cannot say that so much zeal always helped Polish interests. The British Government stiffened against a point of view that was shown up as being too much a French interest. And the Poles realized it well enough.

For that matter, even during the France-Poland honeymoon, no amount of official phraseology could cover up this one fact: that neither the respective economic systems of the two countries, rather dissimilar, nor the leanings of the intellectual milieux, can create a vital interchange of commodities. Political imponderables increased the estrangement. For generations the name of Poland had constituted the sacred Symbol of the religion of freedom.†

---

* Balfour had presided over the Upper-Silesia transactions at Geneva. I met him a short time after on the Riviera and he said to me with characteristic humor: "What a nuisance your line was! We had to find something new, but our secretaries handled the plebiscite results in vain. We always got back to that damned Sforza line."

† My grandfather's eldest sister having, in 1859, been ordered by the Archduke of Austria, who ruled over the Duchy of Modena, to close down

After the resurrection of the country Pilsudski's dictatorship for years found support only in those "patriotic" Parisian papers which, before the War of 1914-18, were subsidized by the Russian Embassies, as the documents published by the Soviet Government have shown us, with names and sums.

It might be useful to compare Polish problems with the solutions applied in Czechoslovakia. There were problems there too, though not so serious as in Poland, due to old grievances, old prejudices. But Masaryk could conceive of Czech patriotism only in the service of general progress. Here are a few of the thoughts he expressed and to which he was always faithful in his conduct:

"Our love for our compatriots should show itself by social laws. . . ."

"Our Czech ideal is, a people without beggars. . . ."

"I will know nothing of an idealism that forgets bread. . . ."

"One should not idolize one's own people. I willingly admit the superiority of other peoples, and this does not wound the love I bear to mine. . . ."

"Whenever a Czech is called, a man should answer. . . ."

This humane conception has thrust back jingo nationalism, has won to the new Slav Republic the respect of the whole world.

---

the popular schools and libraries she had opened for her peasants, sent to a committee of exiled Poles the capital she had formerly devoted to her work in Italy.

But had Masaryk and Benes been Poles, they would probably have spent some time in jail under Pilsudski.

Only a Poland cured of imperialistic dreams can carry out the gigantic task of consolidating a State whose resurrection Mazzini had desired a century ago. But the work will be all the sounder for being less showy and dramatic. It needs much more real courage to undertake with serenity a long and lusterless duty, than to defy death when a blind policy has brought matters to a head.

Such is the price of Poland's life and progress.

And her sad proud history sufficiently proves that she is safe from any danger of absorption by neighboring and more powerful countries.

XVII

RUSSIANS

The most penetrating of the European anti-Napoleonic diplomats at the beginning of the nineteenth century, Count de Maistre, Sardinian Envoy to St. Petersburg, predicted in 1812 to his sovereign, the King of Sardinia, a possibility which became actual fact a hundred and five years later.

"There are," he wrote from Saint Petersburg in one of his dispatches to his small Italian Court, "so many presages of revolution in this country that I quake in every limb to think of them. Can this armed people ever go back peaceably to their original state? Will they lay down arms as easily as they laid down the spade and mattock? Will this scattered peasantry starving in the forests . . . become submissive slaves once more?"

They became so, then; but in 1917, a century later, occurred the revolution, the most violent and most complete of modern times. However, in spite of the Red atmosphere, the old Russian story is still going on.

What else did Trotsky try, in vain, a few years ago, when he attacked Stalin and the other men in power, than to repeat what the liberal bourgeoisie had done to Czarism and what, later on, Lenin himself had done to Kerensky? The only difference probably consists in this:

229

Stalin and his comrades, who now govern Russia, are obliged to offer from the Kremlin a much more serious resistance than the Czar offered to Kerensky or than Kerensky offered to Lenin. Dictators of the Stalin, Hitler and Mussolini type are not "in power"; they have no choice; they are intrenched in power.

But what of the masses?

Mountains of American and European books have described the privations and sufferings of the Russian workmen. The description is exact, the coloring not too overdone, but the books are false. Why? Because they have been unable to show the real feeling of workmen which is still a sort of religious faith in a distant forthcoming communistic Paradise. In spite of tragic deceptions, in spite of Stalin's constant compromises with reality, the workmen still believe that the Leninistic formula, the Dictatorship of the Proletariat, will some day become the key to the enchanting world they hope for.

When confronted with too severe disillusionment, the workmen still say that the great day will come for their sons; that it is their sons who will be happy and free in this life. It is the mystic nature of the Russian soul, with its longing for suffering, that makes this possible. And there is some moral nobility in the fact that when the working classes of Leningrad and Moscow suffer, they find consolation in thinking that they advance the blessed days of universal happiness.

This feeling may fade. But deliberately to have ignored it during the silly years of diplomatic boycott of Soviet

Russia has been the most stupid repetition of the errors committed by the British and German Governments during the French Revolution.

The moral situation is somewhat different with the peasants. They were "communist" after the Petrograd revolution; or, to be more exact, they seemed communist when it was a question of driving the old landowners out of their estates. The peasant movement identified itself with the Lenin *coup*. To tell the truth—and this point is essential to understand the Russian Revolution—the peasants had begun even before the advent of Bolshevism to seize the lands and to slay their *Barin*—their masters. When Lenin grasped powers, he simply put into Marxist words what the peasants had already done with their practical deeds. That is why the peasants supported Lenin, but, like all peasants, without attaching any importance to his written theories.

The same phenomenon took place when, without waiting for orders from Moscow, they opposed so valiantly the Wrangel and Denikin White Russian armies in South Russia. They did so because their own instincts put them on guard against the young officers who were the sons of the landowners they had slain some months before.

On the morrow of the World War, in Constantinople as High Commissioner, I realized at once—and said so to the Big Four in Paris—that the White Russian expeditions were doomed to failure; I felt so especially when the Italian officers in the Crimea reported to me that many of the Russian officers were organizing raids on neighboring properties which had belonged to their families, hoping to take them away from the revolutionary peasants.

All I saw and heard from Constantinople made it easier for me, when in June, 1920, I became Minister for Foreign Affairs, to remain convinced—in spite of what everybody was telling me from London and Paris—that all the White Russian attempts and all the barbed wires around Bolshevik Russia were practically and morally not only sterile and indefensible, but also contrary to the aims pursued.   And I acted accordingly.

Approached for Italian collaboration in a certain anti-Bolshevik action, I declared in Parliament on August 2, 1920: "Attacks from outside will never be a solution.   I believe in liberty and that is why I am against Bolshevism. But the Bolshevist experiment must evolve freely to the end; that is, for as long as the Russians will continue with it.   Bolshevism must live or die of itself; but it must not be a martyr or a pseudo-martyr."

If anyone cared to ask me whether I believe that nothing beneficial can result from the Soviet experiment, I think I should answer: first, as an Italian, that I know too well how difficult it is to discover the truth between the lines of dictatorial documents and statistics and through travels in dictatorial countries; secondly, that the problems deriving from the Soviet experiment cannot be examined on the basis of present facts, even if we did know them all.

To decide whether something beneficial to the moral progress of Europe might eventually proceed from it, is as difficult today as it would have been difficult for some

Roman thinker of the fifth century to surmise whether
the downfall of the Roman Empire would be a success
and what good it would do. . . . Having risked this
comparison I might perhaps add that among the causes
which brought about the fall of the Roman Empire not the
least was the feeling of deliverance roused in the souls of
men through the spiritual revolution induced by Christianity; and that one does not see how the collective moral enslavement reigning in Russia, as in all dictatorial countries,
can aid the upward trend of human spirits as the Christian
revolution did.

Meanwhile, to come to a more practical and concrete
ground—there is no doubt that the entrance of the Soviet
Union into the League of Nations.and, more recently, the
Franco-Soviet Pact which was signed in Moscow in 1935
and ratified in 1936, have brought Russia much nearer to
western Europe. When ratifying their Pact with the
Russians, the French sincerely hoped that the German
Government would abandon the doctrine of the "localiza-
tion of war"—by which Hitler has always meant a free
hand for a German aggression against Russia; and that
Berlin would join the Pact and so accept the principle of
collective security. To Hitler who, like William II, was
always complaining of "encirclement," the French Foreign
Minister Flandin declared in the first weeks of 1936 that
what was being encircled was not Germany but the spirit
of aggression. To this Hitler answered in March, 1936,
with the denunciation of the Locarno Treaty and the
sudden arming of the Rhineland.

An armed Rhineland means the immobilization of the French at their frontier; and the complete freedom, for an aggressive Germany, to launch a war of "civilization" against Russia.

Many Tories in western Europe had been thinking in the first years of the Hitler régime in Germany that, since a rearmed Reich must expand somewhere, it would be better to see the Germans busy against Bolshevik Russia than against anyone else.

Hitler's violence in 1936 and his open disregard of treaties—even when freely signed as was the case with the Locarno Pact—changed all this. The change, of course, was made possible when Stalin swung over from the objective of a loudly proclaimed world-revolution to the more modest and sensible aim of internal economic reconstruction. Given Russia's absorption in her own economic affairs she was no more an alarming fact, at least for intelligent Tories.

In France even those least educated politically have ended by realizing that if Germany is given a free hand with the Russians it will a little later mean German hegemony over all Europe. Remembering Bismarck's diplomacy from 1866 to 1870 the French sigh: After Sadowa, Sedan. . . .

The German schemes toward Russia are the main problem of post-war Europe, just as the fate of Austria-Hungary was the dangerous problem before 1914, at least as long as Germany is ruled by a militaristic dictatorship.

Dictators cannot do without wars.

XVIII

EUROPE AND THE COLONIAL ILLUSION

WHEN the European war broke out, the colonial system
of the powers still seemed at its zenith—first, because of
its extensiveness, but also because of the technical improve-
ments achieved in the art of governing subject peoples,
one of the most brillant examples being that given by
Lyautey in Morocco.

Simultaneously, and despite the parochialism of the governments at home, a sort of international solidarity was
slowly evolving in the colonies. The colonial most jealous
of the exclusive privileges of his country could have no
illusion about it. In fact, if not in law, each European
people felt that in the colonies one had to reckon with
one's neighbors. In her Morocco Protectorate France
had—and still has—to bear in mind all the time what
Spain might, or might not, do in her zone. An initiative
of any kind taken by Italy in Lybia immediately re-echoed
in Tunisia. When the Italian Government decided in 1919
to give a sort of restricted representation to the Arabs
of Lybia, the French felt at once that such a fact was to
have a repercussion in French North Africa.

The treaties consecrated these correlations. The Berlin
Act of 1885, that of Brussels in 1890 and the two Con-

ventions of Berne in 1909 had eliminated certain old colonial abuses and created systems of control.

Out of interest if not out of good will, an embryonic European understanding had at last been found in Africa. We could hate one another in Europe, but we felt that, between two neighboring colonies, the interest in common was as great as between two white men meeting in the desert.

The Negroes of Central and Eastern Africa, endowed with a keener sense of observation than is generally believed, expressed this idea in their own languages. For them all Europeans are *Musango ya Bulaya*. They have always refused to distinguish between English, French, Italians. . . .

This rough attempt at white understanding was rendered vain and sterile by the results of the war, for the World War has destroyed the prestige of the European, of all Europeans. Until the European war, the peoples of Africa and Asia had been beaten everywhere—from the African coasts of the Mediterranean to Afghanistan, from India to Annam, to China even. Adowa, the battle in which, in 1896, some fourteen thousand Italians were surprised and defeated by one hundred and twenty-five thousand Ethiopians is morally no exception. Thousands of Italians fell fighting to their last cartridge.* Italian artil-

---

* The Italian losses were: whites, four thousand six hundred; natives, three thousand. Only one unsoldierlike thing happened at Adowa. The Commander-in-Chief, Baratieri, to explain his defeat which had originated with a mistake concerning the topography of the country, dispatched telegrams to Rome throwing the blame on his troops; which was false

lery continued to fire till all the gunners had been killed
by their pieces. Two of the five Italian generals, Arimondi
and Dabormida, fell on the battlefield; another, Ellena,
was wounded. What matters more, the Ethiopians, who
lost seventeen thousand men, did not advance farther,
attempted nothing against the Italian territory of Eritrea.
Emperor Menelik always expressed his profound respect
for the unparalleled bravery of the Italians. All colonial
wars have shown incidents similar to that of Adowa. If
Adowa became more notorious, it was because it constituted
a turning point in the colonial history of Italy, Crispi's
successors having decided to forego the colonial dreams
of the Sicilian patriot. But in doing so, they complied with
the will of the great majority of the Italians who had
always been hostile to expansion in Africa. This in reality
meant more to Crispi's successors than the fact of the
1896 military reverse. I could quote a hundred documents
of that time to prove that the decision of the majority of
the Italian people was a token of moral courage and no
way due to depression resulting from defeat. Simply by
way of example, here is the manifesto which was issued
after Adowa by the women of Pavia, the city of Adelaide
Cairoli and her heroic sons who fell in the battles of the
Risorgimento:

"The women of Pavia are full of sadness and pity for

---

and criminal. Baratieri was placed under court-martial and the sentence
deplored that "in such difficult circumstances the command should have
been given·to a general so inferior to the exigencies of the situation."

In 1935 Mussolini copied Crispi. In De Bono, his first choice for a new
war with Ethiopia was a general inferior to the exigencies of the situation.

the inconsolable affliction of so many Italian families, and also for the mourners among those other people who are defending their country and their independence. They take part in the anxieties and the tears of the mothers, the wives, the daughters, the sisters of all those who are in battle, irrespective of race or color. They tremble for the fate of their country, to which will come neither glory nor profit from an undertaking not prompted by liberty and justice. They remember all that their city and their Lombardy endured to free Italy from the stranger, and they believe, what their nearest and dearest have taught them, that it is sweet to die for their country. They declare that the heroic constancy of our soldiers, praised today by the whole civilized world and by the foe as well, should not be exercised as a sacrifice to a dictator but should be sacred to the good of the people. They demand that our battalions shall be recalled from Africa and that so many precious lives shall be restored to the land of their devotion. They invoke the memories of modern Italy in which the false glories of conquest have no part, the memories of their Italy that from Columbus to Garibaldi has been the bearer of civilization and fraternal help to the unhappy and the oppressed."

All the worse for Europe, with its literature *à l'image d'Epinal,* if it failed to understand the beauty and nobility of the feelings of the Italian people who disavowed in 1896 what was nothing more than a war of prestige.*

---

* The typical instance of a war of prestige, in modern times, is the French expedition to Mexico. It was the Empress Eugénie, much more

The declaration of the World War found me in Peking. Anyone who could read the eyes of the Chinese knew that they considered our war only a ghastly civil war in which

---

than her flabby husband, who willed it with all her Catholic and Spanish heart.

Some ten years before her death I saw a great deal of her during week-ends at Farnborough Hill. What struck me most was the discovery that not only had the "Empress" vanished, but also the "Frenchwoman." All that remained alive in her was the Spaniard. I believe the reason why she so often asked me to her week-ends, despite her lack of sympathy for the Italians, was my picaresque memories of Andalusia. The more I knew her, the better I realized that her French imperial life had been nothing more for her than an adventure, and the Tuileries little better than the stage setting of a *Midsummer Night's Dream* in which she herself played the leading part.

As a rule I prefer to respect royalties from a distance. If I went to see her so often it was because I felt so distinctly that her rôle of Empress had been for her a stage part. And this added to the sincerity of her conversation—at least with me. I often used to ask her about the Mexican War, the mad expedition which the Italian envoy Nigra described to his government as having been willed by Eugénie—and accepted by Napoleon III—to please the Catholic party and strengthen the régime by a brilliant *action d'éclat*.

She talked readily on the subject. Her sincerity at first struck me as force of character. Only in the course of time did I realize that her frankness in discussing the policy of the Second Empire was, to a great extent, lack of feeling and of imagination.

"It is easy," she said to me one day, "to criticize in retrospect. We staked all on what seemed a certainty to us and to our Mexican allies— the victory of the Southern States in the American Civil War. Had it materialized, the situation in Mexico would have been completely different. The Southern States would have become an independent oligarchic power which would have accepted a common frontier with the Mexican Emperor. In London, the Foreign Office believed as we did in a victory of the South. With the support of English diplomacy and of the Southern Confederation we should have been able to build a solid foundation for the throne of Maximilian."

In reality, the London that had believed in the victory of the South was the London of Buckingham Palace, the Foreign Office and "society." The sensible English middle and lower classes were always convinced that the North would be victorious. I made that remark to Eugénie who merely

each one of us, on either side of the trenches, lost authority
and prestige. The Chinese never saw a valid reason for
our war and decided we were bloodthirsty madmen. But

---

replied with a smile: "Oh, you Italians, you are all the same, always
something of the revolutionary!" I did not pursue the matter further. I
might have pointed out to Eugénie that no vital French interest but only
the prestige of the dictatorial régime was involved in this war, that during
its course French public opinion was blinded and deceived by a muzzled
press. Already on the eve of the war, Napoleon sent Admiral Julien
de la Gravière with the equivocal instructions: "If the sane part of the
population, tired of anarchy, desirous of order, were to be induced by the
presence of our forces to emerge from the social dissolution in which the
country is plunged . . ."

Contrary to what has happened under the dictatorships which have come
into existence in Italy, Germany and Russia, France had managed to
recover a certain amount of freedom of speech in the House of Legislature.
Jules Favre made a courageous speech: "You are going to Mexico as
invaders; beware of the consequences of your successes. You will be
envolved in an occupation and war of indefinite duration."

Rouher, the Emperor's all-powerful Minister, replied with an arrogant
and pompous tirade in which he assured his listeners that future historians
would speak of Napoleon III as "the man of genius who, in the face of
opposition, obstacles and faintheartedness had the courage to open up new
sources of prosperity to the French Nation."

The *Moniteur* on the next day reported "prolonged applause."

The prudent majority, by applauding, prevented Jules Favre from
replying. And Thiers stood up and cried: "You do not want to hear
the truth. You are afraid of the truth."

The truth became evident to the whole world very soon after when
the French Army hastily had to evacuate Mexico, when Maxmilian was
court-martialed and shot at Queretaro and no trace remained of the bloodstained venture—save a wave of dislike and distrust which only long
years of democracy in France managed to dispel. But, for Eugénie, men
like Favre and Thiers remained nothing better than "speech-makers." This
is the term she still applied to them fifty years later in her conversations
with me. For her, they were enemies of "strong government." After half
a century of exile, the poor lady, in spite of her indifference to her "imperial" past, was still repeating the hollow phrases of Rouher. Misfortune
had failed to teach her that a government which simply represents "interests" and is devoid of a human ideal, is no more than a travesty of true
authority and of strong government.

worse came later, when Lloyd George succeeded in extorting from China a declaration of war on Germany and Austria-Hungary. For on that day the Chinese Government automatically acquired full jurisdiction over the subjects of both powers. It followed that a few Portuguese half-breeds of Macao continued to enjoy complete extra-territoriality—which often amounted to impunity, granted the restricted organization of certain consular courts—whereas Germans and Austrians fell under the common Chinese law. There were distinguished scientists among them, men who had often been appointed by the whole diplomatic corps to honorific posts in the common interests of all the Europeans. The Chinese hesitated where we did not. They hesitated as if they were suspicious of the new power which had fallen to them. They feared that, at the first punitive measures, white Europe might change its mind and they would again lose "face" where they thought they were gaining it.

Finally, they did dare.

Germans and Austrians were interned and expelled; the Chinese could confiscate their properties. The diplomatic representatives of a Europe fighting for its freedom a defensive battle that sometimes seemed hopeless, could think only of the fate of their countries—at stake from the Yser to the Piave—and they did not interfere.

The German and Austrian concessions of Tientsin, the German concession of Hankow, were taken over by the Chinese Government. The Chinese Treasury made nothing by the transaction: but the Special Commissioners did

who managed these rich territories. Settled in the former
German and Austro-Hungarian consulates, they must have
said to themselves: "When will the turn of English,
French, Italian concessions come which we can see from
the belvederes of these villas that fell into our hands so
easily?"

And immediately after the Armistice, as if Lloyd
George's mistake in obliging China to join us had not been
enough,* we ourselves added common street broils for the
edification of the Asiatics.

---

* It is worth while reproducing the little-known telegram sent to Lloyd
George by Sun Yat-sen to show that the interest of the Entente lay in
China's not entering the war:

"I owe my life to England; I am grateful to her for it. It is both as
a friend of England and as a Chinese patriot that I have come to point
out to you the momentous consequences that the campaign undertaken by
your agents, urging China to go to war, may have for China and for
England.

"Searching discussions with eminent Englishmen have convinced me
of this, that a breach of Chinese neutrality would be disastrous for both our
countries. China is yet too young, too inexperienced, and might easily
come to disruption should dissensions arise. . . .

"China has always had unbounded confidence in the strength of
England and in her ultimate victory, but this confidence has diminished
since the campaign was started to make us enter into the struggle, a campaign that has gone so far as to insist on sending Chinese troops to
Mesopotamia. All this leads to nothing but a lessening of England's
prestige, for the Chinese cannot understand why the Allies should have
need of them in order to beat Germany. And now, Prime Minister Tuan
has just informed the President of the Republic that the Allies are obliging
the Chinese to fight for them. This does nothing but foment discord
between our statesmen, and might entail serious results, even a rekindling of
xenophobia and, possibly, massacres of Europeans.

"How could the Chinese masses recognize, among the Europeans, those
belonging to the nation they are fighting with? It is to be feared that
everyone would suffer, and particularly the English who have so many
interests vested in the Far East. Another very important fact to be con-

From a moral standpoint, what is the fact of winning a war worth if victory does not teach equanimity toward the loser? It should have been our honor and our duty in China to remember that at the time of the Boxer Rebellion, already a far-off event for us but not so far off for the Chinese. Only one European representative, Baron von Ketteler, feeling the imminence of the danger, fronted it with a stroke of boldness that might have succeeded. The legations were already besieged, but the Tsong-li-yamen had not yet thrown off the mask. The German Minister left his colleagues and, alone in his official sedan chair, went to the Chinese Ministers to try to make them understand the full weight of their frightful responsibility.

He was killed in the street of the Ha-ta-men, five hundred yards from his legation.

A few months later, in 1901, after an expedition which was sometimes severe but, on the whole, honorable, in spite of the bestial order given to Waldersee by a crowned comedian,* the Treaty of Peking provided—by Europe's unanimous will—that a commemorative arch (Pei-lho) be erected by the Chinese on the very spot where Ketteler, whose body was never found, had been murdered. Even more than a monument to the courageous diplomat, it was

---

sidered is that the Mahometans will never admit being obliged to fight their co-religionists. And finally, I believe that the state of anarchy that might break out in China would only cause dissensions among members of the Entente, which would necessarily bring about disasters for the latter. It is therefore quite impossible to ask anything of China but the strictest neutrality."

* "Do not make prisoners!" shouted William II when the German contingent sailed for China.

a permanent lesson to the Chinese.   The inscriptions reminded them of their shame in attacking Ambassadors.   A
Latin inscription, on the Pei-lho, added to the catholic
significance of the monument.

But was not Ketteler a Hun?   Thus thought the
embusqués of the Peking Legations quarter when the telegram announcing the Armistice became known.   And they
rushed to the Ha-ta-men street and tried to blow up the
Pei-lho.   But the international rabble did not succeed in
destroying the majestic monument.   Only a few columns
became loose, thereby endangering the passers-by.   A while
after, the Wai-chiao-pu looked into the danger and wrote
a sweetish note to the diplomatic corps informing it that
the government of the capital city would undertake to
remove a monument which had now become dangerous.

There had been time for thought, but they took good
care not to think.   The diplomatic corps gave in, and the
Pei-lho was moved to a public park, far from the spot
where the brave Ketteler lost his life.   It has only one
Chinese inscription now, and the least that can be said is
that it is ambiguous.   This is its literal translation: "Right
has conquered."   Not one word of Ketteler.   Who worries
over a dead foreign devil?   Chinese casuistry can interpret
the triumph of right as it pleases.

The tens of thousands of Chinese, Indo-Chinese, Indian,
North African soldiers and workmen whom the Entente
had been obliged to call for service in France, brought
back with them, when they returned home, an entirely new
opinion and interpretation of European civilization.   Those

who fought in the trenches felt full of bitterness and hatred
—rightly or wrongly, it matters little—because their bodies
had been used as cannon fodder to fill the deadliest holes.*
In any case, they all, Asiatic and Africans, had learned to
use against other white men the diabolical and murderous
playthings of the masters. What was possibly even worse,
these Orientals were unavoidably put in contact with the
miseries and vices of our big cities. And the subjects of
yesterday, their faces impassive as ever, began to wonder
among themselves if these Rumis, these white men, whom
they had feared and admired so much, were not after all
but as poor things as themselves, and even worse perhaps.

The post-war boycotts, mutinies, rebellions of the subject
races have no other origin. The war destroyed the moral
basis of the ascendancy the Europeans had over Africa
and Asia. I saw China twice, before the war and after.
Few experiences of my life have had that tang. Before
the war, only old philosophers of the type of the venerable
Chang Chi-tung doubted the value of our over-materialistic
civilization. In 1927 and 1928, I could read contempt
on even the faces of the coolies who, a novelty in China,
had learned to pay a few sapeks for the newspaper from
which they expected to learn the failures of the English
and of the Russians.

---

* *"Les conditions actuelles de notre indépendance nous obligent* . . .
*à employer dans notre armée, et en particulier dans le poste de sacrifice
de l'infanterie, des contingents musulmanes importants."* Thus writes a
French authority, General Brémond, in his book *L'Islam et les questions
musulmanes au point de vue français.* If this is the French *point de vue,*
one must admit its sincerity, but one understands why sympathy for the
French has greatly decreased throughout all North Africa and the Near East.

Yes, of the Russians. For those who perceive the hand of the Bolshevik Kremlin in every colonial trouble, unwittingly do the latter a very good turn; for they enable the Kremlin to boast of results which are far beyond the didactic tactics of Moscow.

Certainly it was not Bolshevik propaganda that weakened the Eastern dynasties, guilty, in the eyes of their people, of having compromised with the West. Until the eve of the war, a good many Asiatic peoples were ruled by dynasties—the Osmans in Turkey and the Chings in China, to quote the most illustrious only. By corrupting or terrorizing the dynasts—great or small—it was easy for British and French to secure a hold over the peoples and with these, over their mines, their plantations, their ports. But, following in the wake of the fallen Osmans and Chings, the Mohammedan and Asiatic dynastic forces will be questioned more and more by their subjects who successfully upbraid them with their compromises. This is happening, more or less openly, in Tunisia and in Morocco, as in Annam and Cambodia, where a very clever French policy has endeavored to maintain monarchic forms. It is even beginning to be felt in the far-off autonomous principalities of India.

Let the movement become precipitate, and the peoples will become more and more elusive; and the problem of colonial government more and more arduous, expensive, sterile.

The day is not far off. They know it well who now shut their eyes to the fact. The Roman Church has shown she realized it when she suddenly decided—in the face of a secular tradition—that the bishops of far-off missions shall more and more be drawn from the native clergy, to the great horror of the old Apostolic Vicars in China and elsewhere who, in their hearts, have nothing but suspicion for native priests, most of whom are full of good will but whose souls are unconsciously befogged by Buddhist and Taoist myths.*

Why wonder that it should be so? That the Victorian "white man's burden" should henceforth seem, more even than a hypocritical lie, a pompous boast?

Not only is not one of our colonial empires safe—but not one of them pays. Take Great Britain: no colonial empire is more far-flung, more securely built, more wisely administered. But in India the exports of Japanese textiles have, since 1933, exceeded British textiles; while during the whole nineteenth century the foundation of England's commercial supremacy was the textile exports, especially to India and the rest of the East. Tanganika is now British, but most of the imports into Tanganika are Japanese. The same is true for the Netherlands' possessions of Java and Sumatra. Syria used to be mainly a French market; but the French lost it when, with the mandate conferred to them over Syria, they had a French army in occupation of Beirut and Damascus. The great French possessions

---

* I have attended, in Asia as well as in America, Conventions of Catholic and Protestant Missions. Twenty years ago, colored missionaries were a small and humble exception. Now many young missions in Asia and Africa are represented at such Conventions by a majority of colored people—every year more influential, more enthusiastic, more pushing.

along the Mediterranean are a constant source of economic disorder to France—especially Algeria and Morocco, where French settlers have created a wine industry which, with its low prices, seriously menaces even the home market of the good old famous French wines. Before the war, Germany had colonies in which she was taking great pride—a pride and a colonial mania which were largely responsible for her disasters with the slogan of "a place in England's sun." In 1914 there were not more than twenty-four thousand Germans in all her colonies put together; there were infinitely more Germans, and they were earning a far better living, in Switzerland and Italy. The three Italian colonies of Eritrea, Somaliland and Lybia had some eight thousand Italians at the outbreak of the World War; and the Eritrean plateau had just the same climate and the same soil as the later coveted Ethiopia. There were more than eight thousand Italians within the area of two streets in small Utica, New York, not to speak of New York which is the largest Italian city in the world.

Of course, imponderables are to be taken into account. At the end of the World War, events occurred that might have made the old men sitting in Paris understand that the nineteenth century, with its colonial spoils, had had its day. The awakening of the Arabs might have made France perceive that the mandate over Syria was not so desirable a present. The vitality shown by the Turkish people, as soon as they were delivered from a corrupted dynasty, should have made everybody realize sooner how fatuous that policy was which continued to consider valid the papers that divided Turkey into three zones of influence: British, French, Italian. And warnings were not lacking to the Big Four in Paris. From Constantinople where I had arrived as High Commissioner for Italy after the Armistice, I frankly advised them against a mad policy. It signified, after four years of horrible warfare, starting another war for the sake of Turkish territories the possession of which was worth less, even economically speaking, than friendship with the Turkish Republic now rising on the horizon. Wilson's consent, in compliance with Lloyd George's insistent demands, to the occupation of Smyrna by the Greeks, was probably his grossest blunder, because it was a mean blunder. Having no other means but protest from Constantinople against a decision which would, I wired, be far more disastrous for the Greeks than for the Turks, I felt quite sure that Wilson had come to it out of resentment toward his Italian colleagues with whom—as I have already said*—he had quarreled so bitterly about Dalmatia and Fiume and who had, just at that moment, momentarily left the Conference for an unwise and demagogic trip to Rome.

Equally mean and unintelligently selfish was, a little later, the conduct of the English and the French in distributing the mandates. If the mandates were not a hypocritical form used to cover the ancient imperialism with a halo of undeserved sanctity, but really constituted

---

* Chapter IX.

a new conception of trusteeship,* it was inconceivable that Italy who, in her administration of Eritrea and Lybia, had a record at least as good as France and Great Britain—should be put aside. When, in June, 1920, on becoming Italian Foreign Minister, I found myself confronted with the results of the errors of my three predecessors of the war and Versailles periods, Sonnino, Tittoni and Scialoja, it was too late; everything was over.† Indeed, what I resented was the injustice and the rudeness of our former allies, not the material loss. What I had witnessed in China at the beginning of the war and in Turkey after the Armistice had made me skeptical of the advantages of new colonial acquisitions. I therefore, as duty commanded, maintained the entirety of Italian rights to colonial compensations as provided under the London Treaty of 1915. But I did not press the negotiations. What I had in mind was far more complex. And the little I said to Lloyd George and to Briand immediately proved to me that the time was not yet ripe. The intoxication of war-times had first to be completely dispelled. Today, as I did then, I consider that the only way to preserve Europe's colonial possessions is to generalize responsibilities, to give native representation its due place, to avoid the dangerous tête-à-tête of conquerors and to rule by a sort of European Con-

---

* For the definition of a mandate, see following chapter.

† Sonnino was an unconscious but necessary precursor of Fascism with his nationalistic blunders at the Peace Conference; see Chapter XI and XII and, in my *Makers of Modern Europe,* the chapter on Sonnino. Tittoni and Scialoja became, after 1922, in appearance warm supporters of Fascism. They would have done better to serve the prestige of Italy in deeds when they were in power.

sortium which would yet be respectful of certain acquired moral rights.*   It is needless to point out the part which a renovated League of Nations might play in this, or what a source of strength the League might draw from it for peace in Europe itself.

The law of tomorrow will be that the universal interest shall be more consciously present in each particular State. If, for example, France goes on representing only herself in Syria or in Indo-China or in Morocco, if Great Britain goes on thinking exclusively of British interests in India or in Egypt, the inevitable result will be growing unrest in Syria, in Indo-China, in Morocco, in India, in Egypt. . . . Should the world, or a renovated League of Nations, speak, in all the subject countries, louder than the direct suzerains, the problems of racial expansion and of ownership of raw materials would cease to be causes or pretexts for those colonial wars in which aggressors and invaded are equally bound to suffer for generations from the consequences of decisions even more foolish than criminal.

The way to this conception is essentially ethical.   Even many conservatives who think they hate and mistrust Karl Marx do, in reality, follow him when, confronted with

---

* Discussing all this with Lloyd George, he told me simply that he recognized Italy had been wronged.   But he also tried to convince me that his intentions toward my country had been perfectly loyal; that it was my fault if Italy had no mandate because he had suggested in 1919 our taking Georgia; and that it was because of my opposition from Constantinople that the Orlando Cabinet had finally recalled the military mission it had first sent to Tiflis.   Lloyd George's mistake has been to think he can fool all his interlocutors.

colonial problems, they act as if the economic drive were the most important factor of history. In fact, the colonial field is filled, even more than other fields, with illusions, prides, resentments, anachronistic loves and hatreds. . . .

XIX

MANDATES: FRANCE IN SYRIA

WHAT then is this mandate through which the Covenant hoped to bring a higher moral standard into the colonial system?

Conceived in generosity, like most of the Wilsonian Peace Conference ideas, the mandate was born in sin, as we have seen already.

"No annexation of colonies" had become one of Wilson's Fourteen Points. But the colonies of the vanquished were there, at the end of the war, and there also, the various Arab nations demanding autonomy and perhaps not yet ripe for independence. On the other hand, the League of Nations was only a scheme as yet. What was to be done?

The suggestion of the system of government which the Covenant called the international mandate was first put forward by General Smuts, one of the rare original brains of the Peace Conference, in a pamphlet he published at the end of 1918 under the title *The League of Nations: A Practical Suggestion.**

---

* Before the World War, the word "mandate" had sometimes been used in the case of territories administered by a State responsible to other States. A mandate was proposed in 1906 by President Roosevelt for France and Spain in Morocco, with supervising authority for Italy on behalf of all the Powers; but the proposal was not carried out.

253

Since the most talked of documents are very often little known in their exact form, I shall here give the context of Article 22 of the Covenant which constituted the charter of all the mandates:

"1. To those colonies and territories which as a consequence of the late war have ceased to be under the sovereignty of the States which formerly governed them and are inhabited by peoples not yet able to stand by themselves under the strenuous conditions of the modern world, there should be applied the principle that the well-being and development of such peoples form a sacred trust of civilization and that securities for the performance of this trust should be embodied in this Covenant.

"2. The best method of giving practical effect to this principle is that the tutelage of such peoples should be entrusted to advanced nations who by reason of their resources, their experience or their geographical position can best undertake this responsibility, and who are willing to accept it, and that this tutelage should be exercised by them as Mandatories on behalf of the League.

"3. The character of the mandate must differ according to the stage of development of the people, the geographical situation of the territory, its economic conditions and other similar circumstances.

"4. Certain communities formerly belonging to the Turkish Empire have reached a stage of development where their existence as independent nations can be provisionally recognized subject to the rendering of administrative advice and assistance by a Mandatory until such time as they are able to stand alone. The wishes of these communities must be a principal consideration in the selection of the Mandatory.*

* * * * *

"7. In every case of mandate, the Mandatory shall render to the Council an annual report in reference to the territory committed to its charge.

"8. The degree of authority, control or administration to be exercised by the Mandatory shall, if not previously agreed upon by the Members of the League, be explicitly defined in each case by the Council.

"9. A permanent Commission shall be constituted to receive and examine the annual reports of the Mandatories and to advise the Council on all matters relating to the observance of the mandates."

---

* Paragraphs 5 and 6 deal with mandates in Africa and over the South-Pacific territories. They run as follows:

"5. Other peoples, especially those of Central Africa, are at such a stage that the Mandatory must be responsible for the administration of the territory under conditions which will guarantee freedom of conscience and religion, subject only to the maintenance of public order and morals, the prohibition of abuses such as the slave trade, the arms traffic and the liquor traffic, and the prevention of the establishment of fortifications or military and naval bases and of military training of the natives for other than police purposes and the defence of territory, and will also secure equal opportunities for the trade and commerce of other Members of the League.

"6. There are territories, such as South-West Africa and certain of the South Pacific islands, which, owing to the sparseness of their population, or their small size, or their remoteness from the centres of civilization, or their geographical contiguity to the territory of the Mandatory, and other circumstances, can best be administered under the laws of the Mandatory as integral portions of its territory, subject to the safeguards above mentioned in the interests of the indigenous population."

Mountains of learned books have already been written on the mandates.

It were better to tell my personal experience concerning the most complex and most difficult of all of them, the French mandate in Syria. After all, as the Belgian Rolin once said at the Permanent Mandates Commission in Geneva, "The system of mandates will be in law what it was in fact."

I was in Syria before the war and in 1935, after thirteen years of French mandate.

Sordid alleys; mud creeping everywhere, as at Pera and Galata; variegated souks, but not nearly so rich as the bazaar in Stamboul; gruesome beggars, often infected with leprosy; in the drawing-rooms, ladies who never went out and whose features might have been Circassian had they not sagged under the grease of a lazy indoor life; men who, though conscious of their intellectual superiority, bowed with an obsequious smile to the most brutal Konak Turks—these were my hasty pre-war recollections of Beirut.

In 1935, after fifteen years of French occupation, what a metamorphosis: a capital with wide avenues; beautiful villas; a feverish but well-ordered traffic of thousands of cars going by under the eyes of white-gloved policemen; and instead of the heavy Levantine women who never went out except in carriages, young women who play golf with energy and against whom it is not so easy to measure one's strength at tennis; business men who have, naturally, the same faults and the same qualities as before, but most of whom have acquired the precise and rapid manner of industrialists from Lyons or Milan. . . .

The surprise is just as great when one goes inland. Twenty years ago, there existed one highroad in all Syria. It ran between Beirut and Damascus. Now, all the countries under French mandate, from Aleppo to Damascus, from Antioch to Homs, from Alexandretta to Beirut, are covered with a net of fine motor roads. Everywhere, even in the farthest Druze or orthodox villages, are schools with good accommodations to which one could object only that they are too similar to those of France. Did I not hear fifty black-haired, Semitic-looking young boys, stammering together, *"Nos ancêtres les Gaulois étaient blonds . . . ?"*

There is no doubt, however, that many errors have been committed in the work carried out in Syria by France since 1922.

But there is no doubt either that the task of France in Syria has been infinitely more delicate and difficult than the exercise of the protectorates in Morocco and Tunisia, or of the mandates which fell to England's share.

Why? If attempting merely to list the reasons for the difficulties of the French mandate one would run the risk of writing a whole book only to find in the end that one had left incomplete the count of omissions, paradoxes and potential mistakes which crop up unceasingly in the path, seemingly so fair and straight, of the French High Commissioner. In Morocco, in Tunisia, France found local memories, secular traditions. . . . In Syria, there are nothing but peoples, "nations" with not the slightest bond between them, exclusively imbued with a long tradition of distrust of the successive foreign governments that for centuries have ground them down. In Syria is a vast medley of populations, rootedly different from one another in culture and religion, which seem to live together without intermingling. In Syria, the very highest interests, like those of religious life, become an additional reason for hatred, since even the Christian communities, for fear of losing their autonomies, emphasize their antagonistic rites to avoid risk of closer intercourse. Was it possible to evolve a minimum of common interests, capable of creating a connecting link between so many particularities?

The very formula of the mandate—as provided in London on July 24, 1922*—helped to create confusion.

---

* The mandate was not juridically assigned until July, 1922; but in fact it was at the Supreme Allied Council held at San Remo in May, 1920, under the Presidency of the Italian Prime Minister Nitti, that the mandate was entrusted to France; and only fourteen months later did the Council of the League deliver to the French Government its "Declaration of Mandate" over Syria—and simultaneously to the British Government the mandate for Palestine.

A few French political writers wishing to explain these delays have hinted at more or less secret Italian opposition to the French mandate over Syria.

As I had a part in the first Italo-French conversations concerning Syria, it may not be entirely useless for me to re-establish the truth of the matter here.

At the time of the inter-Allied Conference of San Remo, I was only Under-Secretary of State for Foreign Affairs, but Camille Barrère, the French Ambassador in Rome, often discussed these problems with me. I did not hide from him how skeptical I felt about the joys and satisfactions France would derive from the Syrian mandate. But Barrère knew the friendliness which prompted my remarks. In 1922, when certain French writers were declaring that Italy raised new difficulties, I was Ambassador

For instance, Article 22 of the Covenant juxtaposes, as the reader may have noted already, the most discordant words. It talks of "advice and assistance" which the Mandatory Power owes to the local administration. But a little further on, this task is qualified as tutelage—a word which calls up the idea of an incapable minor.

The official declaration of mandate corrected the fundamental impression of the article of the Covenant since it emphasized the idea of tutelage, in the sense given to the word in civil law and now transferred to international law. But it provided other formulas which were to render the work of France more troublesome. For instance, under Article 1, it declared:

"The Mandatory shall frame, within a period of three years from the coming in force of this mandate, an organic law for Syria and Lebanon. This organic law shall be

---

in Paris. Charged one day to draw the attention of Poincaré, then President of the Cabinet and Minister for Foreign Affairs, to a whole series of meddlesome and useless measures taken by the French Administration in Syria, measures that partly infringed on our rights, I fulfilled my instructions in the most unequivocal manner. But I added: "Do you wish to avoid these thorny and somewhat sterile discussions? Let us, together and with equal good will, study far more essential problems, like the Tunisian problem; and the further we proceed in these, the more I'll warrant you not to mention Syria again."

Ten years later, in the spring of 1933—the story is perhaps worth telling, as it proves with how meticulous a legal precision the lawyer Poincaré wrote, one after the other, the several volumes of his *Memoirs*—the President asked me, on one of my visits to him at the Rue Marbeau, whether my words had been authorized by my government.

"No," I answered; "but they proceeded from the general law of my Embassy as it was known in Rome: to safeguard the real interests and dignity of Italy, and thereby insure an understanding that events might render indispensable for the safety of the Latin world."

framed in agreement with the native authorities and shall take into account the rights, interests and wishes of all the population inhabiting the said territories."

What could the words "native authorities" imply in a country devoid of all legal institutions? And how could the "wishes of all the population" be taken into account in a country where—as in Lebanon—the Maronite village has for centuries exchanged nothing but gunshots with the neighboring Kurd village; in a country where marriage between persons of two different religions is considered worse than a crime?

Under the same article, the declaration of mandate added: "Pending the coming into effect of the organic law, the Government of Syria and Lebanon shall be conducted in accordance with the spirit of this mandate. The Mandatory shall, as far as circumstances permit, encourage local autonomy."

Local autonomies? But which? The only real autonomy was that of Mount Lebanon. That of the Alowites, in the North, was never legal and in any case had been a dead letter since 1856. That of the Druzes was never anything but a *de facto* state established by a bellicose nation against the Turkish *valis* and their tax-gatherers.

One could go on quoting a dozen of the almost inextricable difficulties added by the mandate formula to the already heavy tasks of the Syrian administration.

The French mandate, seen on the spot, recalls the way in which the Roman Empire managed: the same army of occupation, the same religious sects along the sea-coast, the same nomads inland, the same alternative between military expeditions and autonomies . . . with this difference however, that Rome, alone in the world, had to account to no one for her management, whereas France, once a year, must answer to the League of Nations.

Certain Frenchmen whose minds are exclusively set on the past, regret the restrictions provided in the mandate by Geneva. And yet, simply from a selfish French point of view, it is not so certain that these restrictions are always an evil for France—far from it. The French agents in Syria, military and civil, have often struck me as being fairly good; two or three even as being first-rate; but they are men, and it is sometimes good for pugnacious and adventurous young men to remember that brawls in an oasis near the Euphrates may, a year later, be brought up before the Mandates Commission in puritan Geneva. . . .

And what do the Syrians—the Mohammedans of the "Syrian Republic" and the Christians of the "Lebanese Republic"—think after several years of French administration?

A preliminary remark should be made here. The fact that everybody in Lebanon and all the cultured people in Syria speak French—a French which, at Beirut, sometimes seems native—at first affords the French a most natural satisfaction and pleasure. In point of fact, they are beginning to realize, late, too late, that they pay for this pleasure with heavy psychological disillusions. Thinking themselves at home, they have made no effort to search out, in the secret recesses of souls, the essential instincts, so different from theirs. They have been deceived by a false front, by sounds that seemed familiar, but were different—neither better nor worse, different.

One should beware of the expression "the Near East." I have lived for years in both the Near and the Far East, the East of Constantinople and of Beirut, the East of Peking and of Tokyo. The unfathomable depths we feel between us and a Confucian scholar or a Japanese faithful to Bushido help us, at least, not to forget distances and uncertainties; whereas bridge parties at Beirut, at which Parisian slang is the latest fashion, can only lead one astray and render one unfair when one is shocked by mental shifts interpreted—wrongly—as deceit. . . . But Frenchmen will serve the cause of their country if, when they hear in the mouth of Syrians reproachful words which seem to them unjust and untrue, they will do one thing: try to learn what they mean and what lies back of them.

Fate would have it that external events—especially in the countries neighboring on Syria—never were favorable to the French policy; and one understands too well that they contributed to accentuate Syrian aspirations toward complete independence and discontent with the Mandatory Power.

Let us, for instance, consider this especially: on returning from Persia to the Mediterranean, through Iraq, the desert, Syria and her jewel, Damascus, Lebanon and European Beirut, one is struck by a strange diplomatic paradox. The more these different countries are, or seem, benumbed by the great Oriental slumber, the more have they been endowed with treaties and formulas of independence enabling their representatives to sit *inter pares* on the League of Nations with the representatives of France, of Great Britain, of Italy.

Persia with her magical names and sad realities, Persia with more illiterates than Syria, has even given a President —a very distinguished President, for that matter—to one of the assemblies at Geneva.

Iraq, whose social state and intellectual development show marked progress over present-day Persia, already enjoys less international consideration. England has, it is true, given up the mandate she held over the Iraq kingdom and has had it admitted as a member of the League of Nations, but, under the treaty which settled the relations between the two countries at the end of the mandate, she has kept a more or less disguised form of protectorate.

When, having crossed the desert, one arrives at Damascus, the ancient center of Arabian culture, Damascus with its restless class of intellectuals and semi-intellectuals, Damascus with its university where hundreds of doctors of law and of medicine are manufactured every year, one hears Europe declaring, by the mouth of the League of Nations: "Syria is a backward nation incapable of self-government; we charge France to lead her for the sake of civilization."

Is it to be wondered at that the Syrians should think themselves wrongly judged and entertain feelings of rancorous hostility toward France? Especially if one considers the dreams, the ideals which have, at all times, come out of Damascus, probably the liveliest and most feverish center of Mohammendan hopes. . . .

The first time I saw Damascus, I immediately experienced a vague feeling of having seen it before. "But this is Fez!" I exclaimed finally, although nothing, in their appearance, warrants the comparison between the two capitals save the wealth of chiming waters, as in Rome too, and the surrounding greenery which makes them so sweet. Both towns have the same groups of fanatic and somber theologians; and besides them, an identical bourgeoisie, equally businesslike and defiant, convinced, indeed, of the material superiority of the West but despising our conception of life as petty and mediocre.

But Fez is at the remotest end of Moghreb, of the West, whereas Damascus is right in the middle of all the ideas of Islam. From Damascus every year starts that great human torrent, the pilgrimage to Medina and to Mecca, the two Arab cities which Mohammed sanctified. In the courtyards of Damascus mosques, as on the benches of the cafés, every "information" develops which may furnish a new hope to Islam—as, for instance, in the year of grace 1935, the grandeur and power of Ibn Saud, the Arab hero of a war of which Damascus pretends to ignore that the beginnings and ends are far more British than Arab. . . .

To the grudges and reproaches which one feels rising out of this world so foreign to Western mentality I have always held that the only dignified and valid answer that France could make was: "You are right, possibly. But the more Syria may gain in formal political independence, the more she will lose in possibilities of awakening and of economic prosperity."

This is true. But it is true also that a formula of this nature entails duties upon France.

These duties become more pressing still because Palestine, which borders on Syria to the south, enjoys at present a prosperity perhaps unique in the world. The British High Commissioner who at Jerusalem exercises the British mandate—initiated on the same date as the French mandate over Syria—is in no way responsible for that, but the fact nevertheless remains—and it explains the envious and admiring regard the Syrians cast on Palestine where, in the last five years, imports have increased by thirty per cent, whereas in Syria they have fallen by seventy-five per cent.

It is only too natural for the Syrians to forget that the author of Palestinian prosperity is Hitler, with his Jewish persecutions and the resulting flow to Jerusalem of much Germano-Jewish capital and many activities.

The idea of a completely independent Syrian nation is bruited more and more in Syria by the Moslems and disliked less and less by the Christians. But the very idea of a "Syrian nation" is imported—imported from the Italian and Germanic national struggles of the early nineteenth century. Mazzini's idealistic thought has no original roots in the soil of Syria.

A mosaic of races and sects, when will the Syrians understand that their claim to glory should lie rather in the creation of an entirely new formula than in copying old European formulas?

On Syrian ground, divisions into national groups always take on a religious form. For those Semitic races the religious link is the unique principle of all social life and of all national allegiances.

Take the Christians. The most numerous are the Maronites (two hundred and thirty thousand), who hesitated long between the Vatican and the Phanar, who finally rallied to Rome, but who, in essence, are wholly orthodox. Take the Orthodox Greeks (eighty thousand), who, but for the filioque and purgatory, would be very near the Catholics, but whom the Catholics despise. Take the Greeks united to Rome (forty-six thousand), whose loyalty is suspiciously checked by the Propaganda Fide. And take the Jacobites (twenty thousand), for whom Jesus has a divine nature only, whereas he is only human for the Chaldeans (ten thousand)—a sufficient reason for mutual hatred. And yet again, take the Syriacs, who speak the language Jesus must have spoken. . . . The Latins all seem united, and they are united in dogma; but who shall tell the jealousies between Jesuits and Franciscans, Dominicans and Carmelites? . . . And finally, a recent addition, take the nine thousand Protestants. Where do they come from? A few are students from the American University of Beirut, but more are emigrants who have returned with wealth from the United States where they joined a Protestant Church and love it as a symbol of their social rise.

And the Mohammedans? Face to face with the one million one hundred thousand Sunnites stand the hundred thousand Shiites, faithful to the murdered Ali who, in Syria and in Persia, brought into the simplicity of the Islamic religion a violent trend of mystic adoration.

Undoubtedly, the Syrian race has one trait in common, which can be detected everywhere, among the Christians of Lebanon as well as in the Mohammedan plains, and among all the Syrians who have emigrated throughout the whole world: a genius for business.

A passion for business and a love of travel have always been essential characteristics of the Syrians. I have come across them the whole world over, as I have the Greeks—but they are more inclined to enjoy the bounties of life than the Greeks—in Africa and in the United States, in India and even in Mexico. The very Mohammedan religion, which necessarily creates a concept of rest, has not succeeded in destroying the old instinct everywhere. Whence, for instance, in arch-Mohammedan Aleppo, the proverb: Among the Aleppines, even the lame have got to India.

But, in order to create a national soul, a national unity, traits of this nature, be they ever so characteristic, are not enough.

Syria has always lacked a common national thought and sentiment, such as her neighbor Persia possesses to a marked extent. During the centuries of darkest decadence, the Persian ideal endured alive in the immortal poems of Firdusi whose sixty thousand verses are one enthusiastic and magnificent hymn to the glory of Iran (the name which Persia has officially readopted since January, 1935). To Firdusi the Persians owe, not only a charming language, set for ever, but a national feeling which no foreign invasion could ever again impair. Besides Firdusi, Persia has also a very personal and characteristic painting and architecture.

Those are the links which make a people one—the same links that Dante and Petrarch and our painters and sculptors forged for the Italians.

Syria gave less and more—and she suffers from it. She gave, in past ages, the two greatest jurists of Rome, Ulpian and Papinian. She even created the famous Law School of Beryta (now Beirut) of which Rome, for a time, was jealous. But law is a universal, not a national, turn of mind.

I have already said that Syria's claim to glory might lie, not in the copying of European national formulas, certain blind exaggerations of which today threaten to jeopardize Western society, but in seeking a fuller ideal of life which might become the general reality of tomorrow.

Syria was the cradle of the gods. From Syria sprang the three monotheist religions of the world: Mosaism, Christianity, Mohammedanism. If history still has a mission in store for her, it is not to twaddle about formulas of Balkan or Hitlerian nationalism, but to remain true to her old genius for universality.

XX

THE JEWS AND THEIR ARAB COUSINS:
JEWISH COLONIZATION

SYRIA is, geographically, a misleading name. In the days of Rome, of the Crusades, it was a living entity. But it is no longer so today. Syria, like Palestine, is now only a part of the awakening Arab world. And that is another of the many difficulties of the French mandate which the British feel far less in Palestine. Constituted at the same time as the French mandate over Syria, the British mandate over Palestine was probably less active, less encumbering, than the French exercised over a country where they naïvely believed that France was loved. But, above all, the English found a far easier task if only because Arabs and Jews bore them no grudge for their presence, knowing well that it constituted the only possible condition for an armistice between themselves.

What then are the Arabs? Whether they are called Syrians or Mesopotamians, Maronites or Moslems, Druzes or Mutawiles or Ansariis, they are all Arabs. Eighty per cent of their blood is Semitic. Ten per cent, on the Syrian coast, is of Italian and French origin through the Crusaders. Another ten per cent, in Mesopotamia, is half Turkish, half Persian. Few nations have such a complete racial unity; yet eight centuries of Turkish domination have ruined the Arabs. Ruined but not killed—at least not the Arabs of the Mediterranean European world. The Syrians I have met in the United States, from New York to Michigan, were just as alive, intellectually and practically, as their Jewish cousins. Who can predict that in two or three generations Aleppo and Damascus and Bagdad may not once more become important centers, just as they were when the Abassids were giving art and science to the Western world?

But the Arab revival which, to my mind, will certainly come about in the more or less near future, will not necessarily take on an aggressive political character.

Too many people talk of a danger of Pan-Arabism— of a fanatical Pan-Arabism. Does Pan-Arabism, or a danger of Pan-Arabism, really exist as a political element worthy of realistic consideration?

Undoubtedly, if one listened to half the things I heard in many pleasant conversations with important Moslem Syrians in Damascus, during my Syrian travels, one would conclude that it is going to be something serious. And probably the tales which inflamed talkers keep on spreading in the cafés of the Syrian capital, would be enough to make uncritical minds believe that Pan-Arabism is one of the most formidable movements history has seen mature.

It has been my luck to discuss the Pan-Arabic schemes and hopes not only in Damascus but with influential chiefs of the most important Bedouin tribes, the Sbaas, the Beni Kaled, the Fadel. . . .

Strange to say, the romantic nomads who received me under their black tents were much more sensible and matter-of-fact than the French-speaking nationalistic leaders of Damascus. What the Bedouin chiefs admired most in the reports from distant Nedj was that the tribes of King Ibn Saud had settled down at last, had built important cities, had sown corn in the Djouf plains. . . . Never a word about Pan-Arabism.

By the way, there is at present but one problem that interests the Bedouin chiefs: how to give up being Bedouins, *Ahn-Ibls* (camel nomads), how to give up going on with their eternal migrations, with their fortune wholly bound up in camels, the price of which has lowered so terribly since motor cars and lorries have appeared in the desert. Their only hope and ideal is to become *Bakkara* (cattle folk) instead of *Ahn-Ibls*.

Pan-Arabism is little more than a propaganda word for nationalistic agitators in Damascus, Cairo, Geneva. I should be inclined to advise such romantic minds as are tempted to people politics with phantoms of this kind, to remember the rise and fall of Pan-Islamism during the twenty-five years which preceded fatal 1914.

In those days, and with much better reason, a good many statesmen and diplomats believed in the irresistible driving force which the voice of the Caliph would have, summoning the faithful to *Jihad* (Holy War) against the Christians from the banks of the Bosphorus. I asked, with much better reason, if there was not, at the time, a

Sultan-Caliph reigning at Constantinople surrounded by the respect of all the Mohammedans of the world?*

And what did we see from 1914 to 1918? Mohammedans fighting everywhere for England and France against other co-religionists dying side by side with the Austro-Germans. Just as, for that matter—and let us not forget it—on both sides of the trenches, soldiers and bishops and cardinals prayed for four years with the same faith to the same God of War. . . .

For a beginning of Pan-Arabism, there should be an Arab prince, victorious, rich and powerful. Possibly, the part might have been played by Feisal who, when still quite young, died suddenly in Berne in 1933. . . . Feisal (whom I knew quite well, and in whom I appre-

---

*May I insert a personal, and comical, recollection here? I have probably been the one and only human being who, in the second decade of the twentieth century, came near to seeing Pan-Islamism in action. I was Italian Minister Plenipotentiary to China in 1911 and, a few weeks after Italy had declared war on Turkey, I had left Peking for a shooting party in Mongolia. Some distant Mohammedan tribes, having learned of my coming, exaggerated the presence of an Italian camp in the Mongolian plains and decided on an expedition against the Ambassador of an "infidel" country that had dared to declare war on the Caliph of the Moslems.

I was at once warned of the danger from two sides. A brave and modest American missionary rode for two days to inform me of it. And from the south, from Peking, the Wai-chiau-pu (the Chinese Foreign Office) frantically begged me to avoid the "risky danger" and come back at once to the capital. I thought it better not to alter my plans but to have six *carabinieri* from the Legation Guard and a machine gun sent to me immediately from the Legation. This probably soon grew, from mouth to mouth, into an army. It induced the brave Moslems to turn back, not without looting a couple of dozen Chinese villages. . . . The poor villages never guessed that they had fallen victim to the landing of the Italians at Tripoli, some ten thousand miles from the Yellow Sea. . . .

ciated a rare mingling of East and West) held his sway over the imaginations of the Near East by his high intelligence, his realistic sense of politics, his natural genius for that most anti-Arab of political gifts, compromise. One might say of Feisal that he forced himself on his compatriots by dint of gifts which, in a certain sense, made him a stranger among them. This, be it said in passing, is a rather frequent law in political history. Mazarin and Bonaparte ruled France not in spite of but because of their Italian blood. Alberoni ruled Spain forcefully because he was an Italian. Mehemed Ali and his successors were, for generations, the masters of Egypt because they were Albanians. . . .

After the premature loss of the first King of Iraq, the partisans of Pan-Arabism tried to find a new potential chief at Mecca in the person of King Ibn Saud whose prestige had been enhanced by some easy victories over the Emir of Yemen. But Ibn Saud, being a practical man, declined the offer. Evidently he was loath to become, far from his States, the champion of a vague and wordy Syrian or Palestinian nationalism and thereby run the risk of offending the English whose faithful ally he has been for years in the Arab peninsula and to whom, as he well knows, he mainly owes his victory over the Yemenites.

What is the attitude of the Palestinian Jews toward Arab problems and Arab forces? Their mistrust seems, alas, natural enough if one considers the persecutions they endured and the massacres with which they are threatened at every moment, whenever a wave of Arab unrest arises.

But to hate and to despise are the two most dangerous of all political formulas. To my thinking, Jewish immigration, Zionism itself, will find a practical outlet only when some sort of agreement has been set on foot between the Jews and their Arab cousins. This agreement is impossible if the Jewish problem is confined to Palestine. In my opinion, the safest solution for most of the thorny problems afferent to the return of a great number of Jews to their old land, lies in Syria. The Jews, and above all the enthusiastic Zionists, do not very much want to think of it. To the French it seems too daring to think of it. The Arabs, misled by their old contempt for the Jews, do not yet deign to think of it.

First of all:

Do the Jews, the most international of all peoples, really think it so necessary to add another frontier and another flag to those which already make life so heavenly on the Mediterranean shores? With due respect for the enthusiasts of Zionism, no. What the Jewish world wants, with a "national home," is a means to show all the other peoples that the Jews are endowed with the same positive possibilities for becoming agriculturists, producers, artisans as they, if only the Europe that parked them for centuries away from the fields gives them a chance to prove that they are in no way the parasitic types of the anti-Semitic legend.

Can this possibly ever come off completely in Palestine? No. Because Palestine, a sacred name for the Jews— but also for the Christians and the Moslems—has not enough good soil, not enough water, not enough natural resources to enable the Jews to try the experiment under fully normal conditions.

But is there no way to balance, in a tolerable normal life, the return of the Jews with the maintenance of the Arabs and the presence of the Christians—even without expecting the miracle of members of the three religions discussing together at Cordova the philosophy of their eleventh century—and at the same time to give to the Jews who fled from the German persecutions regions in which they may become agriculturists again and feel almost as much at home as in Palestine?

One country alone, as I have said above, can solve this problem: Syria. And in Syria it could be solved in agreement with the Arabs.

I see only advantages for Syria, and even for the Mandatory Power, France, in the realization of a broad Jewish immigration directed toward certain central and eastern zones of Syria which have been abandoned for centuries and are far from all political frontiers. One of the most serious problems of the Syrian situation is the tragic want of proportion between the Mohammedan element, so highly preponderant, and the Christian element. The presence of a new third element, racially homogeneous with the other two, might deaden many shocks.

When I went to Syria to study this problem, I heard the idea commended by high Syrian (Mohammedan) personalities of having a few tens of thousands Jews from Central Europe emigrate to the Euphrates region (the

Djeziree). It seems this region has the advantage of being depopulated and of answering all the moral and economic requisites of the Jewish immigrants.

Another fact—as new as it is strange—might promote Jewish immigration into Syria. The Bedouins, as I have said above, are weary of their everlasting migrations. If, by a wise policy, the Mandatory Power succeeded in making them settle down, the extent of territories needed for the Bedouins would be greatly reduced; and this fact might help on the arrival of an important number of Jewish settlers. Another favorable factor which would not be unimportant is that the Bedouins are, religiously speaking, the only indifferent Arabs. Not the slightest anti-Christian or anti-Jewish movement is to be feared from them if they are satisfied with their lot, even if Jews were to become their neighbors.

It would seem, therefore, that different possibilities converge today to promote the realization of a great idea: the winning back from the desert and from malaria—by imported Jews and by Arabs become sedentary—of the far too numerous Syrian regions that are today abandoned by man and which, in the days of Rome, were among the richest of Asia Minor.

It is probably only in the Syrian eastern plains that this great dream might some day become a reality—the reconciliation of Arabs and Jews united in the common task of reclaiming lands which were theirs when they had not yet divided into two hostile families.

On that day, the ideal might materialize which Feisal

once described in a letter to Professor Frankfurter of
Harvard University: "We feel that Arabs and Jews are
cousins in race, have suffered similar oppressions. . . .
We Arabs, especially the educated among us, look with
the deepest sympathy on the Zionist movement. We are
working together for a reformed and revived Near East,
and our two movements complete one another. . . .
Indeed, I think that neither can be a real success without
the other."

I must add, however, not to look too optimistic, that
the Arab leaders to whom I quoted Feisal's beautiful letter
appeared rather surprised, in spite of their inborn im-
passiveness, that their famous King had gone so far.

XXI

SPANIARDS

WHY the Spaniards last?

Not because, sheltered behind the Pyrenees, they feel safe from European convulsions—possibly a deceptive illusion of theirs.

But because, alone on the whole European continent, they have remained the most individualistic people, the people most completely untainted by nationalistic slogans and prejudices.

An Englishman wrote about France in the days of Napoleon I: "In Paris they have an admirable police force, but they pay dear for its advantages. I prefer to see, every three or four years, half a dozen people getting their throats cut in the Ratcliffe Road, than to be submitted to domiciliary visits, to spying, to all the unbearable machinations of Fouché."

Alone in Europe, the Spaniards still think that way— and they act accordingly.

Even the dictatorship of Miguel Primo de Rivera, which lasted from 1923 to 1930, was no exception to the Spanish rule. Of course, he deported, he imprisoned opponents, he suspended constitutional guarantees and freedom of the press. But every evening, on leaving his office, he would take his one-hour walk in the *calles* of Madrid filled with their noisy crowds—which would have been impossible in Berlin, Moscow, Rome. The dictators of Germany and Italy found States admirably built up, by democracy in Italy, by a lawful administration in Germany. They used them ruthlessly against the citizens and concealed their police necessities under resounding formulas like the one which obtained in Italy: "All for the State; nothing outside the State; nothing against the State."

Both the formula—and the thing—would have been equally inconceivable in Spain.

That is because Spain, in spite of her great past, in spite of her nonchalance, is still one of the youngest national bodies—perhaps the youngest. The strife of the *Reconquista* (fifteenth century) was not a national war, but a series of Western crusades. In Spain, the crusades did not last two centuries as in France and in Italy, but far longer. In a certain sense—were it not for the all-pervading tolerance which now prevails among the Spanish people—one might say they are still in the air. Cervantes, in his immortal *Don Quixote,* tells the story of the "captive" who succeeded in escaping with the beautiful Moorish woman who had fallen in love with him, and landed on the Spanish coast. Full of joy, he goes up to the first Spaniard he comes across, but the latter runs off shouting, "Moros! Moros! to arms," and the whole countryside is aroused—although the scene occurs more than a hundred years after the flight of the last Moors from Spain.*

---

* And this is sufficient to explain what seemed absurd to the cool-headed prelates of the Vatican—that King Alphonso XIII, in his solemn

French thinking is, too often, exclusively built up by the brain. There is nothing unconscious or intuitive about it. Not for nothing Victor Hugo conceived Charlemagne's empire as a French episode and defined it as "a beautiful spectacle to ravish the mind."

In Spain, on the other hand, everything has been instinctive, intuitive; and contrary to England, it has always been thus, with equal refinement in all classes.

In the *Vida del picaro Guzman de Alfareche,** Juan José Martì describes the little lad Guzman boasting to a high Italian prelate of the past of Spain, her legends, her epics, quoting the Cid Campeador and Jaime el Conquistador, the Reyes catolicos and Charles V. . . . The prelate, astonished, asked him how he had read so much at his age, and the young picaro replied: "Yes, I can read a little, and there were even some books at home, but all the lovely things I have just told you are things well known, transmitted by tradition from mouth to mouth. It needs more skill not to know them than to know them."

In Spain, the phenomenon exists no longer of the lower middle classes, snarling, embittered, affected, hating simultaneously both the workmen and the aristocracy, especially

---

address to Pope Pius XI, on his visit to Rome at the time of Primo de Rivera's dictatorship, should go so far as to offer the Holy See the arms of Spain for a crusade against the Infidels, if ever the Holy Father should give the order.

A responsible minister from his former Liberal Cabinets would have spared the King this comical blunder. But dictators need others around them to make mistakes.

*Published in 1602. Others before and after Martì wrote about the popular *picaro* (rogue) type of Guzman de Alfareche.

the intellectual aristocracy—those lower middle classes
which constituted the back-bone of Fascism in Italy and
of Naziism in Germany. For, contrary to a Marxist
theory prevalent in the Socialist spheres of Western
Europe, if Capitalism helped both movements in the beginning, thinking in its stupidity that they would curb the
labor organizations for their benefit, Fascism and National
Socialism quickly became independent forces, the masses
of which were mainly made up of clerks, small professional
men, revolutionary agitators scenting the air, students who
suspected that their University courses, patched up during
the feverish years of the war, would make only dry bones
of them. And, with all this poor crowd, were thousands
of young officers who, having entered the World War as
modest civilians, had got their commissions in the trenches
and hated the thought of going back to their humble and
badly paid bourgeois jobs. How could they be expected
to become post-office clerks again, or teachers or bank-
clerks or shop assistants?

Nothing of the sort existed in Spain.

And that is why nationalism as a religious creed did not
make its appearance there. The Spaniards do not even
understand it.

The essence of nationalism consists in this: the nationalist
may admit that his compatriots can be wrong (and when
they happen to be of a different opinion as to the best
methods of serving the common fatherland, they become
almost criminals in his eyes); but the said nationalist
must believe that his national state is always right, what-

ever it does, in war or peace. This is a diseased state of
mind, indicative of the delusions of grandeur from which
all the nationalisms suffer. A deep and noble American
thinker, Carlton J. H. Hayes, has defined nationalism as
patriotic snobbery. Certainly; but, if one considers the
social training of the nationalistic parties in old Europe,
it is more than that. It is an inferiority complex, seeking
in the intoxicating certainty of belonging to a chosen
nation a remedy for the humiliating depression of a life
of misery and of mediocrity. Italians who are really
conscious of the grandeur of the history of Italy, with
its unparalleled glories and sufferings, do not need to have
the Roman Empire constantly on their lips, like their poor,
naïve nationalists. And the Germans would not have
invented the silly slogan of "racial purity" had they really
been sure of themselves.

True patriotism can be conceived only with some element
of internal humility; because we feel that we are not up
to the purest poetical traditions of our country; because,
absorbed by our task of serving our country, we have
neither time nor wish to despise or hate the other peoples.
It was like that in Italy during the Risorgimento of 1848
and '49, when the Italians valiantly fought the Germans,
but to the tune of the arch-Italian war-song:

"They must go back across the Alps, and then we'll be
brothers again."

In Spain—European oasis of frantic individualism—
patriotism is often felt with the violence of passion, but
never does a Spaniard subject all his ideas and all his

feelings to its sway. This rage for independence is such
that it is even found in the struggle, resumed with bitterness for the past few years, of the old Spanish provinces
against the centralizing tradition of Castile. Under the
kings* as under the Republic, Castile always was, always
will be, the symbol of unitarianism as against the centrifugal forces of the Spanish aggregate. But how identically
Spanish are all these centrifugal forces! Like Catalonia,
for instance, where the very revival of the old Catalan
language is the most Spanish enterprise one can imagine.
(Indeed, the Irishmen who best succeeded in undermining
the power of England—were they not educated in the
English way and was not one of them, De Valera, half a
Spaniard?)

An essential trait that shows how wholly exempt Spain
is from all the European post-war diseases, is disclosed in
the fact that her writers, her spiritual leaders never
counted one traitor to the idea of liberty. (For a writer
who revolts from the idea of liberty betrays his essential
part—to uphold a corporation whose chief cult should be

* And the Spaniards did not feel themselves in the least inferior to
the kings. Back in the feudal twelfth century, the members of the Cortes
were taking the following oath of fealty to the King on entering their
office: "We and you are equals, but we accept you as our king on condition
that you obey the law."

In the twentieth century, my recollection of all the personal friends I
had among those members of the Spanish aristocracy who came into daily
contact with the King is one of absolute loyalty to the King's person (it
was not yet the time when Alphonso XIII had wearied all his friends
with his Bourbon mania for deceiving his councilors and his dignitaries
unceasingly), but downright candor toward the King's political or official
manifestations, candor I have never seen equaled in any other Court.

that of freedom if only because, bereft of freedom, all literature dies out.) Now, whereas Italy had a D'Annunzio, France a Barrès and a Maurras, and Germany the infinite crowd of slave-writers kneeling yesterday to William II, and today to Hitler, all the real Iberian writers of our time—the *Despertadores de Espana**—have remained true to the idea of liberty, of human tolerance, of international solidarity: Ganivet, Benavente, Unamuno, Ortega y Gasset. . . .

All these men defend the concept of personality, endeavoring to harmonize it with the people and, beyond the people, with humanity.

Under these men, and possibly, like Guzman, without reading them, the Spaniards—these people without "lower classes"—unconsciously continue to develop their philosophy of life—a philosophy that laughs at events and at political forms. Its characteristics are fewer material but more spiritual satisfactions—leisure to begin with; a wiser skepticism about what political and religious apostles preach and define as Good and Evil; deeper moral movements, but greater indifference to political movements. . . . There is more wealth in all this perhaps than in the countries which boast—what a pleasure!—that trains arrive on time.

And who knows whether, in the long run, Spanish nonchalance does not have also specific political advantages. One should not be ignorant of the lesson brought out by

---

* The awakeners of Spain.

the relations between Spain and the whole continent of Latin America.

The way Spain remains united to her old colonies of Latin America can be explained only by a persistence of moral force. Latin-American Hispanism is a fact, and it would be rash to assert that it will never have any influence in the political sphere. After the severance of the bonds of sovereignty at the beginning of the nineteenth century, the economic currents seemed to dwindle, the divorce to become complete. And yet, a few decades later, spontaneously—with not the least idea of propaganda on the part of Spain—a refined feeling of spiritual and moral community sprang up, one of the truest and freest creations of the last century and of the beginning of the twentieth century. Distant Madrid, rich in monuments but poor in banks, has a greater hold on the capitals of its old colonies, from Lima to Bogota and Caracas, than all-powerful New York and Washington have on Quebec or Ottawa, Winnipeg or Halifax.

XXII

CONCLUSIONS: EUROPE AND HER FUTURE— THE CRISIS OF THE NATIONALISMS— HOPE OR DESPAIR?

(1)

EUROPE AND HER FUTURE

EVERYBODY, everywhere, is wondering—where is Europe going?

And not only are the answers of adversaries unsatisfactory, but so are the answers of friends.

However, as optimism is the most essential law of life, one might begin with this simple statement, that never in the past was Europe spoken of, thought of, as in this turbid post-war era; and that this is true even of the political writers who are for ever chaffing about the "dreams" of European pacification.

After the violent concussion of the Franco-Prussian War of 1870, Europe came back to the fore; diplomats began to speak of Europe as of an ideal. When I went through that precious Corpus, the *Documents diplomatiques français de* 1871 *à* 1914, it was a comforting discovery to me, as an Italian, to find that Visconti Venosta,

286

by whose side at Algeciras in 1907 I had seen the shadow of the World War arise, shows up, among all the statesman after 1870, as the man most set on the idea of European solidarity.

This idea of European solidarity had not occurred to people after the Napoleonic wars. It had not been necessary. For the victors, cleverer than those of 1918, had taken great care to make the vanquished country, France, feel—or believe—that war had not been waged on her, but on the "ogre" who had led so many of her sons to slaughter. It should, indeed, not be forgotten that the legend of Napoleon's popularity arose only after 1830; and that, after 1815, all the peoples, beginning with the French, sighed with relief when Bonaparte disappeared. Napoleon III would have been powerless against the 1815 treaties. They broke down only through the combined action of two historical fatalities, stronger than any treaties or equilibrium—the unification of Italy, the unification of Germany.

Why, after the Treaty of Versailles, did we hesitate so long, grope so timorously, before we had the courage to feel and assert that we must at last create Europe?

I believe it was due to the nature of the treaty itself. By defining its nature, we shall come very close to the judgment history will one day pass on this famous document.

The Versailles Treaty can be compared—and the comparison constitutes its best definition—only to a bronze statue cast by two teams of workers, laboring simultaneously but independently of each other; each determined to throw quite different materials into the melting, and both agreed on one point only—that they must work fast. The contradictions, the antitheses of the treaty explain a good many post-war hesitancies, for instance those of the Supreme Councils of 1920 and '21 at which I often simultaneously had to adhere to errors I knew to be such, and admit that these errors were—for the time being—unavoidable. Either a wholly Wilsonian peace or an out-and-out "Treaty-of-Westphalia" kind of peace would have produced prompter, more immediate reactions and crystallizations.

But we should not, after all, be overmuch surprised at the long duration of the crisis of which our generation is at once author and victim. The World War was a revolution—and revolutions are long.

The revolution in England lasted half a century.

The revolution in France—the greatest adventure in the history of the last generations—began in 1779; and one may well say that, with the armistices of two Bonapartistic dictatorships and one and a half restorations, it ended only in 1876, when MacMahon surrendered to the will of the electors.

And one may say that the political transformation of Italy, initiated in the eighteenth century by a group of thinkers and statesmen, continued through the years of Bonaparte's invasions and resumed by the men of the Risorgimento and their heirs down to Giolitti, is not yet fulfilled. The Fascist *coup d'état* is proof that this is so.

If the political and social transformations are slow in countries which have for centuries constituted complete organisms, it is not at all strange that Europe should be so long in finding herself.

As regards the really too blatant mistakes made in the hot and flurried casting of the Versailles Treaty, it has often been hinted that they were the consequences of revenge, of hatred, of fear. . . . Of course; but even more than the willful sins of politicians without imagination, they constituted the consequences of an historical factor of which we were the victims, all of us more or less, at the end of 1918.

In 1814 and 1815, London and Vienna had known for a fairly long time in advance that the hour of Napoleon's doom was inevitably about to strike.

Cavour knew, before 1859, that the end of Austrian domination in Italy was certain.

But in November, 1918, victory, from Flanders to the Piave, occurred like an almost unexpected event—at least psychologically unexpected by the peoples. In this our countries paid the price of the stimulants official propaganda had ladled to them.

When, in the summer of 1918, the German troops began to retire almost everywhere in France, the French newspapers magnified—and nothing could have been fairer —the *élan* of the victorious offensives of the French armies with their inexhaustible moral stamina, as well as of their British, American and Italian allies on the French front. But they did not sufficiently bring out that one of the essential elements of the change in the situation consisted in the fact that the German military organization was increasingly compelled to narrow itself down, to draw nearer its bases, that is, to evacuate France. The dis- illusions of 1915 and 1916 had possibly been too bitter a lesson. We hardened ourselves against hopes too com- plete. It should even be acknowledged—for everything then can be accounted for, and otherwise must be paid for —that the discussions of the Reichstag in authoritarian Germany in 1918 showed a more accurate knowledge of truth than those held in the Chamber of Deputies of democratic France. The men who, like Stresemann (to cite one of the best), had in 1914, '15 and '16 shown childish credulity in the pompous lies of their General Staff—the ransom paid for the stultification consequent on Bismarck's dictatorial period—took their revenge in 1918. Defeat is a harsher but more clear-sighted taskmaster than victory.

Misapprehension endured after the war. It was for- gotten—Paris willed to forget—that neighbors never crush one another definitely; that after Rossbach comes Jena; after Jena, Sedan; after Sedan, the Marne. . . .

It was perhaps natural that, at the end of 1918, with the terrible wound of the invasion still gaping, France should be thinking only of bringing her soldiers to the Rhine. It harked back to the policy of the Revolution, but the gesture of 1919 and after was no more than an armistice measure. The moral forces for the expansion policy of the revolutionary Year II were no longer at the disposal of France. In reality, Clemenceau's France merely resumed the policy of her kings—a policy inspired by an anachronistic idea, the duel with the House of Austria. In a world broadened out, with so many strings to her bow, France narrowed her part by seeking on the Rhine a wretched illusion of security, represented by some fifty thousand men scattered along a two-hundred-mile front.

Securities of this sort can even, in certain cases, change into dangerous ambuscades. Gallieni, I believe, unique among the great military chiefs, had an intuition of this; but he had sprung from the transcontinental France of the Third Republic.

The broader the outlook of France, the safer she will be. Safe, let me explain, in the only sense one should desire to be safe. Absolute safety, if it existed, would probably be a cause of decadence, as in the China of the Ching, behind a pretendedly impassable wall. The safety of nations is like happiness in love: a miracle that must be performed anew every day. No philter or ramparts exist that will guarantee either for ever.

In Italy, things were almost the same as in France. The battle of the Piave—the first of the great decisive victories of the Entente in 1918—was a most beautiful manifestation of the collective will of a whole people who, after a great reverse, succeeded all alone in taking themselves in hand and organizing—before any Allied contingent had arrived—a stand that destroyed any possibility of Austro-German success in Italy. But the other side of the trenches was better aware than Italy of the

decisiveness of those days.   Then the movement toward
the national independence of the Slav populations of the
Hapsburg monarchy was hastened.   Had the Italian leaders in the summer of 1918 sensed that, thanks to the
victory of the Piave, the disintegration of the populations
of the enemy monarchy was on the verge of fulfillment, it
would have been easier to enter, even then, into agreements with the post-war Slav neighbors.   In vain I urged
this on Sonnino from the Macedonian front, my only merit
being that I saw things from a more distant vantage
ground—and consequently with easier historical vision.
It was perhaps too much to hope for.   Possibly, four
years of war-hatred and misunderstanding could not van-
ish in a day.   Whence so many futile Italo-Slav quarrels
after the war; whence so many dusty and unreal programs
preached by seemingly futuristic demagogues whose eyes
look only to the past—a past of Roman eagles, Venetian
lions, bloodstained Spanish colonies.   Whereas the simple
and crystalline truth is that any policy of European understanding and of international justice answers, as far as
the Italians are concerned, not only to the human ideals
of the Risorgimento but at the same time also to the most
specifically Italian interests.

Italians who cannot feel the nobility of the policy of
international justice that Mazzini preached, should, out
of selfishness, pretend to believe in it.

The age-old history of Asia has taught Orientals far
more about peace and war.   In China, as I saw with my
own eyes, wars, even when they are waged with ferocity,

never sever all the possibilities of eventual agreements. There is always a confidential agent of the enemy at hand. Shall I own that it was only much later, during the gloomy years of 1917 and '18, that I grasped the full value of a remark Sun Yat-sen made to me when, Italy having entered the war, I left China to return to Europe and serve my country from closer quarters? "When you Europeans fight," he said, "you always forget that all wars end in compromises, must end in compromises."

Useless memories and confessions? Meager, but not entirely useless. We need most to understand what has happened and thereby destroy the legends and myths of which we, the war generations, were the victims.

All the same, despite all our past errors, despite dictatorships and the wars they unloose or threaten, possibilities of European entente are nearer and greater than before the World War and notwithstanding the hatreds and problems it bequeathed to us.

If one considers essentials rather than episodes (admitting, however, that episodes are liable to become very dangerous), one must acknowledge that present-day Europe is far from being more divided, and especially more inexorably divided, than Europe in 1914.

We should, in statements of this kind, beware of current appreciations.

It is indeed true that the 1919 treaties have multiplied the barriers between peoples. We had, in 1914, twenty-six customs systems and thirteen monetary systems. The war has given us thirty-five customs systems and twenty-

seven monetary systems, that is, thirty-seven hundred and
fifty miles of new customs barriers.   The conclusion is easy.
We have a Balkanized Europe, to quote a clever saying
launched by Magyar propaganda.

But in fact, for anyone who can delve to truth without
stopping at semblance, this new Europe, in which there
are thirty Sovereign States instead of eighteen, shows us
the profound reason—new in her history—I shall not
say for union, but for a possibility of union.   I mean the
disappearance of the great monarchies (autocratic and
pretendedly divine), Germany, Austria-Hungary, Russia,
Turkey, Spain.   If one may henceforth contemplate a
union of Europe as being more than a Utopian ideal, it
is precisely because the questions of the Hohenzollern,
Hapsburg, Romanoff, Bourbon monarchies have been
settled.   These families mainly represented the privileged
few who had clustered around them and who quite sincerely—it is so easy to make wish father to thought—
called monarchical loyalty what was only a strenuous
defense of caste.   No doubt these privileged few had
everything to fear from a curtailment, even in the sphere
of international law, of the symbols they used while pro-
claiming to serve the rulers.

Mazzini, whose prophetic soul not only inspired two
generations of Italians of the Risorgimento, but who also,
between 1830 and 1850, succeeded in making all the oppressed peoples of Europe hope in the future—Mazzini
seemed a madman to the European Cabinets when he

dared to announce—Metternich was still all powerful—
that the days of the Hapsburg amalgam were numbered
and that we should witness the resurrection not only of
Italy but also of Poland, Bohemia, Yugoslavia.

It is really too easy to criticize the mistakes made by
the new States, mistakes which were sometimes the fatal
consequence of those committed at their birth by the
Great Powers in 1919.

But the fact remains, nevertheless, that the new European States furnish the solid and permanent material out
of which the new European edifice may be built. The
old monarchies would not even have understood the idea.
A Bethmann-Hollweg or an Aehrenthal at their best might
have offered to help consolidate the "European equilibrium." And we all know what deadly surprises are
latent in this formula, which has belonged to the diplomatic
arsenal ever since the Treaty of Westphalia created an
artificial Europe by dividing it into two rival groups.

In my own mind I cannot help comparing Bethmann-
Hollweg or Aehrenthal, whom I knew so well, with
Masaryk and Benes. The latter also, as is their duty,
value the independence of their country; but they understand perfectly that a reconciliation of Europe, even at
the cost of common sacrifices, is its essential primordial
condition.

It is this new outlook—existing even in those countries
that seem to oppose it most—which warrants the hope of
a common organization of Europe.

History has already shown us two opposite types of concentration of different nationalities in Europe. It has also shown us their results.

One of these concentrations was called Austria, and after 1867, Austria-Hungary. We saw this Great Power at work, with her eight or ten different nationalities linked together only by the interest of the House of Hapsburg. We saw her policy of divisions and jealousies at work— and the final result was the ultimatum to Serbia and the European war.

The other example of an historical supernational formation is given by Switzerland, in which no nationality opposes the other despite the numerical disproportion among her three component elements, German, French, Italian. The three peoples live together in a state of perfect equality, with no shock but those normally inherent in a human society. Every Swiss feels love and pride for his German or French or Italian culture, but he can ally these with a higher Helvetian patriotism, born of a rational interest in union and a common love of liberty.

Our old reciprocal antipathies and our recent hatreds alone prevent us from perceiving that the European feeling has awakened in us Europeans far more than we suppose. And certainly not by our own merits. But because today, new units, the work of Europe, are springing up beside her, which differ from her a hundred times more than the European nationalities will differ henceforth from one another.

Asia was always a world very different from little

Europe, one of Asia's peninsulas. By westernizing the external appearance of Asia we have drawn her nearer to us—but only with material bonds. In reality, now that Asia lies within our reach, we feel our essential collective dissimilarities more than ever.

North America has perhaps contributed even more toward the formation of a half-conscious, half-unconscious European feeling, due to the fact that the American personality has evolved in a manner so much more detached from us during the last twenty or thirty years.

Let those Europeans who are most skeptical over the future of Europe recall their instinctive reactions on their return from a fairly long stay in the United States. Whether they were shocked by the mechanization of American life, or whether, like myself, they loved the warmth and spontaneity so often found over there, even among the most refined—still they feel themselves "back home" as soon as they land in one of our big harbors, Cherbourg or Bremen, Antwerp or Genoa, it does not matter which.

In this the United States has helped us unconsciously. Whoever, like me, has tasted of American life, cannot but have noted that an evening spent with men like Bliss or Butler or Wickersham or John W. Davis was really an evening spent with Europeans. We may enjoy just as much the company of young men like certain very brilliant writers who make New York evenings so entertaining; but we feel they are no longer Europeans. They too may know our philosophers, as Butler knows them, or Shake-

speare like Davis, or the classics like Bliss, or Dante like
Wickersham;* but one feels in them a new mental training
—American, and exclusively American.†

On some future day, it will perhaps be recognized that
even the World War and its four years of slaughter constituted a connecting link between the peoples, if not between their governments. Throughout the war, the instincts of the peoples were found to be so little dissimilar
from one another, in their moral strength as in their moral
weakness, in their hopes for the future as in the disillusions
with which a past heavy with history has laden them. A
day will come—when the wounds and sorrows of war
shall have been toned down by time—when one will realize
with astonishment and fright that the belligerent masses
were led to death, were buried in the trenches, thanks to
a series of assertions which were believed on both sides
equally in good faith: We are fighting for life, for independence, for freedom. . . .

This process of similar thinking does not apply, or not
yet, to the leaders who are, almost everywhere, poisoned
or terrified by nationalisms.

---

*A great American lawyer who died in 1936. Chairman of the Italo-
American Society, enthusiastic lover of Italy, he resigned when he felt
that the Society was being used as an instrument of Fascist propaganda.

†I quoted General Bliss. May I recall a charming personal recollection
of mine? In 1927, General Bliss invited me to lunch at the Century Club
in New York. I arrived very late. I was told that "General Bliss was
in the library." I went to him, apologized. Bliss was busy reading, and
the book which, by a sort of reserve, he put down far away from me,
was a Horace in Latin. Could anything better recall the culture of our
own grandparents?

But nationalism—this caricature of patriotism—bears in itself its own condemnation, because of its violence and its artificiality. The Italian poets and thinkers of the Risorgimento, from Manzoni to Mazzini, preached release from the German yoke without ever a word of hate for the Germans.*

On the day when the various nationalisms will have come to the end of their ephemeral life, we shall not see an unqualified return to the patriotism of 1848, still so pure, in Michelet as in Hugo, in Mazzini as in Manzoni. On that day we shall witness the sudden development of the new European ideality, the symptoms of which are today to be detected only among an intellectual and moral minority.

These are not dreams. To Metternich, who was the master of Europe from 1815 to 1848, Italy was but a "geographical expression." Less than a century later, his imperial and domineering Austria had become an historical memory.

Throughout all the Middle Ages, the Italian communes did nothing but fight each other. Even Dante's genius could not shake itself free from the municipal passions of his day. His apostrophes against Siena and Pisa are laden with more hatred and sarcasm than the "Gott strafe England" of 1914-18. For it so happens that when one hates a neighbor who speaks the same language, the hatred is so much deeper; whence the passionate violence of civil wars.

After all, the concept of the absolute sovereignty of the State was born of monarchic absolutism. It was tempered

---

* See, in Chapter XXI, a verse from an Italian war-song of 1848.

first by what was left of feudalism and later by the liberal currents of the nineteenth century. It has developed again —becoming even more dangerous than under the kings— with the absolutism of democracies. But there is reason to hope that the rhythm of nationalisms suspicious of each other shall follow in the end, that of those religious hatreds which, after having oppressed so many Protestant minorities in France and Catholic minorities in England, have completely disappeared.

Writers who think themselves *real-politikers* scoff at the illusions of the idealists who believe that the recurrence of a European war may still be avoided.

The *real-politikers* forget that, during long centuries, philosophers and theologians believed with the masses that slavery was a law of nature. And yet slavery has not only been suppressed, but more was done toward its abolition in the half-century following the American War of Secession of 1865 than in the ten preceding centuries. That is because there are epochs when certain problems, once laid down, end by being solved.

And we ourselves who have come to the middle of life's journey, have we not seen with our own eyes, in so short a space of time, a great social change, the disappearance of dueling?

There is, therefore, no rational difficulty in admitting that war, as a juridical institution, may disappear.

Does this mean that the great historical revolution is in view?

Certainly not. But what is in sight is a fact which thinking Europe has already understood—and for the first time —that war is a silly and a bad business, and that we must come to an understanding for reason's sake if not for love's.

When ideas of this nature begin to spread, they reach their goal more quickly than skeptics suppose.

In reality there is in Europe but one big obstacle—the tendency of those groups who continue to consider criminal any cession, however trifling, of a parcel of our different national sovereignties on behalf of some idea or organization vaster and more complex than our present States. This is the tragedy of the post-war leaders, men brought forth into a new world, but thinking with old brains and feeling with old passions. The same thing happened during the crisis that followed the Napoleonic wars. The "fatherly governments" which the Treaty of Vienna had given to the European peoples, endeavored for years to check the ever-growing tendencies toward wider economic relations. Their ideal was the town market. In Italy matters came to such a head that conferences for economic developments* aroused popular enthusiasm; it was felt that the unification of Italy was being accomplished there. And the governments finally gave in and disappeared.

History repeats itself, identically, today, but only on a larger scale, that of associations between nations. And the results are equally inevitable, in spite of gloomy appearances to the contrary.

One may even, without being too bold, suggest this forecast: that the organization of Europe, once perceived by

---

* In 1846 and '47.

the people, with its untold consequence—the elimination of war—will progress comparatively more quickly than other changes, as happened with religious tolerance after centuries of wars of religion.   Even the personal concerns of dictators, who can live only in an atmosphere of war, will not, in the end, be able to withstand the moral force which is already in operation.

We are standing at the crossroads.   The Europe of the future—perhaps even the Europe of our sons—will be made by us.

If Europe is made by us, in expiation of the war, we shall be able to pass on to our sons the flaming light of the intellectual and moral treasures which constitute the best and purest heirloom of our national traditions, the lyrical and moral ornament of Europe.

But if we oppose the European ideal as the blind shepherds of the Holy Alliance fought the national ideals, it will mean that we shall become the unconscious abettors of the brutal leveling which the post-war dictators pretend to force on us.   It would not be the first time indeed for the "Conservatives" to prove the most precious allies of the "revolutionaries."

The European ideality was intimately blended with the national patriotism of the Mazzinis, the Michelets, the Hugos.

The nationalities that fill the nineteenth century with their glory were not—with the best of their apostles, the first of whom is Mazzini—an end in themselves.   They were only a step toward a wider European ideal.

Either we shall serve this ideal—in our minds, in our souls, even more than in our treaties—or we shall perish.

And we shall not be submerged by that "revolution" of which the Tories talk with shudders of horror. Ours will be—if it does come to pass—a suicide due to our short-sighted selfishness, to the dread we had of principles of freedom and peace, because we failed to see that it was from these we had to derive the necessary strength to resist the cheap happiness which the Kremlin maniacs have proffered to a weary and hesitant humanity.

(2)

THE CRISIS OF THE NATIONALISMS

The nationalism that saw the light of day toward the end of the nineteenth century has the manner and some of the traits of a religious movement. With this difference, however: that the stronger the religious movements, the more frontiers they crossed. Buddhism gathered to its bosom Thibetans, Chinese, Japanese, more different from one another than an Arab from a Swede. Mohammedanism included in a common faith and common rites the most miscellaneous peoples, from the Chinese of Turkestan to the Moors of Morocco. Christianity dictated to a hundred peoples speaking a hundred languages its universal *Pax hominibus.*

The European nationalisms of the twentieth century, in their religious aspect, link up with the remotest and most childish concepts of the tribes of old, each of whom considered themselves a chosen people. Paul's message is denied: more than ever shall the Jew rise up against the Gentile.

Not one of the old "chosen" people was saved, and nationalism also is beginning to see its doom threatening on the horizon. Conceived, formulated, to reinforce the State, it ends by weakening it wherever it has succeeded in getting the upper hand.

A day will come when we—all of us whom the nationalist inquisition has charged with internationalist heresy—shall have to defend the idea of nationality, and all its rich and fruitful implications, against the wave that will try to drown it in reaction to the crimes and insanities perpetrated by nationalisms.

We should not forget that when Metternich cried out in Vienna, "There is only one question left in Europe, the Revolution," he was really thinking of the national claims. Historians have made us believe that he saw beyond the Napoleonic vogue and the Italian Risorgimento and realized that countries freed from all alien yoke would be destined to become democratic. For Metternich, an Italy enslaved and portioned out, a Germany without union or rights, a Poland despairing of resurrection were so many certainties that the spirit of the Revolution would not wake up again.

One of the fatal errors committed by Marx was that he failed to understand that national feeling and love of freedom are inseparable. He did not understand because, in this gloomy prophet whose style was similar to that of his ancestors from Jerusalem, hatred prevailed over love. I have already described* Marx's attitude toward the Risorgimento. Lassalle, so much more human, understood it better. When, in 1859, Prussia worried over Napoleon III's action in Lombady, Lassalle was practically the only man who gauged fairly what part of idealism lay beneath the intervention of the French.

At that time, Lassalle, a good German, added: "Of course, if Napoleon III should afterward attempt to do violence to the German nation, she would defend herself even with uprisings of the masses." For those who draw a parallel between the development of power by the people and a diminution of national loyalty, commit a very petty mistake. The patriotism of the Athens of Pericles was not based on conservative forces; on the contrary. And one of the weightiest causes of the downfall of Rome lies perhaps in the failure of the Gracchi and their ideal: a rural democracy including all the Italians. The rurals, small landowners, would have withstood the barbarian invasions; whereas the avid and selfish patriciate sank and disappeared amid the indifference of a crowd who felt it had no duties toward a country which had given it no rights.†

As Metternich had feared, the rise of nationalities, which Mazzini had preached, caused the overthrow of the absolutist monarchies, one after the other.

---

* Chapter VI.

† One might recall here that the nationalists in France were disappointed, at the time of the Ruhr invasion, by the patriotic loyalty of the German workmen. They clung to a country which had given them their "social laws."

But—and it is always thus—a principle, an idea (a myth if you please) renders, at a given moment, a radical service to the cause of human progress—so radical that situations alter and with them the myth should alter too. If the idea evolved, it would continue to live; but it most often becomes set in its past glory; and people continue to bow to it until they perceive it has become a lifeless formula. The petty violence of nationalisms has almost made us forget that the most clear-sighted apostles of the idea of nationality in the nineteenth century never considered the nations as an end in themselves. In the thick of his struggles for the unification of Italy, Mazzini never ceased to aver —as I have said before—that nationalities were only a pause on the way to European union.

Although they do not actually reject these precepts, the élite today show, in practice, a natural but dangerous hesitation. Natural, because certain tendencies toward the didactic German formula of an all-powerful *Superstaat* justifies the fears; but dangerous, because union must be achieved by the democracies or else we shall slide back to anarchy or fall under dominations excluding national equalities.

England, with a political sense which only centuries of freedom can develop, has understood this clearly. Under the myth of the Crown, which secures to the island the appearances of a metropolis, the British Empire is now made up of Dominions all equally free. As an anticipation of the international era, let us call to mind that the French Canadians have steadily risen in numbers and prestige while they have, at the same time, become citizens more and more loyal of the British Commonwealth.*

The nations which will lack England's courage may imagine they serve a patriotic ideal. In reality they are merely looking back like Lot's wife; and, like Lot's wife, they risk coming to a dead standstill.

If the National States continue to shirk and ignore their new duties, the rising generations will recover from the nationalist intoxication only to recoil from them. And this not in order to enlist in Communism, the scarecrow which Conservatives brandish so gladly.

The danger is far more serious than all the bogeys used on "right-thinking" people. It really lies in a despondent collapse into intellectual and moral torpor, which a life without issue might occasion.

Disasters of this kind have occurred before now. The Pax Romana was not destroyed by the advent of a few hordes of barbarians. It collapsed because all hope had died out, and all faith.

(3)

HOPE OR DESPAIR?

Those who fear that the light of freedom has been dimmed for ever, and with it the drive toward human brotherhood and peace, cite the fact that there are no more popular revolutions.

---

* See Chapter VIII.

Of course, the movements which are usually called revolutions—the Soviet, the Fascist—have been nothing more than *coups d'état*. Revolutions were made in the days when the guns were the same on both sides of the barricades. Machine-guns have consigned them to the kingdom of past shadows. But, under other forms, the sacrifices and heroisms have continued, all the more vital because they are often unknown—like the devotion of the young Italian poet Lauro De Bosis who, in 1931, knowing he would be shot down, flew over Rome in a tiny airplane to throw down leaflets summoning to freedom. He had learned to fly just to die. His story, in other times, would immediately have become the theme of a legend. But Italy has a long memory. It took three hundred years for a statue to be erected on the Roman Campo di Fiori where Giordano Bruno was burned. It will not take generations to see the Italians revere the memory of the young poet who, at thirty, handsome and beloved, went to his death because—as he tells us in his extraordinary *Story of My Death,* written on the night before the flight and posted a few minutes before he climbed into his cockpit—"I shall be of more account dead than alive" to the freedom of Italy.

And elsewhere in the *Story,* which all the children of Italy shall know by heart one day: "During the Risorgimento, there were thousands of young people ready to die for the regeneration of the Italians. Today there are but a few. Why? It is not that the sum of courage has gone down. It is because nobody takes Fascism seriously, and

everybody expects its inevitable fall. Wrong! It is necessary to die." And he died.*

Besides, the feeling of human solidarity which we should
learn to combine with national loyalty is already far deeper
than one might think to judge from the newspapers, which,
all—those for the rich and those for the poor alike—
emphasize only manifestations of hatred.

I shall go even further. No one in Europe, save a few
crazy brains, believes in war any more—in the advantages
of war, I mean. And if so many groups have taken on a
bellicose air, it is mere sham for reasons of home politics,
of defense of caste interests. But even those groups hate

---

* Among his lyrics there is a noble poem, *Icarus,* written a year before
his death (translated into English by Ruth Draper). It gives us De Bosis'
idealization of flying as the liberator of a pacified humanity. G. M.
Trevelyan wrote of De Bosis in his foreword to *The Golden Book of
Italian Poetry,* a posthumous work of the young Italian poet (London,
Oxford University Press, 1932):

"He was a man of rare personality. In some respect his idealism of
thought and character reminds us rather of Shelley and the young leaders
of the Italian Risorgimento than of our own disillusioned generation. The
ardors of his soul; his strong love of life and its joys, of earth and its
beauty; his claim to individual freedom as the birthright of man; his
classical scholarship and his intense devotion to the poetry of Greece,
Italy and England, all seem to spring from an older tradition and to
reincarnate an ancient faith. But in some respects he was most modern.
His great interest in the discoveries of modern science and the speculations
of modern philosophy and the relation of the two, put him in the ranks of
those who go forward. As a poet he felt the universe revealed by science
and philosophy to be a harmony. Modern speculation and science brought
him round to the ancient faith in man's destiny, in the presence of which
he felt his own to be of small account.

'The lover of life
Holds life in his hand.'

"Untouched by considerations of material interest, he combined intellectual fervour with a remarkable balance of mind. . . ."

war; they would very much prefer to talk about it all the
time and never make it.   There is the French bourgeoisie,
for instance.   In spite of its *Action Française,* in spite of
its *Croix de Feu,* it is not at all keen on war.   It has as
great a horror of it as the Socialists have, whom it hates.
It trembles at the thought that its children might war or rot
in trenches.   It has not the slightest desire to see taxes
rise tenfold.   But   .   .   .   but they think, the French
with their big bank-account, that the fear of war, the idea
of war, constitutes for *le peuple* a sort of potential lesson
in favor of hierarchy, of authority, of discipline.   Something like what Monsieur de Voltaire used to mean when
he wished for "some religion for the under-dog."

The same holds good for Germany, for Italy, even for
Russia.   A certain danger of war seems, to the powers-
that-be, an additional excuse for the severity and the extension of their power of control over the whole life of the
nation.

When the hegemony and the privileges of the upper and
middle classes were accepted by the *plebs* as a law of nature
—that is, in the first half of the nineteenth century—nothing was more unpopular with the rich in Europe than wars
or policies conducive to war.   In France, under the Restoration and under the monarchy of Louis-Philippe, the
bourgeoisie always strove against any danger of war.
Chateaubriand carried off his expedition to Spain only
against the almost universal opinion of the country.   When
Napoleon III, urged on by the oath he had taken as a young
Italian *carbonaro* and by the future of glory and power

Cavour had dangled before him, entered in 1859 on his campaign in Lombardy, he had almost the whole French bourgeoisie against him.

It was only when the twentieth century brought out in the masses a spirit of social emancipation coupled with internationalism, that the upper classes all, everywhere, became warlike in appearance. This enabled them to say, from Paris to Tokyo, from Rome to Berlin: "Social reforms? Perhaps. But first we must save our country, threatened, encircled. We must bend to a supreme national need."

But besides the selfish motives of caste which drive so many good and peace-loving people to put on "a war face," to use the old Chinese phrase, there are—a novel and admirable fact—millions of Europeans who have cast aside all computation of caste interest and entertain an ever increasing horror of the idea of war. Their strength was seen in 1932 when Paris as well as London, New York as well as Brussels, had to own that the League of Nations— then the victim of a series of errors due to a lack of living faith in its leaders and especially in the leader of British diplomacy, Sir John Simon—was powerless before the Japanese invasion of China. This quasi-religious force was measured again in 1935 and 1936, when the population in England was roused, honestly, sincerely aroused outside of selfish considerations of British interest (which existed and were at work) against a war to which its main objection was—that it imperiled the rising principle of international solidarity that alone can insure a permanent peace.

INDEX